**A Step-by-Step Master Class
for People Who Want to Deliver on Their Dream Projects**

Six sets of questions to help you review and refine your vision, skills and experience

Hundreds of tips, terms and "lessons learned" from a 3-time Inc. 500™ CEO

Your idea could be a part-time business or a Silicon Valley startup, a small-town storefront or an internal project at your current company.

The only person who can define your Dream Project is you. *From Dream to Delivery* will help you do just that, by leading you through a guided conversation with yourself.

Section by section, you'll record your answers to these carefully chosen questions. Then we'll use your unique personal responses to build the customized roadmap you need to go out and turn your Dream Project into Reality.

Techniques to utilize, traps to avoid, terminology to understand. And how to fit it all into your life without damaging your family or your future.

Never started a business or a big project? We'll give you a "crash course" introduction. Skip past what you already know, dig deeper on things you want to learn.

It's the one book you need to go from Dream to Delivery.

Also by Don Daglow

Indie Games:
From Dream to Delivery

A parallel volume to this book, written for people creating independent games outside the large publisher ecosystem.

From Dream to Delivery

From Dream to Delivery

HOW TO DO WORK YOU LOVE, LOVE WHAT YOU DO, AND LAUNCH YOUR DREAM PROJECT

DON L. DAGLOW

Sausalito Media, LLC
Sausalito, CA

ISBN 978-0-9967815-4-1 (Paperback), 978-0-9967815-3-4 (eBook)

Published by Sausalito Media LLC, PO Box 1035, Sausalito, CA 94966. Sausalito Media is a trademark of Sausalito Media, LLC. All Rights Reserved.

Cover design by D.V. Suresh

This book is dedicated to my wife Marta, without whose support and encouragement this Dream Project would never have been delivered.

Contents

PART I

BIG DREAMS

"CHASE YOUR DREAMS
TILL THEY GET TIRED OF RUNNING AWAY.
JUST TAKE CARE OF YOURSELF AND YOUR FAMILY ALONG THE
WAY, BECAUSE ONCE THE FIRST DREAM IS CAPTURED THERE WILL
BE MORE TO FOLLOW."

— Don Daglow

CHAPTER 1

Getting Started

A Book About You

Most books tell a story about someone else. Their adventures, their hopes, their dreams.

When you and I finish this process, this book will be about you.

It will talk about what you want for your career and for your life. The obstacles you face and realistic, practical plans for how you'll overcome them.

This is not the Big Lie that says, "Imagine the road to riches and success will come to you!"

This is, "Let's find a realistic way for you to do work you love to do, and then let's refine those plans and strategies to make it happen."

So please think of this book as a private discussion between you and me.

Wait, check that. Think of this book as a private discussion between you and you. A chance for you to talk openly about your hopes, dreams and fears. No judgment, no criticism, no worrying about anyone else's feelings.

When you've finished answering each set of questions, I'll share how to turn your answers into productive next steps. We'll start writing your own script for your career instead of accepting chapters other people have written for you.

That's why I opened this book with my mantra to "Chase your dreams till they get tired of running away."

If you stick with the process and give yourself thoughtful and real answers to the questions, I think this story will have a happy ending.

Giving Ourselves Permission

Anyone can create a dream project. Your gender, ethnicity, religion, background, education, personal characteristics and location are not an issue. Your product or service will speak for itself.

In fact, if you're not "the typical entrepreneur" it may help you stand out in the crowd.

You'll need to follow the community standards of the locations, media and channels in which you work (e.g. no hate speech or personal attacks). Apart from these basic safeguards, if you start small there are no gatekeepers you have to please, no prestigious schools you have to attend and no exclusive clubs you have to join.

It's just a matter of whether you're willing to learn the necessary skills and do the work to create your dream project. And then do still more work to find a way to get it into the hands of people who will love it.

There's a quote from Agatha Christie (although it's often credited wrongly to Mark Twain) that provides a central theme to this book. Her wisdom is simple:

"The secret of getting ahead is getting started."

To start this book, I had to give myself permission to spend a few hours plotting out the questions I would ask. One thing led to another, and after several stages of work the book is now published and in your hands.

We often talk ourselves out of starting things, for reasons I'll discuss below. This means we sabotage our chances to finish work that we would be proud to share with the world.

At some point in the process we may decide to drop an idea that isn't working. This often chain reacts into another, better idea.

But we still have to *start*. If a voice in the back of your head tries to talk you out of starting your Dream Project, ignore it. Your idea may or may not eventually lead somewhere valuable, but we have to give ourselves a chance.

The alternative is to accept failure, which I refuse to do.

Your idea may be a part-time side business, a full-time startup or a bold new initiative inside your current company.

Whatever your goal may be, what's the one thing you'd have to give yourself permission to do in order to start your Dream Project? And I mean starting it now, not next month or next year.

That first step is often just sitting down to think, organize your notes and write down your ideas. Once you take that simple step, you'll have achieved more than the legions of people who never start at all.

This book will help you do it.

What You'll Need

How do you like to write down your ideas? A notebook or journal? An iPad or laptop? A yellow pad?

If you're comfortable and it's a quiet time and place where you can write down your thoughts as they come to you, the method doesn't matter.

I do, however, ask that you do two things:

Commit that you'll write down your answers, not just think about them. The process of writing things down forces us to clarify our thoughts, and is the enemy of wishy-washy indecision.

Since you're writing this ONLY for your own eyes, commit to yourself that you'll answer with complete honesty. Before you can discuss your plans with family and friends you need to decide how you *really* feel.

How to Use This Book

Each section of this book has three themes: "Questions," "My Story" and "What to Do with Your Answers."

The questions follow a logical sequence. We'll start by talking about your Dream Project and your vision for it. Then we'll discuss part time and full time work, and the issues of projects that involve teams ranging from small to large. We'll cover the different ways to organize your project and to make plans for the work to be done.

In the second half of this book we'll gradually move into the issues of starting and running a business, from small part-time ventures to ambitious startups.

Please answer the questions in each section before moving on to that section's "What to Do with Your Answers." You'll always give yourself the best ideas if each question is fresh and new when you respond to it.

Not every question or discussion in this book will be relevant to you and your objectives, and the content is designed so you can skip the parts that don't fit into your plans.

For example, if you don't plan to hire anyone to work with you, just skip the questions about building a team. Use your best judgment as you proceed, and the story you create with your answers will bring your dream project to life.

How All This Started

Most writers start with a book and then move on to presenting their ideas at conferences.

From Dream to Delivery started as a series of conference presentations that were built around ten questions. Each audience member wrote down brief answers that no one else would read. After each question I'd provide suggestions on how to follow different paths, and shared mistakes I'd made on similar issues.

After the first few presentations at games industry events, it became clear that this process was helpful to people who were planning new startups or even small side projects. So I presented these ideas to companies and leaders from a wide cross-section of industries at Meetups and at business accelerators in San Francisco. More people reported that the sessions gave new momentum to their projects.

So I wrote this book for that multi-industry audience, and the list of questions grew from ten to over 80. I later added a parallel volume for people planning projects in the games industry.

I continue to refine these ideas based on lessons learned on my own projects and from working with both new and long-term clients. If you'd like to explore working together I can be reached at ddaglow@gmail.com, and my personal website is at www.daglowslaws,com.

CHAPTER 2

Big Dreams: The Questions

QUESTION 1.1

What Dream Project or Projects have you been thinking about that inspired you to read this book?

Don't worry about refining your thoughts into the perfect concept — just write down a basic summary of your Dream Project. Your idea may involve:

- Making some extra money from a hobby

- Starting a new company

- Launching a new initiative within your current company

Please take your time, write down your responses, and answer fully from your deepest thoughts. Think only about your own opinions, not about what others may want you to think or do. Do not look ahead to other questions until you have finished this one.

QUESTION 1.2

When did you first become interested in the segment, category, topic or profession that lies at the core of the Dream Project you want to do?

What parts of the Dream Project most interest you?

Example: If you wanted to found a small business to create garden hoses from recycled fast food containers, when did you get interested in garden products, and what first inspired that interest?

When did you become interested in plastics, and what inspired that interest?

When did you become interested in recycling, and what inspired that interest?

Please take your time, write down your responses, and answer fully from your deepest thoughts. Think only about your own opinions, not about what others may want you to think or do. Do not look ahead to other questions until you have finished this one.

QUESTION 1.3

What makes you passionate about this Dream Project?

Please take your time, write down your responses, and answer fully from your deepest thoughts. Think only about your own opinions, not about what others may want you to think or do. Do not look ahead to other questions until you have finished this one.

QUESTION 1.4

Is this your first big Dream Project?

Have you pursued lots of Dream Projects in your life?

Have you worked on many new initiatives or startups where the size of the venture was similar to your Dream Project?

QUESTION 1.5

Dreams change as we live our lives. What is a Dream Project you once really hoped to do but that is no longer as important to you?

Please take your time, write down your responses, and answer fully from your deepest thoughts. Think only about your own opinions, not about what others may want you to think or do. Do not look ahead to other questions until you have finished this one.

QUESTION 1.6

What Dream Project do you think may be important to you a few years from now that isn't as important to you today?

Why will you care more about it in a few years than you do now?

QUESTION 1.7

If your Dream Project is a restaurant or retail store, what will make your business stand out compared to other similar businesses in your area?

If you plan to open a store, how will it compete successfully with internet retailers?

Please take your time, write down your responses, and answer fully from your deepest thoughts. Think only about your own opinions, not about what others may want you to think or do. Do not look ahead to other questions until you have finished this one.

QUESTION 1.8

How specific is your vision of your Dream Project?

Is there a way to take your product idea and expand the concept into additional products or services that can be introduced if the first effort is a success?

Example: If you planned to do a startup that would design, manufacture and sell new styles of leather purses, are you also interested in leather briefcases? Leather clothing? Leather jewelry? Leather upholstery?

Could you enjoy working on silk and satin purses as well as leather, and purses made from new industrial materials and synthetics?

Please take your time, write down your responses, and answer fully from your deepest thoughts. Think only about your own opinions, not about what others may want you to think or do. Do not look ahead to other questions until you have finished this one.

QUESTION 1.9

Is it the craft involved in the making of your Dream Project that interests you?

Or is it the raw material that is used to create a product or the unique methodology used to perform a service?

Or do you take joy in using the finished product and watching others use it?

Some combination of the above choices?

Example: Your new app shows the closest coffee shops to users. You could most enjoy:

- Programming. Anything that lets you code and make money sounds good.
- Coffee. You're preoccupied with coffee, exotic blends, the search for the best barista and the best latte-foam art.
- Audience. You keep looking over people's shoulders to see if they're using your app.

Please take your time, write down your responses, and answer fully from your deepest thoughts. Think only about your own opinions, not about what others may want you to think or do. Do not look ahead to other questions until you have finished this one.

QUESTION 1.10

How would you describe your Dream Project to a stranger in just one sentence that would fascinate him or her?

How will your Dream Project draw attention in a crowded market?

Is this a new idea, or are you improving on a product or service that already exists?

Please take your time, write down your responses, and answer fully from your deepest thoughts. Think only about your own opinions, not about what others may want you to think or do. Do not look ahead to other questions until you have finished this one.

———————

QUESTION 1.11

What are the three most important features of your Dream Project that will make someone want to buy your product or service?

———————

QUESTION 1.12

One of the first people to use your product or service has lunch with a friend. What do they say to the friend about their experience with your product?

Note: We're not looking for them to describe your product or service. We're looking for their description of what they felt like when they used it.

Please take your time, write down your responses, and answer fully from your deepest thoughts. Think only about your own opinions, not about what others may want you to think or do. Do not look ahead to other questions until you have finished this one.

QUESTION 1.13

What kinds of people will want to buy your product or service? What do your most important target customers have in common with each other?

QUESTION 1.14

What other companies offer a similar product or service?

How is yours different? What makes yours better?

Please take your time, write down your responses, and answer fully from your deepest thoughts. Think only about your own opinions, not about what others may want you to think or do. Do not look ahead to other questions until you have finished this one.

QUESTION 1.15

How would you feel if The New York Times, Wired magazine, Oprah Winfrey and your best friend's mother all said your Dream Project sucks?

QUESTION 1.16

You just won a mega-million-dollar jackpot in the lottery! You've cleared your to-do list and taken a 3-month vacation at a series of your favorite cities and resorts.

You return happy, rested and all caught up in every phase of your life. There's no to-do list for work, and nothing at home that needs to be cleaned, straightened, fixed, watered, painted, re-arranged or put away.

You no longer need to work, nor does your spouse or partner. If you have kids, however, they still attend the same grade of school and they still have to do their homework. Some things can't be changed by money!

From this moment on you can do whatever you want to do each day. In this "perfect world" how would you spend the first month when you got back?

Please take your time, write down your responses, and answer fully from your deepest thoughts. Think only about your own opinions, not about what others may want you to think or do. Do not look ahead to other questions until you have finished this one.

CHAPTER 3

My Story: The Big Company in Chicago

I've been part of several Silicon Valley startups, in roles ranging from engineer to manager to advisor to CEO. The most successful was Electronic Arts, where I was an early employee at a new company that ultimately went public.

When I was growing up in the San Francisco Bay Area, however, there were no careers in video game development. The games industry did not exist.

I was not one of "the popular kids," and I was shy. More accurately, I was shy until you wanted to discuss world history or theatre or science fiction. Those were passions where I would talk your ear off. And what I loved to talk about most of all was baseball.

I'm blind in one eye, so I could never play the game at an advanced level. Whenever my homework was all done — and sometimes when it wasn't — I would play a board game called *All Star Baseball*. Usually I played by myself, managing both teams.

I grew up in a loving family with inspiring parents, but recurrent medical problems cascaded into alcoholism. For years many evenings were full of anger and conflict as my parents argued. Things got better after I started my career, but many nights as I was growing up that board game was more than a distraction or a hobby – it was the safe place I could retreat to where I could shut out an angry world.

If it were baseball season and the San Francisco Giants were playing I'd listen to the real game on the radio as I played the board game. If there were no game I'd do the radio play-by-play for myself as I narrated the action in my own board game on the desk in my room.

So what does this have to do with big dreams?

All Star Baseball was a very simple game, because trial and error had taught the designers that a more complex version didn't sell.

The round game cards for different big league players were placed on a spinner that would point to a spot that determined the outcome of the play, accurately simulating the hitting of my heroes Willie McCovey, Willie Mays and Stan Musial.

But there were no pitching cards in the game, so Juan Marichal and Nolan Ryan were no more intimidating on the mound than a rookie pitcher.

This frustrated me until at age 15 I figured out how to fix it. Calculating the probability differences, I created a second set of pitcher cards to complement the hitter cards and get far more accurate results.

I remember thinking, "I should send this design to the big game company in Chicago that publishes *All Star Baseball* and see if they want to buy it. This modification keeps the game simple but solves its greatest flaw."

But, of course, my next thought was, "I'm just a 15-year-old kid. The big company in Chicago is never going to listen to me."

So I never wrote to them.

I never tried.

Four years later in 1971, I was one of the first college students to gain unrestricted access to a mainframe computer. I started using the mathematics I'd developed at age 15 for simulating baseball in a board game to program a far more accurate computer game.

The system worked, and although I didn't know it at the time I had written the first interactive computer baseball game in the history of what became the games industry. I went on to work with Hall of Famers Earl Weaver and Tony La Russa on baseball simulation titles that bore their names and won Game of the Year awards.

Ultimately I became CEO of a company that (among other titles) published computer baseball games, a smaller version of the big company in Chicago that published *All Star Baseball*.

But the lonely 15-year-old boy had no way of knowing that all this would happen. I thought that being part of professional baseball was just another impossible dream.

I've been very, very fortunate in my career, and I'm grateful for all of that good luck.

But what if that 15-year-old version of me had sent this new version of *All Star Baseball* to the big company in Chicago?

They'd probably have sent me a "no thanks, but you're a great kid" letter without even looking at the design. They might have ignored me. They might have loved the idea and sent me a check.

But we'll never know, because I didn't try.

Once I became a professional game designer I always remembered this story. I couldn't always take financial risks. I couldn't leave a job that paid the bills.

But I resolved that the adult Don would always remember what the 15-year-old Don did not yet know:

If you believe in something there will always be some reasonable way to try to bring it to reality. There's always a way to pursue your Dream Project.

Sometimes individuals like you and me really can do better than the big companies in the big cities.

But we can't give up before we start. We have to try.

CHAPTER 4

What to Do with Your Answers

"EVERY GREAT DREAM BEGINS
WITH A DREAMER."

— Harriet Tubman, heroine of
The Underground Railroad

If you have not yet written down your answers, please go back and do so. Writing your thoughts down – even when you're the only one who'll ever read them – will produce far more insights than just answering silently to yourself in your head.

1.0.1 The Recipe for Long Term Success

I am a great believer in seeking balance in our lives. In my career as an entrepreneur I've tried to follow this recipe:

> 2 lbs. (900 grams) Personal Passion
> 1 lb. (450 grams) Common Sense
> 1 lb. (450 grams) Personal Experience
> 1 lb. (450 grams) Healthy Skepticism
> 8 oz. (225 grams) Patience
>
> *Take Passion, Personal Experience, Common Sense and Skepticism and mix liberally. Season repeatedly with patience as needed, and keep practicing new variations. Repeat as necessary.*

I'm having fun with the way I express this idea, but here's the serious thought behind it:

Personal Passion drives everything that's worth doing. Getting up every morning to go work at a job you hate really sucks. Doing work that you believe in and that you believe to be important feels like fun as well as work. And work you love is far more likely to be done well and to make you happy when you come home.

Personal experience reflects the businesses, hobbies, and interests where you have insider knowledge. A Dream Project in that space will give you advantages you won't have elsewhere.

Common Sense guides us to be logical, to look both ways before we cross the street. Common sense reminds us not be so carried away by passion that we start to do dumb things.

Healthy Skepticism stops us from being victims. When you see an ad that says, "Make a Million a Month with My Secret Formula!" your skepticism stops you from sending the scam artists your money.

I see other books proclaim, "You can quit your job, tell off your boss and become independent!" They open with stories of people who successfully did all those things. It may not be as obvious as the million-a-month scam, but it's still a trick used to sell books.

These authors never talk about people who told off their bosses and then boldly sailed into financial disaster. Your healthy skepticism reminds you to be careful with big changes in your life. My job in this book is to prepare you for the work required to plan any Dream Project, and to encourage you to do that research and preparation.

I'll also keep reminding you to retain your healthy skepticism as part of the overall process. That's what drives strong research and planning.

Patience is like salt. You need it for everything to taste right... but too much ruins the meal. A lack of patience in the planning stage can sabotage our plans. Being too patient — waiting year after year for the perfect moment to start our Dream Project — can mean we never start at all.

Balancing the "flavors" of Passion, Experience, Common Sense, Healthy Skepticism and Patience will produce a Dream Project that is uniquely well-suited to you.

The Passion-Process-Product Method. In the pages that follow I'll give you a framework for this approach, which I call "The Passion-Process-Product Method."

You'll start with your passions and develop a practical way to do work that leverages your personal strengths and talents. When it feels like you've found the right recipe for success, you'll be ready to create a product or service that inspires passion in others.

I'll share lots of advice in this book. Always remember, however, that figuring out how to balance these values in your life is a recipe only you can perfect.

1.0.2 The Meaning of "Dream Projects" & "Dream Jobs"

I wrote this book to help people from a wide variety of backgrounds launch a diverse range of projects and companies.

Here are some examples of people who could use this book and what they could do:

An engineer and a graphic designer who feel bored in their jobs at a huge telecommunications firm. They have an idea for a useful new mobile app, and they want to start a new company to build and sell it.

A successful real estate agent who finally has given himself some free time to pursue his passions. He has always wanted to write, illustrate and publish books for children, and is now ready to start the process.

A manager who feels that her company is slipping from being vital to being banal. She has a great idea for a new initiative that could open the door to new revenue streams for the firm. She doesn't want to start a new company. She wants to make her current company more successful.

Each of these examples features people who have a dream of some kind. Some of those dreams involve people striking out on their own, while others are visions for transforming the company where the person already works.

Some are full-time, others are part-time projects that someone wants to undertake.

In the pages that follow, I use the term "Dream Project" to describe what it is that you most want to do. I chose this term because it is so broad, and could refer to everything from starting a tech company that serves the whole world to starting a part-time gardening service that serves your home town.

You're the one who decides if your dream is part-time or full-time. You're the one who decides if your dream is a project or a job, and where and how you want to pursue it.

1.0.3 The Difference Between a Hobby and a Profession

It is absolutely vital to think about – and listen to your feelings about – what activities you enjoy as hobbies and which you would enjoy as your profession.

Whenever a family member has a birthday I'm usually the one who makes their favorite kind of birthday cake. I really enjoy the process.

As much as I enjoy baking birthday cakes, however, I know that if I tried to do it even part time I'd be miserable in two weeks. Starting with the fact that I don't like getting up at 3:00 or 4:00 AM every day, which is what real bakers have to do. Nobody wants day-old bread, cookies or cake.

As we go through this process together, please keep this thought in the back of your mind: what are the things I enjoy as hobbies, and what do I enjoy as my profession?

1.0.4 Three Kinds of Dream Projects

There are three major kinds of Dream Projects, each with a million variations, and it's important to know which one you're after:

The One-Person Initiative. You could be writing mystery novels, making leather purses, serving as a personal assistant to disabled seniors, or any of a million other things. The goal of the Dream Project is to build a part-time business that is fun and earns some extra money, or to earn enough to pursue the business full time.

The Small Team Dream Project. It might be anything from creating and selling a new smartphone app to opening a native plantings nursery. It may be an internal team building a new product line at an existing company. A small group of friends may work on the project part-time, or enough money may be scraped together (or budgeted by an employer) to make a go of it full time and see if the business gets off the ground.

The Investor-Funded Large Dream Project. This is the dream popularized by the American television show, "Shark Tank," and by success stories like Steve Jobs and Steve Wozniak at Apple.

I have been a part of several such companies, and worked for other founders. Despite all of the publicity when things go right, only a small percentage of such ventures are funded, and most of those companies fail.

My goal here is not to discourage you from trying this path. Just be sure to consider all three kinds of Dream Projects, since the first two categories have produced millions of success stories.

1.0.5 Some Dream Projects Aren't About Money

Making money with your Dream Project is a major theme in this book, but not all projects have profit as their primary goal. Exceptions might be:

- An insurance agent writing a book about insurance planning that can be given for free to prospective clients as part of the sales process
- A singer-songwriter recording music and making it available for download, solely to share joy and self-expression
- A grandparent self-publishing a book of family recipes to share

with close relatives and friends

If your Dream Project lies in this category there will be many sections below that you can skip, while many other questions will be highly useful.

1.0.6 Assembling the Rocket

When it comes to figuring out how to build a Dream Project, there's a lot we can learn from space scientists.

To launch a rocket a long series of decisions and commitments need to be made. They aren't done all at once, and if the engineers come up with a question they can't answer there will be delays.

As with a new rocket for the space program, there are multiple points in the planning of every Dream Project where you either discard the concept or re-commit to the idea and set about pushing ahead to the next stage.

In all of those early phases you're not "on the launch pad" and committed to doing anything. You're doing a series of self-assigned steps that may lead to the decision to launch your Dream Project.

Starting out a Dream Project (or doing the whole thing) as a part-time activity makes it easier to consider all the possibilities. If it's a good idea, the moment will arrive when you realize that you are in fact "ready to launch."

As we start this journey together and discuss your ideas, remember that we can take our time and make sure you feel good about what you're doing before we proceed to the "launching" steps that we'll reach later in this book.

1.0.7 No "Hail Mary" Plays

In American football, the game is over when the time on the clock runs out. The team with the most points at that moment wins the game

If a team is losing the game and there is only time for one more play, they have to bet everything on that one opportunity. They run one last wild, long, almost-impossible play. It's almost certain to fail, but if it succeeds they will tie or win the game.

It's called a "Hail Mary" play, because you say a prayer and hope it works, even though it will probably just make the final score worse.

I regularly see articles that seem to recommend that people in the world of business try for Hail Mary plays. They'll say something like:

Jane Hernandez started her chain of 256 flower shops by taking the last $200 in her savings account and using it to pay for a booth and flowers at her local Farmers Market. Just six years later, she's used these five powerful rules for business success to build an empire valued at over $100 million!

I'm very happy for Jane Hernandez (whose company I just made up) but in our story she got a great result from using a terrible strategy. That's as rare as winning the lottery.

Her five powerful rules for business success are probably excellent advice, but they won't enable me to turn $200 into $100 million. That's a copy-writing trick taught to marketing students, an inferred promise used to get people to buy books and magazines.

Launching your Dream Project is not about backing yourself into a corner and then desperately trying to achieve your goals with some dramatic (and usually foolish) exercise.

Launching your Dream Project is about figuring out what you deeply want to do, and then experimenting with ways that you might be able to do it. Piece by piece, you learn enough from those trials to make the most of your chance to do the kinds of work you love.

There may be a moment when you've saved up some money and decide to take a risk on a bigger experiment. But you do so when you feel you're well-prepared and coming from a position of strength.

Here's a more practical version of Jane's story that features common sense instead of desperation:

Jane Hernandez started her flower-selling business six years ago by saving up an "experimentation fund" of $1,000 to try out her ideas. Each Saturday morning she brought a different mix of flowers to her booth at her local Farmers Market. She studied the flowers that sold well at other booths, and kept charts of which flowers sold best for her.

After three months she was bringing in a profit of $500 a month. And she was having a great time doing what she loved.

She repeated the process each month as different flowers came into season. By the end of the first year she had turned her $1,000 investment into $7,500 in pre-tax profits. More importantly, almost half of that money came from her first two wedding assignments, a key market she'd need to crack.

After three years Jane was earning enough that she made the jump to making flower sales and flower arranging her full-time job, and she works from a small warehouse space near her home. She continues to love this new career.

There may not be a $100 million payoff to this Jane Hernandez tale, but it's the kind of story I've seen happen in real life, over and over again. The punchline is that the person is doing work they love and making a living at doing it. All because they launched their Dream Project.

There was no dramatic "Hail Mary" decision where Jane had to risk losing her car or home in a made-for-Hollywood gesture of self-sac-rifice.

It wasn't necessary, because Jane had saved up the money she risked and guarded that money carefully as she explored what did and did not work. She started out part-time and then made the jump to full time.

What would you do with the money if you followed Jane's strategy and saved up your own "experimentation fund?"

CHAPTER 5

Your Dream Project (1.1-1.6)

DISCUSSING QUESTION 1.1

What Dream Project or Projects have you been thinking about that inspired you to read this book?

This topic is most relevant for: Everyone

1.1.1 Focus on the Journey, Not Just the Destination

Answering the questions in this book may deepen your commitment to your Dream Project.

It's also possible that your ideas will change as a result of this process of discussing your Dream Project with yourself.

The key is to let your thinking take you where your passions and your common sense want you to go. There's nothing wrong with changing your mind as you consider something. You may rearrange your priorities and change your focus several times.

I've always liked the advice of poet Ralph Waldo Emerson, who coined the phrase, "Focus on the journey, not just the destination."

When it comes to Dream Projects, that advice is not just useful. It's critical.

Let's say that you're planning to start up a part-time business selling solid bronze sculptures you design, each representing one of the Greek gods.

If you refuse to consider any alternatives to this precise objective you can block out lots of opportunities:

Alternative Materials: The high cost of bronze and its weight might push your price point and shipping costs sky-high. By experimenting you might find that using resin instead of brass or changing to hollow casting would allow you to produce high quality works that collectors love... and that they can afford. But you'd have to be willing to do those experiments.

Alternative Content: What if another major movie based on the comic book character Thor is released? For six months you might be able to sell more statues of Norse gods than you can for those of Greece. But only if you're willing to consider changing your initial focus.

Alternative Market: Two of your designs might coincidentally resemble major historical figures from China, and your style of sculpture could be popular there. With a few changes in the character and costume designs you could sell 1,250 copies of each sculpture to a distributor at a nice profit. But you have to be open to changing the initial product market.

Examples like this remind us that by making the journey our focus, not the destination, we can have an adventure guided by research and experiments.

1.1.2 Stay Out of the Shadows

Once we get immersed in a project it's easy to lose track of the original objective. Be sure to watch out for these traps:

- We keep adding features to a simple, easy-to-use product, so it becomes a complex product that's confusing

- We try to do something that's too big, get bogged down and never ship a product or launch a service

- We have lots of written plans and beautiful slide shows, but we never actually start creating the key components of the product or service

Finishing your product, launching it and getting feedback from your initial users are the three keys that open the door for the success of your Dream Project.

If you have a clear plan and then drift off into the shadows, be ruthless about getting back on the path that leads to completing version 1.0.

DISCUSSING QUESTION 1.2

When did you first become interested in the segment, category, topic or profession that lies at the core of the Dream Project you want to do?

What parts of the Dream Project most interest you?

This topic is most relevant for: Everyone

1.2.1 Which Angles Matter Most?

I have met many people who have a deep love for books.

Some love great writing and devour every word.

Others gravitate to "coffee table" books with striking photos and illustrations.

I've worked with artists who would feel the pages of a book and tell you all about the paper that was used to print it, and how it absorbs and reflects light.

In the example for this question I suggested that someone who made garden hoses from recycled fast food containers could be interested in gardens, plastics, recycling or some combination of all three.

Which parts of your Dream Project drive your passion for the work? Does more than one interest play a part?

It's important to understand these factors, because they often reflect your greatest strengths, as well as the parts of the project where you may lose perspective.

1.2.2 Which Version of Me is Really Me?

Our lives have different phases. Our interests change. Old friend-ships fade away and new friendships are made.

Our skills grow, and with them our perspectives. We learn from our mistakes, and from our successes.

Why think back to when this Dream Project first excited you? To ask yourself the question, "Are the things that excited me back then still exciting to me now?"

Is the market opportunity for this product or service as great as when you first came up with the idea? Or have competitors already filled this niche?

Is there a twist on the old idea that would make it more relevant to an audience now?

Is this really your passion, or is it someone else's dream that you've adopted?

Give yourself time to consider these questions over the next few days while you're in the shower, driving to work or walking the dog.

DISCUSSING QUESTION 1.3

What makes you passionate about this Dream Project?

This topic is most relevant for: Everyone

1.3.1 Knowing You Can Finish What You Start

Completing any big project is hard work.

When the early excitement wears off and the finish line still looks far away, even the most dream-worthy of Dream Projects can become a grind. If you're testing an early version of your product or service and improvements come in sets of "two steps forward, one step back," it can be exhausting.

Author and marketer Seth Godin refers to this discouraging middle zone as "the dip," and that's exactly what it feels like. Everyone who creates and then sells products for a living can recognize the feeling. Godin's book, called *The Dip: A Little Book That Teaches You When to Quit (and When to Stick)*, is well worth reading.

What keeps people going until the goal is finally in sight and the positive momentum starts to build?

Passion.

What makes people continue to do quality work when they're tired and distracted?

Passion.

If you're unsure about your level of passion for this Dream Project, go back and write in more details about why you want to pursue it.

Make sure your answers are coming from a passionate fire inside you, not from an intellectual idea that you think will earn money.

If all you see is interest, not passion, what would you have to change about your Dream Project to make you excited about doing the work?

Would you need to modify this idea, or jump to a completely different Dream Project?

1.3.2 What von Moltke Understood About Business

Helmuth von Moltke was a senior German general and military strategist who was born over 200 years ago. He entered military service just after the fall of Napoleon.

Despite being separated from life today by centuries, he is the source of a famous quote that applies to business as well as it applies to armies: *"No plan survives contact with the enemy."*

Modern pundits have twisted this line into *"No business plan survives contact with customers."*

What can you do about this problem? Take advantage of it.

After working for many years on teams that build and ship products, I can tell you that von Moltke was right. We are not mind-readers. Stories about teams that connected perfectly with an audience on their first try are either lies or wonderful good luck.

I have on a few occasions "nailed it" on a product on the first try. But I have over 100 products listed on my professional credits, and direct hits are rare.

The key to success lies in taking the "pretty good" first version of a product or service and continuing to tune and improve it until you have something that's really great. That slow, painful process is how you make a product that's 900% faster (or easier, or lighter, or...) and that users prefer 5-1.

We'll discuss these ideas in depth later in this book.

DISCUSSING QUESTION 1.4

Is this your first big Dream Project?

Have you pursued lots of Dream Projects in your life?

Have you worked on many new initiatives or startups where the size of the venture was similar to your Dream Project?

This topic is most relevant for: People who are pursuing a project that feels challenging to them.

1.4.1 What Kind of a Dreamer am I?

Some of the company leaders I work with are savvy veterans of previous startups. Others are launching their first company after years of experience in other businesses. Some are recent university graduates whose school project spontaneously turned into a company.

But many people who start Dream Projects are none of the above. They're individuals with unique skills looking to do work that they love.

All of these kinds of leaders can succeed, but they face very different challenges. It's important to understand where you are in your career, and what excites you.

If you're a startup veteran, are you really excited about going back into the trenches again? Is this unique concept truly compelling to you?

If you're leading your first new venture, is it the project itself that drives your passion, or is it the opportunity to captain your own ship for the first time?

If you're a recent grad, is it this idea that motivates and drives you? Or is it the excitement of finally getting out of school and getting to work on real projects for real paychecks?

If you're an individual setting out to make money doing what you love to do, are you ready to do the extra work required to go into business? Or do you just want to spend more time at a favorite activity?

DISCUSSING QUESTION 1.5

Dreams change as we live our lives. What is a Dream Project you once really hoped to do but that is no longer as important to you?

This topic is most relevant for: Everyone

1.5.1 Learning from Our Past

I'm asking this question for a number of reasons. Here is a short list of the issues that your answer might raise:

Could the past idea, once you think about it, still be interesting to you? Could it be more interesting than what you wrote down as your Dream Project?

Why did you lose interest in this older idea? Could you lose interest in your current idea in the same way? Or is your current Dream Project fundamentally different?

Did you abandon the prior idea because of some change in your life or in the business climate? Could you come back to it now?

DISCUSSING QUESTION 1.6

What Dream Project do you think may be important to you a few years from now that isn't as important to you today?

Why will you care more about it in a few years than you do now?

This topic is most relevant for: Everyone

1.6.1 Spinning Our Own Web

We often temper our dreams with the need to be practical.

We say to ourselves, "What I'd really love to do is run a soccer school for kids, but that would never pay the bills. I'll do something else I enjoy as my Dream Project. I'll open my own real estate agency instead of working for someone else."

So the soccer school gets filed in the "10 or 20 years from now" department, even though it's the passion project. The real estate agency is interesting, but not compelling.

The title of this book is, "From Dream to Delivery." It's not "Plan your way to the next thing you think you ought to do, or that other people tell you that you should do."

We choose what we do each day, each week, each month. But our dreams tend to choose us instead of the other way around. They make themselves known via our hearts, and then our heads have to listen.

If our hypothetical Realtor were passionate about opening her own real estate office this could be an excellent choice, because she's doing something she loves and making money.

But if her passion lies with teaching soccer and she dreads going to the office each day, there might be other choices that don't involve risking her family finances:

She could cut back a few hours a week in order to start a part-time after-school soccer program.

If winter is a slow season for real estate, she could use the time to rent a gym and teach an indoor soccer camp each afternoon.

Agents spend a lot of their time looking for new clients. If she occasionally gains new client referrals from the families of her soccer students, she could devote more time to teaching soccer.

None of these cases may apply to you, and your current Dream Project may be one that you're pursuing passionately.

But if your 20-years-from-now Dream Project is more exciting than the one we've been discussing, is there a way to pursue it now instead of later?

CHAPTER 6

Projects in Places (1.7)

DISCUSSING QUESTION 1.7:

If your Dream Project is a restaurant or retail store, what will make your business stand out compared to other similar businesses in your area?

If you plan to open a store, how will it compete successfully with internet retailers?

This topic is most relevant for: Dream Projects that are stores or restaurants

1.7.1 Location-Based Businesses

Most of the principles in this book apply to Dream Projects that are housed in a shop or storefront as well as to online apps or physical products. However, businesses that have a storefront present additional challenges to the entrepreneurs who want to run them:

Marketing Experience. Being an insider is valuable in any business, but in retail it's especially important. New stores and restaurants will get some business from walk-in traffic, but almost every such business owner discovers that they have to go out and promote their company.

Attending meetings of the local Chamber of Commerce, Rotary Club and other organizations. Running (expensive) ads in print and online media without wasting money. Handing out free samples at the bus stop.

You'll read a lot about the need to go out and aggressively market your business in this book, and when you have a local audience that marketing has to be even more personal, focused and intense.

If you don't have experience in marketing a business to the local community, where could you work to learn these skills before you take the risk of starting your own business?

Restaurant Experience. If your Dream Project is to open a restaurant, have you completed culinary school or a professionally accredited restaurant management program? Have you worked in the restaurant business for several years and learned how to run both the front and the back of the house?

If you don't have that training or experience, consider if you're willing to work for someone else to learn the trade. It's the only way to know in advance if starting such a business yourself would be a Dream Project or a nightmare.

It's not enough to have one person who is a wonderful cook and another who's a wonderful host. The subtleties of cash management, ordering, food storage, pricing, prep time, designing high-quality recipes that can be made quickly even when the house is full, payroll processing, constant cleaning, training, detailed health inspections, alcoholic beverages license, liability insurance, staffing for busy and slack periods etc. are difficult to learn out of a book.

Could you enjoy collecting and selling prepared foods or pre-packaged items instead of running a kitchen?

Launching a serious challenger to major restaurants in a busy downtown or resort area might require a budget in the millions of dollars in many American cities.

That crowded area, however, might not have a specialty chocolate shop, as was the case in one busy San Francisco neighborhood. Instead of being just one more restaurant, the chocolate shop founders became the only store of their kind within a mile in any direction. You won't be surprised to hear they're doing well, and doing so without having to run their own kitchen.

Another San Francisco chef leased the small deli space inside an upscale fine food and wine store, where he limited his rotating menu to just four dishes at breakfast and eight sandwiches or soups at lunch. The small physical space kept his costs down, and the short menu kept food costs and storage needs under control. Finally, running a deli that closed at 3:00 PM meant he could spend evenings with his family.

Best of all, sales went up at the food store because of all the customers coming to buy from the deli. There's no better way to keep your rent from going up than to have your landlords make more money with you than they did without you!

Restaurants are often a family business, and once people realize how expensive it is to hire a staff they try to do as much work as possible themselves. This can lead to long, grueling hours and pressures that go home with you at night.

Working together under this kind of schedule and financial constraints can change families' lives in negative ways. It can especially impact the lives of kids whose parents both work in such a business.

If you have training and experience in dining and hospitality you have hard-won insider knowledge. How can you use that expertise to create both a successful Dream Project and an acceptable quality of life?

Local Reviews. Everyone who sells a product or service deals with user reviews in today's world of business. This book will have user reviews listed on Amazon and other websites when it's published.

For local retailers, especially restaurants, reviews can be frustrating and difficult to control. And they can have a very real impact – positive or negative — on your business.

A couple has a fight during what was supposed to be a romantic dinner out. You didn't start the fight, but your trattoria or taco shop may get a 1-star review on Yelp. Sometimes angry people that that anger out on innocent bystanders.

A busload of tourists arrives with no advance notice and suddenly your store is swamped. You have a great day at the cash register, but that night two customers, irritated by the crowd and waiting in a long line, leave you bad reviews.

Two 5-star reviews and one 1-star review add up to an average of 3.67, which won't put you into any of the "best restaurant" or "top shops" charts. It's not fair, but it's how the system works.

You can pay lots of money to companies that promise to protect your online reputation, but most of these firms serve attorneys and doctors who can afford their high fees. Some of the tactics used by the more aggressive firms (e.g. publishing counterfeit positive reviews) have backfired and lowered the client's reputation instead of helping it.

Some owners read their online reviews each day, study everything about them and use the data to make their business better. This is how any company can turn negatives into positives, though I admit that I feel bad when I read anything less than a great review.

Leases. The internet and shared work spaces have made offices less critical and expensive for many kinds of businesses, but for location-based businesses the rules have not changed.

There's an ancient cliché that says, "The three most important things for any store or restaurant are location, location and location!"

This is one cliché that remains true. Your storefront has to be located where there are lots of people with money to spend. And they have to be the right kinds of people, ones who will want to come inside and spend that money with you.

Having a door that you open to the public in the morning and lock up at night means you have to have a lease, an expense that you'll have to pay every month.

Businesses can often handle expenses that decline when things are slow and ramp up when more money is being made. A lease is the worst kind of expense, because you have to pay it every month – good or bad — or the landlord can change the locks and close your business.

That lease will be priced at a rate per square foot per month or per year. Other charges, however, can complicate things, so you need to read all the fine print and object if something doesn't look right:

- Utilities may or may not be included, and for restaurants and some retailers they can be expensive
- Trash hauling may be covered with an extra fee
- Janitorial services may be included, may be covered by a separate flat monthly fee, or may be excluded so you have to pay separately for the services you need
- Some leases require tenants to pay a prorated share of the property taxes for the building
- I've seen draft leases where landlords were trying to charge tenants for maintenance and repair expenses for the building
- Some landlords want business owners to personally "guarantee" a lease, which means being personally liable for all of the payments in the contract (don't do this!)

Resist the temptation to take a long term lease when you're starting out, and look for a spot that screams, "location, location, location!" without needing expensive remodeling (called "tenant improvements" (or "TI's"). In some cases expensive equipment, counters or other fixtures may still be present, and you can acquire the right to use it as part of the lease.

Be careful on how long a commitment you need to make in order to get such a deal. Keep an eye on all the lease terms and make sure the grand total cost per square foot isn't above market rates. We'll talk more about leases and business terms in a later chapter.

Remember, if your space is small and your tables or aisles are usually full of people, everyone assumes you're a great place.

If you're serving twice as many guests but the room is half empty, walk-ins may turn around and walk out.

1.7.2 Opening a Store

If your Dream Project is to open a store, you have one huge and critical question you need to answer:

Why will people buy from me instead of just ordering from Amazon and having free delivery within 48 hours?

To come up with a good answer to this question you'll need to have a specialty, a unique expertise, or a theme or style to your "brick and mortar" business that cannot be reproduced by online competitors.

Here are some examples I've seen in our local community:

Be a Destination, Not a Store. A small, three-outlet San Francisco bookstore chain called Book Passage offers a steady stream of author appearances and readings at each of their stores. These events draw people from around the area and turn the stores into social gathering points where people meet and talk with old and new friends about shared interests.

Amazon can't re-create this experience without opening their own physical store in your town. The smaller your neighborhood or city, the less likely it is that they'll ever do so.

Many booksellers have used this "café and events" strategy, but there is no shortage of cafes so this can make things worse instead of better. Making a shop a destination requires holding high quality events most nights of the week, not just hosting a local book club once or twice.

It's a lot of extra work, and that will be true of almost any retail strategy that empowers you to compete successfully with Amazon.

Sell something that's best when it's super-fresh. You can buy donuts, flowers and tomatoes online, but they won't be fresh like the ones at a specialty bakery, flower shop or market.

You may have a booth at the local farmer's market or a bakery and café with big ovens in the back. If what you produce is super-fresh – and super-good – your customers aren't going to be checking out Amazon to see if their prices are better.

Sell something where people want to personally pick out the exact item they buy. Watch how people buy mushrooms or tomatoes or bananas in the grocery store and you'll see many shoppers who peruse carefully before choosing the precise item or bunch that they want.

This can also extend to craft items as diverse as hand-painted holiday ornaments, hand-carved pecky cedar wooden bowls, and flower arrangements.

Location (again), Location, Location. It isn't enough to have a location where there's lots of foot traffic. If you put a farm equipment store in Times Square in New York City you'd see lots of people walking outside your windows... but you wouldn't sell very many tractors.

I mentioned the small San Francisco area chain Book Passage above. Two of their three bookstores are adjacent to ferry terminals and the third is a half mile from another such facility. Airports are crowded with book stores for bored passengers, but Book Passage is the only book store serving ferry passengers who need something to read on their trip.

Historical locations. If lease rates are reasonable, having a store or restaurant in an historic building or neighborhood will draw visitors that would never pay attention to a row of concrete storefronts built in 1982. Unfortunately, landlords are also aware of these patterns and are prone to overcharge per square foot, which erases the benefit to the retailer.

"Click and Mortar" retailing. If you're selling something that customers can't buy on Amazon, could you use Amazon, eBay, Etsy, Square, WooCommerce or some other systems to sell your products online? The specialty chocolates shop I mentioned above created custom-boxed mixes of chocolates from different high-end suppliers, which during holiday periods were high-margin top-sellers.

Craft and Culture (1.8-1.9)

DISCUSSING QUESTION 1.8:

How specific is your vision of your Dream Project?

Is there a way to take your product idea and expand the concept into additional products or services that can be introduced if the first effort is a success?

This topic is most relevant for: Everyone

1.8.1 Is It a Product or a Company?

Very few products and services remain popular and profitable for more than a few years. That's why even highly successful companies like Apple, Google, Facebook and Amazon are continually trying out new ideas.

It isn't just a quest for additional revenue. These companies know that they continually need to offset the inevitable revenue decline of older products.

Investors often tell CEO's after a pitch, "You have a product, not a company."

What they're saying is, "You have one good idea. But when that strong product eventually fades, there's no plan for what happens next. Your success may last for a few months or a few years. But we only invest in long-term, sustained value."

Products have life cycles. They are born, they grow, they start to age and eventually they die. If your plan yields just one product, consider how you could turn it into a product line.

Here's another reason why we have to keep thinking of new ideas, twists and products: big rivals can and will copy *your* features into *their* product with their own added improvements.

They will (usually) carefully ensure that they do not infringe on patents, trademarks or copyrights, and when they do so it's entirely within the law.

Business strategists refer to this when they say, "New companies have to develop innovations that are defensible."

Products have to be so different that new competitors can't make subtle changes to avoid narrowly defined patents. If your product is completely unique, the patent for it can be broader and harder to circumvent.

Brand positioning has to be so unique that your product without your logo doesn't attract buyers. I could spend millions making a beautifully crafted cartoon about a mouse with big ears, but it could never challenge Mickey Mouse in marketing power.

How could you make your Dream Project so unique or iconic that it's defensible?

What line extensions or completely new products could you pencil in now as possible downstream introductions to give you new revenue streams as your first product matures?

DISCUSSING QUESTION 1.9

Is it the craft involved in the making of your Dream Project that interests you?

Or is it the raw material that is used to create a product or the unique methodology used to perform a service?

Or do you take joy in using the finished product and watching others use it?

Some combination of the above choices?

This topic is most relevant for: Everyone

1.9.1 The Recipe or the Ingredients?

How can you create multiple products without turning your Dream Project into a nightmare?

We want to start from your personal passions, since that's the key to producing great new products. For example:

If the craftsmanship in hand-made leather purses is your passion, instead of making the same purses year after year, you could add new designs and "retire" others. If other designers developed similar styles they'd be focused on your old ideas, not your new ones.

If you love fine leather in any form, you could expand your line of high quality purses into briefcases, luggage, leather jackets and other clothing.

A master knife sharpener could team with a local chef to offer combined classes in cooking and knife skills. The events would bring in new revenue and new customers, and differentiate each artisan from her competition.

The owner of a dog kennel could add dog training services, or expand their grooming options to position it as a canine spa. They could offer special rates for day-visitor dogs for customers with long work schedules.

Keep thinking of how these follow-on products or services could be adapted to your Dream Project.

1.9.2 The Post-Disruption Economy

There are lots of articles about "the Disruption Economy," the new patterns and methods in business since online apps starting gobbling market share in every segment.

We've lived through multiple eras during a very short number of years:

"The traditional way of doing things," where retail stores, newspapers, software publishers, record companies and television networks did not face online competition.

"The coming of Disruption," when Apple's smartphones and Google's search engine fueled growth for Amazon, Facebook, Netflix, eBay, Spotify, Uber and other companies that improved on old ways of doing business.

"The Post-Disruption Economy," where it's now clear that the new businesses and their audiences have ousted the traditional leaders in each category.

I use the term "Post-Disruption Economy" to say that the battle is over. The genii aren't going back in their bottles. The old world is not returning.

If you consciously decide to operate as a citizen of that new, forever-changed world, you'll have an advantage in every phase of your business.

1.9.3 K.I.S.S.

The old saying, "Keep it simple, stupid!" (usually abbreviated as K.I.S.S.) applies intensely to the process of building a Dream Project, especially if this is the first time you've started a business. This issue comes in multiple flavors:

Start with the concept of a micro-business. Endless articles about Steve Jobs and Elon Musk keep encouraging us to try to start huge global companies. If you wanted to build a treehouse for your daughter, would you start with the blueprints for Hearst Castle?

Step one in the creation of any project is to picture a micro-business, typically a one-person company or a very small team. It won't work for every Dream Project, but the concept of trying to "start micro" helps us focus on building a small but solid foundation.

It's worth noting that Muhammad Yunus, an entrepreneur from Bangladesh, won the Nobel Peace Prize in 2006 for developing the concept of micro-businesses. They made bank loans available to small farmers for the first time by treating them as micro-businesses, while all other banks rejected them for not being big.

Start with a simple product or service. Teams get in trouble when they envision big projects like "create personality profiles of everyone in the US to predict their business and personal travel behaviors..." Teams that start with grandiose visions that would challenge a big company often never ship their Dream Project at all.

Make your initial mission as simple and small as you can while still meeting the need you'll address in the marketplace. Then you can leverage what you learned on the initial product to grow your business to the next stage.

Complexity creep. For Dream Projects that are software programs or services it's easy to keep inventing new "bonus features." All too often, though, those new ideas don't justify interrupting the truly important, highest priority work. Resist the temptation to divert your plans to add anything less than a compelling feature or correct an important shortcoming.

Keep doing your best work. A critical skill for an entrepreneur is to discipline yourself to do your very best work every day. I know that if I worked late last night I can walk into the office feeling tired and worn down.

The standard we have to meet in order to succeed does not lower itself when we're tired or upset. That's why, as hard as it is, we have to keep insisting that we and our team keep aiming high on the quality scale in everything we do.

My mother was a professional illustrator and painter, and she learned about these issues of focus and distraction through her work. She told me the following fable that relates to how we challenge ourselves in our careers.

1.9.4 The Juggler and the Fifth Ball

Once upon a time, my mother told me, there was a young man who learned how to juggle. His father taught him to keep three balls in the air at once and he amazed everyone in his little village.

The boy moved to the big city and a local street performer taught him how to juggle four balls. It was difficult, but the young man made steady progress.

One day the young man asked his mentor to teach him how to juggle five balls.

The grizzled old man shook his head. "You are not yet ready," he told him. "You must master four balls before you juggle five. Do not stop when you achieve success. Seek mastery."

The boy protested, "I'm getting better every week! I know I can do it!"

Against his better judgment, the mentor relented. He taught the boy the techniques for keeping five balls in the air. The young man practiced hour after hour, and after just a few days he kept all five going while the old man counted to ten.

The wrinkled juggler nodded his approval.

That weekend, the mentor and the student performed together in the town square. The young man juggled four balls in the air, earning applause from the crowd.

Although the old man had forbidden him to do so, the boy suddenly pulled a fifth ball from his pocket and kept all five balls flying with his graceful movements. The crowd started to cheer, but then something went wrong.

A ball tipped off the boy's fingertips and fell towards the cobblestones. He lunged for it and two more balls eluded him. Soon all five balls had rolled away in all directions.

The crowd wandered away. Soon the old performer and the boy stood all alone in the empty plaza.

"I'm sorry, sir," the boy told his mentor. "I should have waited to try to juggle five balls at a time in public."

The old man smiled. "It's all right, son. I knew that this would happen. But I wanted you to learn the most important lesson I could ever teach you."

"What's that, sir?" the boy asked.

The old juggler pointed to the balls scattered around the town square. "That's the lesson," he said. "When you reach for one too many of anything, you don't just drop that one. You drop everything else you were juggling before you went too far."

CHAPTER 8

Your Project Vision (1.10–1.11)

How would you describe your Dream Project to a stranger in just one sentence that would fascinate him or her?

How will your Dream Project draw attention in a crowded market?

Is this a new idea, or are you improving on a product or service that already exists?

This topic is most relevant for: Everyone

1.10.1 The Great One-Liner

This kind of statement is called a "high concept" or "the x-factor" in some media businesses, or a "positioning statement" in other segments. It may also just be called "the one-line pitch."

Here are some examples to inspire you (written in my words, not those of the original marketers):

For the Apple iPhone: "A cell phone with a built-in computer, camera, iPod and touch-screen so you can have voice and video calls, access the Internet and listen to music anywhere."

It's hard to remember that just twelve years ago the biggest phone screen was only about two inches wide, and you couldn't watch video or search the web.

Google: "A search engine that pre-screens websites for quality so you don't have to wade through pages of junk."

We take this for granted now, but before Google a web search turned up lots of pages filled with useless links designed to fool search engines so they could sell ads.

Tesla: "A luxury-class electric vehicle that accelerates like a sports car and has a range of over 200 miles."

PayPal: "Makes paying for items on the Internet easier and more secure than using a credit card."

Amazon: "Buy almost anything at just one website and have it delivered for free within 48 hours."

Writing one sentence may seem simple, but I can tell you from experience that honing your one-sentence summary to perfection is something that takes a lot of editing, thinking, re-drafting and hair-pulling.

1.10.2 The Loud Party

Here's an exercise I use to teach this process:

Imagine you're at a party, and that you're single. The music is loud, so you have to raise your voice and you don't hear every word of what people are saying.

A friend introduces you to one of the most attractive people you've ever met. You control the urge to stammer awkwardly when you say hello. The new person says, "I hear you're working on a really interesting project! What is it?"

At that moment someone across the room calls out to your new friend. He or she waves back and says, "Be there in a moment!" Then they turn back to hear your answer to their question.

You have just one sentence in which to describe your Dream Project in a way that will impress this gorgeous person and make them want to circle back to talk with you. The room is loud, and their friend is waiting impatiently.

What do you say in just a few very clear words to make your project – and you – sound fascinating?

1.10.3 Your Best Friend Who Lives Next Door

As I've noted, most discussions of the business side of Dream Projects will be found in the second half of this book.

But there's one business topic I want to bring up early on. It's so central to the success of your project that you'll want to start thinking about it in the earliest stages of your planning.

Some really lucky kids live next door to their best friend. They go to school together, go to soccer practice on the same team and double date to the junior prom.

No matter how fascinating your answer to "How will your Dream Project draw attention in a crowded market?" may sound, you need to recognize that you need "a best friend next door," too.

Hint: It will be the person who leads the marketing for your Dream Project. Marketing is the discipline that has to work hand-in-hand with product development through every step of the process.

If I just published this book and did nothing else to promote it I know what would happen. The mighty power of Amazon, Barnes &

Noble and Ingram would produce almost no sales at all, because this book would be lost in a sea of other books.

As small business entrepreneurs we are often responsible for our own marketing. We are faced with two choices:

- Spend long hours doing online research to learn what other small businesses have done to get their products noticed. Go to Meetups, conferences, etc. to meet others and learn from them. Or...

- Find and work with one or more people who have experience in successfully promoting new products without risking a lot of money.

As we discuss the next few questions in this section I'll raise a number of the key steps and issues involved in marketing to help you plan for both "sides" of the process.

Which brings us to The Elephant in the Room for those of us whose Dream Projects' success hinges on the power of our software.

1.10.4 The Elephant in the Room: User Discovery

There are over three million active apps in the iOS App Store alone as of this writing. Google Play's store has 2.75 million apps. There are over ten million websites and the number is growing rapidly.

But for Dream Projects based on the Internet – or those that need to use the Internet to reach their customers — there's an "Elephant in the Room," a problem so big that it cannot be ignored but that many people never talk about.

These statistics, with their story of millions of apps competing for attention, tell us that this exciting wave of opportunity and innovation brings with it major new problems. They all fit under the heading of "User Discovery."

We may work for months or even years to reach the point where we're ready to share our vision for our Dream Project, this unique piece of ourselves that we want the world to love.

All too often, however, when we launch those Dream Projects into the world something very frustrating happens.

No one has heard about the product. Because no one has heard of it, no one has tried the product. Because no one has tried it, no one can tell their friends about the product.

It just sits there in your online store or in the Apple or Android marketplace. You check it every half hour and nothing changes. No sales. Day after day. No sales.

It's a terrible feeling.

Most new Indie apps and websites today never find a significant audience and never make much money, if any at all.

Most new Indie apps and websites today are created without a real marketing plan, which is one (but not the only) reason why they never make much money.

The big publishers, who count their annual revenues in the billions of dollars, already have the email addresses of millions of users. They control the ad banners in their current products and have the big budgets needed to buy ads everywhere else.

For small startups there is no ready-made legion of existing users to whom we can promote our new products. There are no big marketing budgets. When a team ships its first app or launches its website it's like moving to a new town and starting classes mid-semester at a huge new school. You're surrounded by a sea of faces but no one knows or notices you.

There is no easy recipe for solving this problem of User Discovery, even if you're paired up with an excellent marketer. I share a lot of experiences and suggestions in the pages that follow, but I can't tell you how to guarantee success.

I can, however, tell you how to guarantee failure.

If you ship a product that is *not* compelling and useful, that you have *not* tuned so it is easy to learn and exciting to use, you're virtually certain to fail. You'll make very little money.

Building a really great product or service opens the door to success but does not guarantee it. Building anything less than a great product is a waste of time.

So why do we even try? When the odds are so tough, why do so many people still create new websites and apps? Why do people open new shops and stores when local consumers are loyal customers of existing places?

Because it's work we love to do. We know that *some* great products from new teams will find ways to get noticed and make money. Some of them will make a lot of money.

I'm working on a new product in parallel to writing this book. I don't share the statistics above to discourage you.

I share them so you go into the process with your eyes open and you're ready to manage the risks as well as the rewards. So you're ready to embrace strong marketing and strong marketers.

If you're building a new website or app because you've been told it's a relatively easy way to make good money, whoever told you this was misinformed... or lying.

If you're building a new website or app because it's what you love to do and you're out to create a great product, I'm here to help.

If you're with me, let's keep going.

1.10.5 The Advantages of Small Companies

Big corporations have many advantages, but there are key advantages for small startups, too.

Short Approval Chains. I once worked with a software publisher where it took 23 different signoffs to approve the marketing materials for a product. You can imagine how long it took to complete that step on each title!

Small teams can accomplish as much going out to lunch as a big company can accomplish in a month with 22 meetings.

Deeper Commitment. Small startup teams have a lot more freedom of action, a lot more individual impact on the product and many more potential rewards than the teams at the big corporations. They're not just doing a job and picking up a paycheck, they're doing work in which they deeply believe.

Sharp Focus. Managing one product makes everyone focus on the details. A big company with a catalog of 136 products lacks that same across-the-board attention to detail that makes customers admire a company.

Freedom to Do Something New. Big companies have to make big profits every quarter and every year in order to maintain and grow their stock price. They can't do projects that feel risky because stock analysts value predictable revenue and profits. Small teams operate under none of these restrictions, which is why they're the source of so much of our technical and creative innovation.

Lower Costs. Big corporations have long term leases for large office complexes. Small teams can work in less expensive settings without long term commitments.

Fast Reaction Times. If all five people in a company work together in one room and a product is constantly being returned to stores, they'll keep attacking the problem until they find a way to fix it.

If someone in a large company notices the returns, however, questions arise:

- "Will my manager be angry instead of grateful if I share this when we're all supposed to be focused on next year's budget?"
- "If I try to solve the problem will I waste a lot of time without getting anyone to do anything?"
- "I'm in operations and this is a design problem. Will anyone even listen to me?"
- "Is there a senior exec who will be embarrassed and angry if I try to fix this?"

Researcher and analyst Dr. Chris Argyris of Harvard Business School wrote a landmark article about this issue, *Double Loop Learning in Organizations* (which you can find online via Google). He pointed out that large organizations have layers of resistance to receiving bad news.

Each manager in the chain considers whether there will be a negative backlash to addressing the issue. The initial report of "40% of the widgets we sell are being returned!" is diluted at each layer. If it reaches the top at all the message is, "We need to refine the widget marketing materials to clarify our positioning."

If you don't hear about problems you can't try to fix them, and small teams excel at this important skill.

1.10.6 The Two Acceptable Market Positions

Years ago I worked at Electronic Arts, which even in its infancy had an all-star marketing team. Our CEO, Trip Hawkins, had been Director of Marketing for Apple, starting there not long after Steve Jobs and Steve Wozniak launched the flagship Apple II personal computer.

Hawkins,, Marketing VP Bing Gordon (now a partner at VC firm

Kleiner Perkins) and his Marketing teammates David Grady and Stan Roach all joined with us in Product Development to operate informally as a single team, debating issues in a climate remarkably free of politics and ego.

All of these guys are brilliant, and they taught me many important business lessons. One of them is especially critical:

There are only two acceptable market positions for a product:

- First
- Best

If you're the first successful product in the marketplace, you define the rules. Like Google ("I'll just Google that and find the answer!"), your brand is the name consumers use for the entire category, not just the product. That makes it harder for competitors to persuade customers to leave you and buy from someone else.

If you're the best product in a category, you stand out. Any buyer looking for the highest quality is likely to go to you. New and recurring sales come to you the same way that water flows downhill.

But what if both those positions are already taken? What if there's already a First and already a Best in your chosen market?

The classic "formula" for creating new product categories – where there are no entrenched leaders — is to cross-breed existing brands. If I judge a pitch competition I may hear two or three of these hybrid messages in one night.

Saying "the style of Ferrari mixed with the power of Cuisinart!" does not mean your team can design things as well as Ferrari, nor manufacture them as well as Cuisinart.

Gasoline-engine food processing is not a step forward for consumers.

This "hybrid" technique can be effective, but beware of ideas that produce good slogans and bad products.

1.10.7 New and Improved!

Invading an existing category by creating a dramatically different new product can be a great way to take that "best" position in your segment. Cell phones with screens existed before Apple introduced the iPhone, but everyone forgot about them once they saw Steve Jobs demo its dramatic new features.

But not all improvements on old ideas are that dramatic. I often hear entrepreneurs say things like these (fictional) examples:

"We've developed a social network that links friends as effectively as Facebook, but is encrypted and fanatically protects users' privacy!"

"We've designed a new messaging service that's faster than Twitter and has far fewer restrictions!"

"We're like Zappos, but we only sell really comfortable shoes!"

Let's look at the "improvements" promised by our sample entrepreneurs:

"We've developed a social network that links friends as effectively as Facebook, but is encrypted.,.."

It's too late to invent a social network that's better than Facebook. Every potential customer knows that all their friends are already on Facebook, so even a "better" network can't pull them away.

"We've designed a new messaging service that's faster than Twitter ..."

You can follow millions of different people on Twitter. You're not going to go someplace "a little better" that has a tiny fraction of the content.

"We're like Zappos, but we only sell really comfortable shoes!"

Zappos has hundreds of varieties of really comfortable shoes, legendary service and millions of happy repeat customers. Those users have no reason to look for another online shoe store.

If your Dream Project feels like it's a little bit better than existing products, what could you do to make it dramatically better?

1.10.8 The Blue Ocean and the Green Swamp

Every few years a new best-seller comes along that tells us about better ways for startups to innovate.

These books often have real value, and in fact I refer to several of them in this volume. But their simple terminology can hide traps, even as they unlock treasure.

One such book is *Blue Ocean Strategy* by W. Chan Kim and Renee Mauborgne. The authors point out ways in which companies produced products that were so unique, so different that they created entirely new categories. Instead of trying to be better than existing competitors, they chose segments where they had no existing competitors.

One of the "Blue Ocean" examples is the Apple iPhone, which changed the definition of "phone" in the first year after it was introduced and helped make Apple the largest company in the world.

Another well-known example comes from the games industry. In the mid-2000's Sony and Microsoft were locked in an ongoing battle to produce the most sophisticated video game console, designed around complex hand controllers to serve the most discriminating players.

Nintendo realized that their rivals were so focused on the high-end audience that an even larger audience was not being served. People who liked playing video games but lacked the time or interest to play for many hours every week were being left behind.

So Nintendo produced a new system called (improbably and perhaps inexplicably) the Wii. Instead of using controllers covered with buttons it let you move a smaller, lighter remote in the air, so to play golf you swung the controller like a golf club. It had simpler graphics, just a few buttons, and cost far less than its rivals.

And for over two years the Wii confounded Sony and Microsoft by outselling their sophisticated game consoles, forcing them to add the same functionality to their machines. The Wii was a huge surprise hit.

With these great examples of brilliant Blue Ocean strategies, why did I mention a Green Swamp?

Let's say that I'm going to open a new restaurant. I'm all excited as I tell you about my brilliant Blue Ocean idea. My restaurant will have:

- No salads on the menu. Everyone has salads.
- No burgers. Fast food places have burgers.
- No sandwiches or pizza, default lunches for many people. Same for seafood, noodles and soups.
- No fatty foods like bacon or sausages or deli meats, no eggs, no sweet breakfast dishes or desserts.
- Nothing Italian, Thai, French, Indian, Japanese, etc. because those niches are saturated.

This is a Blue Ocean strategy, because my restaurant is not like any other restaurant. But this approach forgets a key fact:

Making a small audience very happy with any product or service doesn't work if you don't earn enough money to keep the business operating.

My hypothetical restaurant would be great for the small audience that likes my unique menu and original recipes, but it probably won't draw enough customers. Soon I'd have to close the business.

Blue Ocean products serve large groups of users that were being ignored or forgotten by existing companies. Green Swamp products serve small groups that will generate relatively little revenue, and they are usually fatal to the startups that produce them.

1.10.9 New Kinds of Shelf Space

Later in this book I'll discuss at length the issues you'll face if your Dream Project is a product you plan to sell in stores. But such businesses aren't always as different from online startups as we might think.

There are lessons that physical goods can learn from their online cousins. Let's frame the discussion with some traditional business terms.

As you sell more and more of a physical product and buy components in larger quantities, the cost of each unit goes down. The one millionth light bulb might cost you 40% less than the first one that rolls off your assembly line. This is referred to as the "incremental cost per unit."

Unlike physical products, you can sell a million additional copies of an app, and each one after the first will be almost free. You may spend millions producing that first great copy of your app, but the incremental cost per unit for the second copy is almost nothing.

Smartphone apps and reference websites are marketed in an environment where "shelf space is infinite."

When shelf space is infinite, the market becomes supercrowded. It isn't hard to get your product into these new kinds of online stores. It's incredibly hard, however, to get your product noticed.

This explains why we've spent lots of time in this section talking about how you spread the word about your great new product and inspire people to try it out.

But new technology also offers some of these dramatic new opportunities to physical goods as well as online products.

Items that are small enough and light enough to ship at acceptable costs can actually benefit from Amazon's disruptive technology and business model.

Let's say that your Dream Project is bottling and selling your grandmother's fabulous barbecue sauce.

25 years ago there might have been three or four barbecue sauces in any given supermarket. Apart from some small stores in your home town, you'd have had a hard time getting grandma's barbecue sauce onto the shelves. A handful of mass market brands from big companies controlled the shelf space.

But what does "mass market" mean? It means a product that is intended to sell to millions and millions of people. A mass market barbecue sauce can't be too spicy or too chunky or too different from what we're all used to tasting. You can have vanilla, chocolate or chocolate chip ice cream but not mint pecan flavor. Pecan mint isn't popular enough to appeal to millions of people.

The more unusual and unique your product, the lower its potential to become mass market.

Two changes have taken place in recent years that have opened new opportunities for entrepreneurs.

First of all, retailers discovered that some customers would pay more for higher quality, less generic items. Those higher prices created opportunities for new companies to produce variations on the plain-mass-market standards.

In today's supermarkets you might find ten different barbecue sauces. Some will be extra spicy, with flames bursting from the letters on their logos. Others might claim to perfectly recreate the authentic local flavors of Kansas City, St. Louis, Memphis, South Carolina, Louisiana, Texas, Georgia or Alabama. Still others might tout being organic, sugar-free or no-artificial-ingredients.

Yours might just say, "Made from our secret family recipe!"

But if you think like an app or website company, you don't have to be one of those ten brands on the shelf to build your business.

When I went to Amazon.com and typed in "barbecue sauce" this morning, the computer quickly brought up a full page of choices. And another page. And another.

When I got to 180 different barbecue sauces I stopped counting.

With the almost-infinite shelf space of Amazon and other online retailers, a low-shipping-cost item can have several different custom recipes, each precisely tuned for different tastes.

Separate sauces for pork, beef, lamb and salmon? No problem.

Low-sodium sauces in the five most popular regional styles? All five can easily appear on the "shelf."

There's one more advantage to the online shelf that you don't get with the brick and mortar store: subscriptions. If a customer's family goes through one bottle of barbecue sauce each month, they can set up an automatic re-order that will ship every 30 days.

If your grandma's sauce is the one the subscriber chooses, you get more than the regularly repeating sales. You also know that your competitors on the physical shelf are not getting the sale, because with your auto-shipped product arriving on time each month they have no reason to go shopping elsewhere for barbecue sauce. You're not just locking in your repeat sales. You're also locking your competitors out.

It's important to remember that all the issues we'll discuss later about health department certifications, inventory costs, warehousing costs, customer returns, etc. still apply to physical goods. These are intrinsically different business models than the app and web companies I'm comparing them to.

But if your Dream Project is to sell grandma's barbecue sauce, you have more paths to success today than your mother or grandmother ever had.

App developers are often told, "to draw users you have to specialize in a single valuable service, customize your app for different kinds of users, and find ways to personalize the relationship by allowing people to post photos or decorate their personal pages."

How can you apply these principles of "specialize, customize and personalize" to make your product a success?

If you haven't already done so, skip back a few pages to where we first started discussing this question. Read through the advice for apps and websites, and picture how you could use those same attitudes and approaches to sell on Amazon and other online stores.

It's a crowded space, but the opportunities are there if you have the right Dream Project and you market it in the right way.

DISCUSSING QUESTION 1.11:

What are the three most important features of your Dream Project that will make someone want to buy your product or service?

This topic is most relevant for: Everyone

1.11.1 After the One-Liner

The one-line description is designed to make your Dream Project appeal to people in two important ways: logically and emotionally.

In the words of Bill Reichert of Garage Ventures, we're going for the "Wow!" factor. The one-line description tries to capture all that "Wow!" in just a few words.

Once we have people's attention with that one sentence, we need to keep them focused on what we're saying. After the drama of a "Wow!" statement, the best way to keep their interest is with facts.

Look back at the three features you listed for your Dream Project. Are they the three things that are most likely to make someone want to buy your product or use your service?

Do they make you stand out as the very best product in your segment? Or as the first product of its kind, a pioneering invention that creates a new segment?

Here's an exercise that I have used a number of times to help refine my thinking on these issues:

Ask friends or associates who are familiar with your Dream Project to tell you what they think are the three biggest product features you should list on your website.

You may give them a list of ten potential important features, but don't tell them in advance which ones you think you should emphasize.

If you're like me, you'll get some very different answers from the ones you chose all by yourself. Sometimes I stick to my own ideas, other times I recognize the input is on target. Either way, the exercise is valuable.

CHAPTER 9

Your Project's Audience (1.12-1.13)

DISCUSSING QUESTION 1.12:

One of the first people to use your product or service has lunch with a friend. What do they say to the friend about their experience with your product?

This topic is most appropriate for: Everyone

1.12.1 It's Not Just What People Think

As innovators we are anxious to hear what people think about our new product or service.

What's actually most important, however, is how people *feel* after they try it.

Author Nir Eyal (who is a great speaker if you ever get the chance to see one of his sessions) has a great book called *Hooked: How to Build Habit-Forming Products.* He discusses how our brains do not start with logic. We do not think, "This is an excellent breakfast cereal. I've decided I like it a lot."

What researchers have found is that we have an emotional reaction to the smell, appearance, taste and texture of the cereal. We spontaneously harvest the feedback from all of our senses and mix them all into an emotion.

Then, with the emotion already defined, our brains step in and start trying to explain the emotional decision that has already been made. "I really like this cereal," the brain says. "It smells like cinnamon and it has a crunchy texture. And the box says it has 5 grams of fiber and it still tastes good with only 8 grams of sugar."

In other words, our brains try to make us feel like we're being logical, but in reality it's the emotions that control much of what we do.

Our brain can also contradict feelings when it comes to products. I taste the cereal and love it, but then see that one bowl in the morning will cost me 900 calories. As much as I love the flavor, I now hate the cereal.

But wait! "Hate the cereal" is also an emotion! And it's one of the emotions we most want to avoid in our customers.

After you make a list ranking the key features for your product or service (and those for your key competitors), take the process one step farther and look at how people *feel* after they use the product.

In some cases multiple features might each drive a separate emotion: "The car was fun to drive because it accelerated so well, and I even loved waiting at stoplights because the sound system was so great."

1.12.2 Start with the Heart

When you're looking for customer feedback, always start by asking the "how do you feel" questions. Don't move on to "What do you think?" until all the questions about emotions have been answered.

Researchers found that discussing opinions can "erase" our memories of feelings as we make that transition from emotional reaction to logical self-explanation.

We want to record as many of those feelings as they remember before we switch gears to the opinions.

DISCUSSING QUESTION 1.13:

What kinds of people will want to buy your product or service? What do your most important target customers have in common with each other?

This topic is most relevant for: Everyone

1.13.1 Looking Past the Mirror

For years we would talk about this topic as "Audience segmentation," "Target markets and customers," and similar terms. In the last few years the people working on Lean Startups have started calling it "Product-Market Fit."

Whatever you call it, the process is vital to our success.

I typically see three kinds of teams when I work with startups:

The team driven by a product vision. They're building something they'd love to use themselves, and they think that lots of other people will want to use it, too.

The team driven by an opportunity vision. They're building something that's so superior or so unique that they think that many people will want to use it. They may or may not enjoy using the product themselves, but they think that other people will rush to pay for it.

The individual or team driven by an artistic vision. Painter or glass-blower, clothing designer or sculptor, game developer or novelist, they all have a vision for something they're proud to make. They hope and theorize that other people will want to own the works that they produce, but they're driven at least in part by an internal artistic compass rather than a focus on making the most money on sales.

Each of these styles of product vision is valid and has its advantages. But each also has its pitfalls:

- The team building something they'd personally love to own or use may be so focused on their own tastes that they miss the mark with the general public
- The team trying to please a target customer can never deeply understand the user experience in the same way as someone who is a member of that target audience
- Artistic visions are by definition driven by the internal standards of the creative team. They may or may not resonate with others, and are the least likely to earn money for their creators

As you look at the answer you wrote down about the audience that will love your Dream Project, ask yourself this question: Have you researched what kinds of people respond best to your product? Have you investigated how many such people are out there in the world?

Are there other groups, other demographics that might be interested in your Dream Project whom you have not yet considered? How could you reach those additional potential customers?

1.13.2 Lessons from Great Marketers

Whenever I think about these issues I remember two secrets of great marketing that I was taught many years ago:

Pick a Person. When we try to picture a million people who might like out Dream Project, there aren't any faces in the image. Many kinds of products and services have "targetable audiences" of millions of people, but we wouldn't recognize any of them on the street.

I was taught that what we need to do is to picture just one person. If your friend Amy would use and love the Dream Project you're building, then picture Amy when you're thinking about your audience. Go so far as to put her picture on the side of your computer, to remind yourself of who your audience is.

It's a lot easier to discuss, "Would Amy like this feature?" than it is to discuss, "Would millions of people all over the world like this feature?"

This approach gives you a concrete goal instead of a fuzzy one.

Practice the Most Critical Skill. I was taught that the number one skill in marketing isn't being a great communicator or a great strategist.

The most valuable skill in marketing is being a great listener.

Great marketers won't just compile lists of features and specifications for competition's products. They'll go onto social media sites to read what people are saying. They'll read all of the competitors' forums and their Amazon review pages. They'll do deep searches on consumer or business websites.

Great marketers will sit silently and watch the users who first get to experience your Dream Project. They'll watch people use competitors' products the same way.

If consumers discuss the product as they use it, the marketers won't respond or comment. They'll just sit and listen to what people say about their experience and their feelings.

I always want to explain, to clarify, to help those first consumers.

But I know from working with great marketers that the most valuable skill is to keep my mouth shut and be a great listener.

1.13.3 Social Media Influencers

The emergence of popular celebrities, bloggers and social media stars as "influencers" is a major trend of the last few years.

The phenomenon has changed the face of marketing for fashion, cosmetics, music, software, games and many other categories. A sizable number of previously-unknown individuals have 10,000 or more followers who regularly read their Twitter feeds or watch their live or recorded video streams, and a handful of leading voices have millions of followers.

A Google search on "top beauty influencers," "top tech influencers," "top marketing influencers" and the influencers for your product or service category will give you lots of examples.

Other, even larger media influencers are reality, music, sports, film or television stars who may have millions of Facebook, Instagram, Twitter or YouTube followers. Some of the most visible current examples are Oprah Winfrey, Ellen DeGeneres and the Kardashians, who have leveraged their (very different) television shows into large endorsement and branding businesses.

Top musicians and groups now use YouTube, Vimeo and other channels the way that their predecessors used MTV and VH-1 in the 1980's, driving concert ticket and record sales as well as earning advertising revenue. As of this writing, Justin Bieber, Ed Sheeran, Eminem, Katy Perry, Taylor Swift and Rihanna all have over 30 million YouTube followers.

Social media newcomer or established star, if one of these influencers discusses your dream project online and tells their audience they like it, thousands of people – or hundreds of thousands of people – may see it. That's a big boost for your dream project.

Getting attention from superstars is often a matter of luck, but everyday people with dream projects can still work effectively with influencers. You do have to be careful, however, and it's not for everyone nor for every dream project. Risking your entire budget on a single high-profile endorser can easily sink a startup.

If you're a small company, look for free support instead of paying an influencer. It takes time to meet people and build relationships, but there are lots of "influencers" with small to mid-sized audiences, and great products can be reviewed and streamed for free. Why? Because the influencer may love your dream project, and they're looking for interesting content that will bring them an even larger audience.

Look for streamers who have featured other strong products from your industry or category, and pitch them to showcase "a great new idea from a startup team living off ramen and pizza."

Don't just look for people. Look for channels. Not all influencers are a single individual. Some are small teams building social media channels centered on topics, interests or themes. Food products might get attention on recipe and cooking blogs and streams (and there are a lot of them). Exciting new fashion or beauty items could appeal to many channels. If your product fits their needs for programming, the fee you pay to a YouTube channel or a Twitter thought leader may be small, or they might feature your content for free.

Consider how the social media outlet fits the product. Items for a younger audience might do best with an influencer based on Instagram. A product that earns strong word-of-mouth recommendations might do great with Facebook-based influencers. YouTube supports huge, diverse audiences with a wide range of interests.

If you have a budget for influencer sponsors, look for a small number of influencers who each have a few thousand followers. Their fees will be far lower than the big guys, and they may be easier to communicate with. You're looking for collaborative people who want to draw the best audience for them and the best sales results for you.

Try working with these smaller influencers one at a time, so you can measure the sales increase from each event and learn what works and what doesn't work with your audience. The data may show that subtle differences in influencers produce dramatic differences in your sales.

Take the time to research influencers and their audiences carefully. Do they cover products that appeal to your dream project's target audience? What impact have they had on prior items in your category? Have they engaged in weird online behavior (such as openly racist comments) that could offend your users?

Once you learn the fee structure for a potential influencer, run spreadsheet projections on how many additional units you'd have to sell in order to make a profit on the deal. Does that increased sales volume feel realistic and possible? If not, don't spend the money – there are many other ways to promote your dream project.

If you consider one of these deals you may be asked to pay an influencer's fee before you know exactly how they'll promote your dream project, and before you know if and how they'll inspire users to buy your product. Do not commit until you have such information in writing.

Be transparent, not tricky about your promotional activities. Ethical influencers will label content they create on your behalf as "sponsored." Openly state that you're paying for these activities and endorsements. Consumers will recognize the patterns and figure it out anyway, and transparency is always the best policy. In some jurisdictions laws may formally require that you make and document these disclosures.

1.13.4 Your Dream Project's Web Page or Website

Every dream project needs to have a professional-looking website dedicated to presenting and promoting it. You can have one site for your product or service and another for your company, or combine them both into one. You'll use your website(s) as a home base to reach out to potential users and to communicate with existing customers.

Buying the domain name for your dream project (and. If different, for your company name) is an important step to take once the official product or brand name is identified. Unclaimed domain names are inexpensive, so if the name changes before it's released you can usually get the revised domain name.

For example, if your dream project is a new kind of cough drop called Cinnacrushers, your domain name might be "cinnacrushers.com" and the URL for your product would be "http://www.cinnacrushers.com" – the address you type into your browser to display the page.

Domain names are paid for by the year, so you can sign up for one year at a time, or longer. The companies that offer these services are called domain registrars, the largest of which is GoDaddy. Any registrar can secure your domain name for you.

If your domain has a common suffix like ".com" (which is by far the most effective for ranking highly in Google searches) it should cost less than $15 per year to register. If it costs more than that, then exit the page and find another registrar. GoDaddy often has sales that make domain names especially inexpensive. (Note: I have no business relationship with any of the companies mentioned in this section aside from being a GoDaddy customer.)

If you're not already experienced in building websites, there are some easy ways to get going. My favorite approach is to create a WordPress site, an open standard that produces websites that are easy to use and that search engines love.

With WordPress you choose a "theme" (which can also be free or purchased for a fee), and that theme defines the standard layout, colors etc. for pages on your site. "Plug-ins" are code modules (some free, some sold at relatively low prices) that can be dropped almost seamlessly into a WordPress site, and there are many highly useful plug-ins.

If you Google "WordPress hosting" you'll see a list of companies that will host such a site for you on the cloud, including Google Cloud's own offerings. Costs are based on storage and bandwidth used per month, and you don't need to buy larger plans until your visitor traffic requires them.

For most small companies cloud hosting is far better than hosting a WordPress or other site on your own computer or server and dealing with all the security, bandwidth and storage hassles. Basic-featured WordPress hosting sites will offer free hosting, but more sophisticated options will charge a fee each month.

An alternative to using WordPress is to use Squarespace, Wix or Weebly, online services that allow you to choose options from menus and then assemble the selected style, format and font choices into a website. They will then host the website for you in the cloud in return for a monthly fee, which is how they make their money. The downside here is that you don't have the freedom to choose your hosting company as you do with the open standard of WordPress. If you change suppliers you'll have to re-do many aspects of building your website elsewhere.

Services like Feedblitz. MailChimp and others (which each operate in different ways) allow you to invite site visitors to opt in for email updates, which lets you create an immediate and highly valuable link with users.

The web presence for your dream project can be anchored by:

A product page on your company website, which helps build web traffic for your company since busy sites rank higher on Google searches. This is best if you plan to have multiple products, and people are more likely to know your company name than the name of any single product (e.g. Ford, Lockheed, CBS).

A separate product-specific website, which allows you to use the name of the product as the site domain name and URL This works best if you have one or more products that are (or will be) very well known, so people are more likely to search for a product name than to search for your company. You can also add a separate company website with general information, but don't duplicate the same content on both sites – this will lower the search rankings for each site.

If you host the product page on your company website you'll still want to buy the domain name that goes with the product name (at a minimum the .com version). This prevents someone else from buying it and creating confusion for search engines and users.

There are two skills you'll need to learn in order to maximize the effectiveness of your website. Both represent dynamic subjects where best practices can and do change every few months. In each case you'll want to do online searches for recent articles to keep abreast of these continuing changes. The two categories are:

SEO (Search Engine Optimization) – We're all familiar with how Google searches give us prioritized links to valuable information. The algorithms they use in this process are updated continually, so if we want our website to rank on the first page of any search (and most users never read farther than that first page) we have to study the current wisdom on best practices for Search Engine Optimization. Then we modify the text, layout, etc. of our site to give ourselves the best chance to rank highly.

"Mobile First" is a key principle of current SEO, because more online searches now come from smartphones than from desktop computers. The term means, "If you have to choose, make sure the mobile version of your website is prioritized in your SEO."

A WordPress plug-in called "AMP" (among others) will facilitate optimizing your website for mobile users.

Keyword Analysis. Every page on a website can have a keyword attached to it, and Google uses these keywords as part of how they pick the best pages to show to users. Using WordPress to create and maintain your site makes assigning keywords especially easy.

The process of choosing the right keywords for each page is highly dependent on what keywords similar pages are already using. You'll never outrank Apple or hundreds of other big companies if you want to use the keyword "iPhone" to draw people to your page. But you'll find fewer big competitors for a term like, "mobile cooking game," which could put you high on the front page of a search for that term or a similar one.

Whether it's a free-standing website or a page on your company site, you'll want to do consistent updates. You can then post links to the new content on Facebook, Twitter, etc. (discussed below). When users click on those social media links they'll be brought to the appropriate page on your website. This makes your page the center of information for the product, while using the same content (text, link, photo, video, etc.) to do updates on all of your social media platforms.

Elements you should consider adding to your product or service's web page include:

Text. Whatever you write about your dream project on your website has the potential to help market your product. It may be anything from a single sentence describing the product features to quoting early reviews from influential journalists, but it needs to be concise and easy to read. We want text that makes people believe that your dream project will solve a problem or fulfill a need, which are strong emotional motivators. Text will also be the largest component of how you tune the SEO strategy for your site,

Screenshots make great updates for apps and software projects, or to showcase highly visual products like clothing or jewelry.

Videos can likewise be used to show off music from new artists, visually appealing products, or the dramatic lifestyles lived by the people who use them.

FAQ pages, hints, tips, etc. If you have a complex dream project, an app or website with this kind of content can dramatically reduce the number of emails coming in to your customer support email address. (FAQ is an acronym for "Frequently Asked Questions.")

Links to great reviews or stories in the press, which can be highly effective marketing tools.

1.13.5 Almost-Free Marketing on Social Media

We've talked about various ways to market dream projects, and how some of those methods can be very expensive.

Social Media is a proven category of marketing for drawing attention and potential customers to your product. If you already have a large number of Facebook friends, Twitter followers etc. it can cost relatively little money to publicize your dream project through these channels to start the ball rolling. This won't make new products get noticed by millions of people all by itself, but it's a great start.

What if you don't have lots of social media friends or followers? Use the time while you're developing your dream project to start creating your "presence" on social media. Reach out to friends, write interesting posts, tweets etc. about products and/or services you like and respect, and comment on quality posts and messages you see from others. The only way to create good neighbors in the online community is to act like a good neighbor yourself.

These methods do take time, and to be effective they require that you update your chosen channels consistently. Many entrepreneurs start out with good intentions but then postpone updates, giving potential customers the feeling that the project may have been abandoned. This can undermine the power of these methods.

Most successful online marketing programs will involve multiple channels, although picking the most effective media is important. A musician's album or a toddler's animated toy need to be promoted with video, regardless of the outlet, and many social media platforms now support video. A new line of jewelry might benefit most from a series of images posted on Facebook, Instagram and/ or Twitter.

One downside of social media platforms: they all keep changing the rules on us. The algorithms for what gets shown at the top of the page, what gets shown at the bottom and what doesn't get shown at all keep changing. The only thing worse than having to deal with all these changes is giving up on social media, which is almost always a terrible decision for dream project marketers.

Before you start revealing your dream project via any method on any channel, consider when to start this kind of publicity.

You want to start early enough to give yourself time – sometimes several months before the product is released – to build interest and have a significant number of people who want to buy it the same day it becomes available.

You don't want to start too early, and give competitors time to speed-develop a similar product or service that can ship before you do.

You don't want to start the process until you have something compelling to show that has the "Wow!" factor that will draw people's attention.

If you aren't already a member, join each of the popular social media sites, find friends, and play with the various systems. As you watch the people around you and the content that appears each day, you'll start to understand which services are best-suited to promote your product or service.

Social media sites to consider include (in alphabetical order):

Facebook – The largest outlet and the one with the most diverse demographics, Facebook has the power to share a wide variety of assets and links, including high quality photos and video.

In recent years, however, Facebook has forced accounts belonging to businesses to become "pages" instead of having all the same features of individual accounts. Content posted in these business pages has a much lower priority than your cousin Irving's cat pictures, which means that until your dream project has a lot of followers you have to buy Facebook ads to publicize it. Those ads are highly targetable and effective, but can also be expensive.

If you're posting from your personal Facebook account these limitations don't matter, but personal accounts are capped at 5,000 friends. Business pages can have millions of followers.

Instagram – Instagram excels at reaching a younger, millennial audience, and its image-driven content is ideal for products where screen shots or videos will interest teens and young adults. Instagram is owned by Facebook, and is following in the footsteps of its parent in requiring businesses to advertise in order to grow their following.

Unlike the other systems discussed here, with Instagram users can't click through on links. You can create an awareness for the product, but potential customers have to do a separate online search to actually find your website.

LinkedIn – LinkedIn is a professional network rather than a social one, although a lot of friendly messaging goes through their system. The LinkedIn news feed mimics the Facebook format. It can be a useful place to post if you have a network of friends on the service, especially journalists. If not, your energy is better spent on other sites.

Pinterest – The audience here is dominated by women, so it's prime territory for products aimed at female audiences. Pinterest works best if your dream project has striking photos, since its users create and copy from boards of favorite images. You'll want to update your images frequently for maximum attention, and Pinterest is likewise making it harder to build large audiences without buying paid advertising.

Twitch – Twitch is the #1 video channel for getting video games noticed, but is of far less value than YouTube for most other categories.

Twitter – Like Facebook, Twitter can feature text, screenshots and videos. Unlike other channels, however, your tweets can quickly be buried by the high volume of traffic seen by active users. Twitter is experimenting with how to solve this problem, but the traditional remedy is to repeat tweets every few hours for a short period of time to maximize exposure without angering or boring your audience.

Remember that Twitter is also a two-way system for interacting with your audience. By tweeting messages with a @yourproductname tag players can send you public messages as well as direct private direct tweets about your dream project.

YouTube – YouTube is the king of video social media, despite the efforts of Facebook and Twitch to lure its audience. There are many companies and influencers streaming product features and reviews on YouTube.

1.13.6 Writing a Press Release

There are many excellent online articles about how to write a good press release. I will not cover that ground here, since guidance is readily available via a Google search.

I do have three guidelines for your press releases that you may not read somewhere else:

Remember that your new product's launch announcement is only news once. If you want the press to publicize the product or service, you'll get one shot to convince them to do so. If you send a press release before your dream project looks and feels interesting, no one will write about it. Not now, and not later.

If you send out a release and then send along more information later, your dream project is no longer "news" when that second mailing arrives. It will be much harder – though not impossible — to get journalists' attention.

Don't do mass mailings. Treat every outreach to a journalist as a unique personal communication. If you build a list of fifty journalists, bloggers and social media influencers it's tempting to do a mass mailing. You could send the same cover note, documents and links to everyone on the list, since it will save a lot of time.

We've all tried it. Once. Because it almost never works.

Journalists are like you and me: they want to be treated with respect as individuals, as real people. Take the time to research what each person has written, or what their podcasts or streams cover. Then write an individual personal note that discusses the products they've been covering and why your dream project would fit well with their other content.

This strategy won't always get a wave of coverage, but it will get far more responses, and higher quality stories, than the best mass mailing.

Beware of Swag. Many startups have sent journalists press kits packed in what looks like Indiana Jones' suitcase. They've sent collectible Darth Vader helmets, autographed NBA basketballs and special edition boxed sets of every kind. All of these (often very cool) items can be referred to as "swag."

With astonishing frequency, startups also send journalists cheap electronic doo-dads that are embarrassing to the sender, annoying to the recipient, and damaging to the environment because they're tossed into the trash and go into our landfills.

If you're a billion dollar company this might be worth doing once in a while. But leading journalists get so much swag that a lot of it gets discarded, left in the lunch room for people to take home to their kids, or passes through multiple hands and then gets sold for cash on eBay.

Leading journalists are looking for great stories and for great products to review, not swag.

This doesn't mean your product introduction or marketing have to be boring. I've seen beautifully-written material packaged in illustrated envelopes and folders that just screamed, "This is really cool! Open and read me now!" These kinds of initiatives cost far less to pull off, and can have an even more dramatic impact on your visibility in the press.

CHAPTER 10

The Competition (1.14-1.15)

DISCUSSING QUESTION 1.14:

What other companies offer a similar product or service?

How is yours different? What makes yours better?

This topic is most relevant for: Everyone

1.14.1 Start by Doing the Homework

I bet you weren't surprised to see these questions. If we set out to sell a product or service we know we have to understand the competition. Even more importantly, we have to understand their customers.

If you're an industry expert you have a big advantage. You already know the right questions to ask when you talk to users about different products' strengths and weaknesses.

These steps are critical when challenging existing products in the marketplace. And much of the process can be done by one person by investing time, not money.

1.14.2 "I Could Never Do That!" Syndrome

Charging ahead without doing research is hazardous for entrepreneurs. But the opposite approach has its dangers, too.

There are many people who have deep expertise in an industry, come up with a great idea for a new or improved product, but never do anything with it.

"I could never take on Proctor and Gamble," they say, as they keep following the same boring work routine for 25 years. "You can't win against a big guy like that."

A few years later Proctor and Gamble invents a similar product, and the industry expert grumbles that he or she had the same idea years before. And they're right.

Now, I agree that competing with Proctor and Gamble is very hard to do. They're a big company and they hire some of the best marketers in the business.

But if you have a great idea and you never explore your Dream Project, all you're doing is guaranteeing that someone else will implement the idea instead of you.

Maybe there really is no way for you to create this product or service. But I believe that you have to explore, try things, look for ways to push your idea ahead.

Trying and failing feels bad.

Never trying and watching someone else succeed feels worse.

DISCUSSING QUESTION 1.15:

How would you feel if The New York Times, Wired magazine, Oprah Winfrey and your best friend's mother all said your Dream Project sucks?

This topic is most relevant for: Everyone

1.15.1 What My Mother Taught Me

Yes, the answer to this question is obvious. Any of us would feel awful, terrible, gutted, humiliated and a lot of other horrible feelings if this happened.

My mother, who was a professional artist, taught me something very important about doing work that has your name on it. In fact, it's advice I've thought of often as I write this book.

"If you sign your name to a painting, or a story, or something you build with your hands," she'd say, "you have to be ready to accept the consequences. If you love what you did and other people love it, too, that's great."

Then she'd look me in the eye and say, "But if you love what you did and other people don't like it, you have to be willing to live with that. You can't be an artist if someone criticizing work you're proud of will make you stop doing any work at all. You have to be able to learn from the criticism, get better at what you do and keep going."

I have no idea if people will like this book when I finish it, but I'm going to write it anyway. And even if they don't like it I'm going to learn from this experience, improve my work and write another book after this one.

I think some readers will criticize my advice to "take care of yourself and your family financially and emotionally while pursuing your Dream Project." They'll say it contradicts the Silicon Valley stereotype of complete, self-sacrificing "burn the boats after you land on the beach!" commitment.

This book reflects over three decades of Silicon Valley experience. I've seen friends become millionaires and I've seen friends lose their marriages and their families and their homes. I can live with criticism that says that the approach I recommend is too cautious, because I believe I'm giving good advice.

Having people attack your work – and you – sucks. It feels terrible. But, as my mother said, when you put something out there with your name on it you have to accept those bad days as part of the deal.

Each time you ship something new you'll find that it gets easier to see criticism of your work. The harsh words don't change who you are and what makes you unique, and the feedback will help you grow as a creative professional and as a leader.

That's why I ask this "How do you feel..." question: to get those feelings out on the table so you can look at them, recognize them.

And once you recognize them, then your next job is to make a conscious decision not to let those fears stop you from pursuing your Dream Project.

CHAPTER 11

A Fun Idea (1.16)

DISCUSSING QUESTION 1.16:

You just won a mega-million-dollar jackpot in the lottery! You've cleared your to-do list and taken a 3-month vacation at a series of your favorite cities and resorts.

You return happy, rested and all caught up in every phase of your life. There's no to-do list for work, and nothing at home that needs to be cleaned, straightened, fixed, watered, painted, re-arranged or put away.

You no longer need to work, nor does your spouse or partner. If you have kids, however, they still attend the same grade of school and they still have to do their homework. Some things can't be changed by money!

From this moment on you can do whatever you want to do each day. In this "perfect world" how would you spend the first month when you got back?

This topic is most relevant for: Everyone

1.16.1 Where do Dream Projects Come From?

Let's imagine that your Dream Project is a great new smartphone app for hotel chains.

You were standing in a long line at a hotel, getting more and more frustrated as clerks fumbled to see which rooms had been cleaned and were available. Guests held up the line by cutting in to complain that they'd been given the wrong kind of room.

Ever since that moment you've been dreaming about creating a great new app that allows hotels to check guests in twice as quickly as current systems. You've been thinking of starting a new company to bring this great, sure-fire idea to life.

When you answered this question about how you'd spend your days after you won the lottery, what was it that you planned to do?

Did you see yourself sitting with your team and hand-crafting the world's best hotel guest check-in management app?

Or did you...

- Envision yourself on a beach in the Caribbean, planning where to take your next dive to explore the infinite colors of the tropical reef?
- Dream of writing the Great 21st Century Novel from an antique table on the balcony of a hotel suite in Venice, Italy?
- Start planning a tour of the 50 best restaurants in the world?

When you answered that question about winning the lottery you wrote down what you'd most like to do if you had all the time and all the money in the world.

How did your post-lottery-win plans relate to your Dream Project?

If they tie together in some way, that's a good start. But what if the stories don't match?

What if your big idea is to build the world's greatest hotel app, but your post-lottery dream is to open a bed-and-breakfast in Brooklyn?

Then you have to ask yourself some more questions.

1.16.2 Sometimes We're Stuck

There are times when we're stuck due to financial obligations and we have to tough it out for a while.

I deeply support the real-world thinking that goes into these "I can't quit this job right now" decisions, especially when we have children and other family members who depend on us for support.

If we recognize that sometimes we have no choice other than to work at a boring or frustrating job, what does that mean for our Dream Project? Could it be a slow-but-sure side project that gets worked on as time allows?

1.16.3 For Love or Money

Do you have more than one passion? Is one passion more financially rewarding, while another is closer to your heart but will earn less money?

Most people don't have just one narrowly-defined kind of job or project that they could enjoy doing. If your Dream Project is #2 or #3 on your "Top 10 favorite things to do" list you may get great joy from working on it.

Or are you horrified to realize that your Dream Project and your post-lottery dream just don't match? Not even close.

Doing something that you don't really care about just for the money often turns into a miserable grind.

As painful as it sounds, I know from my own experience that giving up on an ill-conceived project can be a good thing.

Discarding an old idea opens the doors of creativity to a different initiative that may combine both personal passion and the potential to make money.

But you have to stop working on the old dead-end idea in order for the new dream to crystallize in your mind and in your heart.

PART II

GREAT PEOPLE, GREAT PROJECTS

CHAPTER 12

Great People, Great Projects: The Questions

QUESTION 2.1

Will you be working alone at the start of this project, or will you need to start with a small team?

Please take your time, write down your responses, and answer fully from your deepest thoughts. Think only about your own opinions, not about what others may want you to think or do. Do not look ahead to other questions until you have finished this one.

QUESTION 2.2

If you're working solo on your Dream Project, is this something you've done before? How recently?

If you'll be leading a team on your Dream Project, is this something you've done before? How recently?

Please take your time, write down your responses, and answer fully from your deepest thoughts. Think only about your own opinions, not about what others may want you to think or do. Do not look ahead to other questions until you have finished this one.

QUESTION 2.3

Is your Dream Project a mobile app, PC app or website that will require support other than standard customer service after launch? Will you be running a "Live Team?"

If so, what kinds of team members will you assign to the Live Team?

QUESTION 2.4

Are you planning to work full time on your Dream Project?

Is anyone else planning to go full time with you?

Please take your time, write down your responses, and answer fully from your deepest thoughts. Think only about your own opinions, not about what others may want you to think or do. Do not look ahead to other questions until you have finished this one.

QUESTION 2.5

Is there a way for you to pursue your Dream Project part-time and still make progress towards your goal?

Do you have potential team members who could work on the project part-time as well?

What parts of your Dream Project could you complete even if you were just working on it part-time?

QUESTION 2.6

If you have a team, will your group all work together in a big room?

Or will you build a virtual team where you each live in different places and communicate electronically?

If you chose this latter option, how often (if ever) would you want to get together in person to work through issues face to face?

Please take your time, write down your responses, and answer fully from your deepest thoughts. Think only about your own opinions, not about what others may want you to think or do. Do not look ahead to other questions until you have finished this one.

———————

QUESTION 2.7

Of all the people you've worked with in your career, who's the one person with whom you'd most like to work again?

What made them so special to work with?

Would they enjoy working on your Dream Project?

———————

QUESTION 2.8

In which past job you held was it the most fun to come to work each day?

Was it the project itself or the people you were working with that made it special?

Please take your time, write down your responses, and answer fully from your deepest thoughts. Think only about your own opinions, not about what others may want you to think or do. Do not look ahead to other questions until you have finished this one.

QUESTION 2.9

What is the best-organized company you've ever worked for? What did they do that made you feel that way?

Where did you work in your career thus far where people got the most done each day, week, month and year? What was it that made the team so productive?

QUESTION 2.10

Regardless of how efficiently the team worked, and regardless of how much you enjoyed the process, what is the project you've worked on in your career where you were most proud of the product or service?

What was it that made you feel so proud?

Please take your time, write down your responses, and answer fully from your deepest thoughts. Think only about your own opinions, not about what others may want you to think or do. Do not look ahead to other questions until you have finished this one.

QUESTION 2.11

How would you feel if you never went back to your current work environment again?

How would you feel if you never saw the people you work with again? Are there some people you'd never miss and others you'd think of constantly?

Are there other perks or activities involved in your current work that you'd be sad to lose?

Note: We are just talking about hypothetical feelings, and are not planning or taking action.

Please take your time, write down your responses, and answer fully from your deepest thoughts. Think only about your own opinions, not about what others may want you to think or do. Do not look ahead to other questions until you have finished this one.

QUESTION 2.12

What other parts of your life would bring you joy if you could just magically make them go away? Some of these may seem obvious (the IRS?), but writing them down still helps you organize your thoughts.

What other parts of your life would bring you anguish if they were suddenly taken away (e.g. your family, your church, close friends, places you like to go, activities you enjoy etc.)?

Make a short list of things you would and would not like to leave behind, and if you feel especially strongly about any of the people or items on that list, write down why.

Please take your time, write down your responses, and answer fully from your deepest thoughts. Think only about your own opinions, not about what others may want you to think or do. Do not look ahead to other questions until you have finished this one.

QUESTION 2.13

Is there anything or anyone in your life now that you need to get away from, so the idea of starting over someplace new sounds especially great?

Is there a bad memory you're trying to escape by moving to a new office or even a new town?

Is there something pushing you towards making a complete, across-the-board clean break and starting over in a different job, a different industry, a different place or with different people around you?

Please take your time, write down your responses, and answer fully from your deepest thoughts. Think only about your own opinions, not about what others may want you to think or do. Do not look ahead to other questions until you have finished this one.

CHAPTER 13

My Story: Lost Dreams and Those We Just Misplace

My father received his degree in Anthropology from the University of California. He was passionate about field research, and his future looked bright.

Then the stock market in the United States collapsed, ushering in the Great Depression. Tens of millions of people lost their jobs, and the funding for scientific research dried up. There were no jobs in anthropology for recent graduates. My dad worked his way through school a second time and earned a second degree – this time in Business and Accounting.

When I was a boy I asked my dad a lot of questions about how businesses worked. He'd give me thoughtful answers.

But then we'd watch a show about the great herds of buffalo and the lives of the Plains Indians. Or about the cultures of Athens and Sparta. Or about the Maori of New Zealand.

If I asked him about any of those topics his eyes would light up like Christmas morning. He'd walk over to the bookcase and pull out one of his old textbooks. He'd take off his glasses, balance the book in his big hands and flip through the pages until he came to the section he wanted.

He'd show me the illustrations, his face beaming, and tell me about the subject. I enjoyed those conversations, although after a while as a young boy I'd be ready to go play.

Dad's business card said he was an Accountant. But his eyes told you he was an Anthropologist.

There are lots of books about how to choose a dream to pursue in your life. I think they've got it all wrong.

Our dreams choose us. We don't have to pursue them. They're right there all the time, waiting for us to notice.

As a boy I told my parents that when I grew up I wanted to do accounting, just like my dad.

Each time I said this my father would look at me and shake his head. "You don't want to be like someone else," he'd tell me. "You want to be yourself. You want to find what *you* love to do. I had limited choices because of the Depression, but you can experiment and try things and choose what you want to do."

My mother was a professional artist who also had to change careers because of the Depression. She became a corporate executive at a time when few women were promoted to those levels. She would tell me, "Make sure you put a roof over your head, but find a way to do what you love when you go to work each day."

It's one of the great gifts my parents gave me, the idea that only I could decide where my passions lie.

We can't always pursue our passions when we want to, or in the way that we want to do so.

But if you never pursue those dreams at all, you give away a piece of yourself, a piece that can also bring joy and value into the lives of others.

That's not something we should abandon willingly.

CHAPTER 14

What to Do with Your Answers (2.1-2.3)

"THE SECRET OF MY SUCCESS IS THAT I'VE BEEN LUCKY ENOUGH TO HAVE BEEN INVOLVED IN GREAT MOVIES AND TO HAVE WORKED WITH GREAT PEOPLE."

— Harrison Ford

If you have not yet written down your answers, please go back and do so. Writing your thoughts down – even when you're the only one who'll ever read them – will produce far more insights than just answering silently to yourself in your head.

DISCUSSING QUESTION 2.1

Will you be working alone at the start of this project, or will you need to start with a small team?

This topic is most relevant for: Everyone

2.1.1 Solo Project or Initial Team

Some visions can be solo efforts: writing a book, programming mobile apps, creating websites, many forms of fine art, crafts like making jewelry or doing leather work, home services, etc.

Other plans take a team. Most companies that are planning to market nationally or internationally require the collaboration of different disciplines.

Hiring only the people you truly need is an essential part of any team's management plan, since it's critical to spend as little as possible and conserve cash.

What does an ideal small team look like? In a perfect world you all...

- Have worked together before, and done so productively
- Have complementary strengths, experience and training

- Have an individual specialty that is unique on the team and vital to the company's early success

The world isn't perfect so most teams don't have all of these advantages, but try to cover as many of them as you can.

If your Dream Project requires money from investors they will have other criteria as well, and we'll discuss those issues in later chapters.

2.1.2 And Now, a Word from Our Sponsor, "Cash"

A few paragraphs ago I used the phrase, "It's critical to spend as little as possible and conserve cash."

I cover this point in detail, with lots of suggestions, later in this book.

But I wanted to give you a short preview of those comments here, much earlier in your planning, because it may be the most valuable advice in this entire book if you're running a business.

It's advice that often sounds exaggerated and wrong, which is why so many people end up in trouble.

Never *ever* personally guarantee a lease, a bank loan or any other loaned money. I'll explain all the reasons why in a later chapter.

Guarantees are legal commitments (often just a single line in the small print of an agreement) where you promise to pay back money if the company you manage cannot do so. They can easily lead to unexpected problems – even financial catastrophe – for you and your family.

Most companies succeed or fail based on how well they manage cash. Conserving your cash is the single most important skill to acquire for a first-time business leader.

Most entrepreneurs are surprised the day they run out of cash. They are even more surprised by all the bad things that happen in the days that follow.

Most cash crises are triggered by coincidences where expected cash does not arrive and/or unexpected payments have to be made.

Late cash arrival and unexpected cash departure are both routine in business, especially small startups.

Avoid cash commitments as often and as long as you can.

- Adding employees adds salaries, benefits and payroll taxes, and laws require you to pay all of the above on time
- Leasing an office adds a non-negotiable cash commitment each month
- Running up your credit cards creates a later cash crisis when the payments grow into hungry monsters eating up your bank account

Cash is King. Thank God I was taught this early on by a mentor, because I would never have lasted long as a startup CEO without this lesson.

We'll discuss all of these issues – with specific examples of how surprises happen and how to avoid them – later in this book.

2.1.3 The Thing About Terms

I attended a business class many years ago where the instructor started the day with a fun activity.

"I will pay one million dollars," he announced, "to the first person who will give me a pen."

We all had cheap hotel pens and note pads right in front of us. One man almost fell flat on his face leaping out of his chair to give his pen to the instructor.

"Thank you, sir!" our teacher proclaimed. "I am now obligated to pay you one million dollars, and everyone in this room heard me make this oral commitment to you."

We all looked at each other. He couldn't possibly be serious.

The man went back to his seat and the instructor approached him. "Here are my terms for the deal," he said. "I will pay you a penny every 25 years until the debt is paid off, and the debt is personal, non-transferable and non-assignable, so you can't collect after I die. Here is your first payment."

And he handed the man a penny.

"If you learn just one thing from me today," the instructor told us with a gleam in his eye, "this is it. Everyone focuses on the total value of a deal. But what really matters are the terms. Keep your eye on the terms of every deal and you'll do well in business."

I did keep that lesson in mind, and every deal I've ever done has reminded me that he was right.

DISCUSSING QUESTION 2.2

If you're working solo on your Dream Project, is this something you've done before? How recently?

If you'll be leading a team on your Dream Project, is this something you've done before? How recently?

This topic is most relevant for: Everyone

2.2.1 What Kind of Adventurer are You?

People who feel driven to create Dream Projects are determined to achieve a goal. I think of us as adventurers pursuing important missions, working diligently for something in which we deeply believe.

We all have different ways of setting out on these missions, and it's important to understand your natural work style and how you like to get things done.

In my case, I'm good at doing solo projects but I like being around other people. Given the choice, I prefer working as part of a team over being a purely solo performer.

I have a couple of friends who are happiest when they're holed up by themselves at their computer, creating something all by themselves until it's time to get feedback on their work.

I have other friends who would go stark raving mad ten days into a solo project. They simply have to be collaborating on something to enjoy work each day.

If you're considering a one-person Dream Project as a full-time activity and you have never worked alone before, look for an opportunity to take a practice run for at least a couple of weeks before you fully commit. It's hard to know your real preferences and limits until you try them.

2.2.2 First Time Managers and Rookie CEO's

Ask any successful startup CEO about the first time they ever led a team and you'll hear some fun stories about naive mistakes that they made.

There are some parts of being a manager that you can learn from a book. But many parts of managing you just have to learn by doing it. You have to figure out your own personal style. You'll learn from your successes, and grow even more when you make mistakes. I learned a lot of important wisdom the hard way as a first-time CEO.

It's not a great rarity for new teams that are started by first-time managers to grow to be larger companies. It's harder for a new manager to get to this stage than for a veteran leader, but it happens all the time.

If a team is going to be involved in your Dream Project, ask yourself before you start out, "Is leading this team what I really want to do? Should I have someone run the day-to-day business so I can work in my professional specialty?"

We'll discuss these choices in more detail later in this book.

2.2.3 Having Veteran Advisors at Your Side

If you'll be leading a team for the first time on your Dream Project, it's worth the time and equity to enlist the help of one or more experienced advisors who have fought these battles before.

I have played that role for clients many times, and as a CEO I've had great mentors who played that role for me.

Regardless of how well a potential advisor's experience may fit your business category on paper, you need to interview them to see if there's a personal fit.

If one of you is a quiet and respectful listener, and the other's style is to interrupt and yell, "I'm just jumpin' in here 'cause I just thought of something very cool!" you might drive each other crazy.

There are many variations on this theme of "our styles are like oil and water, and they don't mix well."

Resist the temptation to hire the wrong advisor because they're well known or have a great resume. If you're working in the fashion business, that auto industry executive who's an old family friend is not likely to give you relevant advice.

DISCUSSING QUESTION 2.3

Is your Dream Project a mobile app, PC app or website that will require support other than standard customer service after launch? Will you be running a "Live Team?"

If so, what kinds of team members will you assign to the Live Team?

This topic is most relevant for: Everyone whose project includes an important mobile app, PC app or website

2.3.1 Living the Live Ops Loca

Live ops is short for "live operations." Once any app, program or website goes live and people are using it there are two sets of issues that arise:

Problems:

• Bugs

• Confusing interface on a specific screen

• Incomplete or unclear documentation

• Powerful features that no one is using

• User complaints

• Contact form entries go unanswered

• Contact form entries are answered, but make users angry, not satisfied

Opportunities:

- Discovering where users disappear (se we can keep them)
- Researching user paths so we find why they aren't using features, etc.
- User suggestions and complaints
- Announcing sales and special offers
- Creating "events" where users have to act within a specific time window to earn special rewards
- Upselling users to additional features
- Testing different menu styles etc. to see which one get best user response
- Testing preliminary functions of new features with selected opt-in users
- Managing user communities to build committed relationships

You'll notice that QA, Product Development, Marketing and Community Management are all involved in live ops.

2.3.2 Get Off to a Good Start

Live ops is not something we start thinking about as we near the launch of a product or service that includes web and smartphone components. It's something that has to be top-of-mind on the first day of work on the project.

- A user data policy has to be created so everyone on the team understands how different forms of user data have to be treated under U.S., European and other regions' laws
- Data has to be tagged if it is or is not user-identifiable under those policies
- Telemetry has to be built into the app to collect data on user paths through the product's screens and states, not just their

spending patterns

- A procedure for adding new data points and telemetry has to be defined, since even modern data bases don't like having new data classes added in a variety of ways

- Systems and procedures have to be created for running events, so that teams can script sales, promotions, special content pre-sentations, themed promotions etc. with little or no modifica-tion of the code to support each instance

- Tools and dashboards have to be created so that when the app goes live the team can examine all the collected data, not just a pre-defined subset

- Tools and dashboards have to be created for Customer Service to examine (and potentially correct) user accounts when ques-tions arise

It's tempting to say, "We'll think about those things once we get the functionality hammered out and the design feels solid."

Unfortunately, that's like saying, "We'll figure out where to put the elevator shafts after we've erected all the steel and poured all the concrete in the building." You've missed the chance to do things properly and you'll be hacking crude fixes forever to get the func-tionality you need.

Data, telemetry, metrics and analysis all have to be planned for in the original structure of the code for the app, program or website. We'll talk more about how to look at that data in a later chapter.

2.3.3 Live Teams and Events

When the first version of an app is released where users are spend-ing real world money, a transition happens. The development team that created the product integrates with the community manage-ment function and transitions (with some people swapping in or out) to become the live team that manages the product.

As they collect data on actual usage patterns, user retention, what parts of the app generate revenue etc. the live team makes running improvements to the code and assets. If they do so effectively they can build an audience that week-by-week is more and more committed to the product.

If the product is successful the live team may continue operating for years, evolving the content and features as they go.

The centerpiece of operations for most live teams is events. We have (at least) one official holiday in the U.S. each month throughout the year. Every thirty days you get an excuse to do something different in your daily life, energizing boring routines, and you might even get a day off.

Events have the same function in apps and websites, and by keeping things feeling fresh and new they alleviate boredom and make users want to stay involved.

Events have these critical needs:

Motivate users to enter the app or come to the website right now. They may already be using your product every day or they may not have logged in for three weeks. We just want to give them a reason to come back right now.

Marketers call this kind of activity a "call to action," because it gives the user a reason to stop waiting and act. It may be a giveaway, a contest, a sale, an announcement or anything else that grabs their attention and moves them to log in.

Be Worthwhile. Whatever the perceived value of the sale or opportunity is to users, you have to deliver. If an interesting event inspires you to return to the app but what you find there is boring you're much less likely to respond to any further offers.

We don't need them to spend money on every visit (and trying to achieve this can produce user resentment and backlash), but if we want to grow our base they can't ever be allowed to feel like it was a mistake to have logged in.

A Time Limit. Users need to enter the app or website within a defined set of days to participate, and the deadline is real. Some aspects of the event may endure (e.g. special items may be bought in the store after the chance to win them for free has expired) but the experience ends at midnight.

Diverse Themes. A once-a-month "Weekend Sale" will lose its luster quickly. Major holidays (and informal holidays like The Super Bowl and The World Cup) give you an excuse to create themed announcements and custom graphics for users as they enter the app. When the calendar doesn't cooperate you can make up your own mythical holidays to celebrate.

Reusable Assets. Our budgets aren't just finite, they're often tiny. Events have to use existing digital assets whenever possible. When necessary we want to re-decorate screens and settings rather than starting from scratch.

2.3.4 The Need for Strong Product Managers

Live teams are built around both software developers and marketers (the latter often called product managers or PM's), since their objective is to sell the product or service to users.

PM's are integrated into the leadership of live teams to drive the vital work of attracting users, not to mention attracting revenue to the company. Product Managers often join a dev team long before the product goes live, so they can work to pave the way for a strong initial launch.

In some companies (especially on mobile platforms) the PM's direct the live team's work and manage the other disciplines. In other settings PM's are paired with a producer, and there are many variants in these reporting arrangements.

2.3.5 "Hey UI, I'd Like You to Meet UX!"

In his landmark 1993 book, *The Design of Everyday Things* (which he recently re-issued with many updates), Donald Norman shared the term "User Experience Architect." This was the title he'd chosen to replace "User Interface Architect" on his business card at Apple.

Norman defines UX — the now-accepted abbreviation for User Experience – as being more than just the functional design for software products. UX also includes graphics, the interface, the physical interaction with the device that's running the software, the documentation, and even the service you get if you contact the company looking for help.

The introduction of the smartphone, with its hyper-competitive online stores, pushed UX to the forefront of the Silicon Valley vocabulary. UX principles instruct development teams to:

- Optimize every aspect of how the user interacts with the software

- Reduce or eliminate every possible source of frustration a user could feel towards the app or the company that publishes it

This is the same integration of Product Development, Marketing, Customer Service and Community Management that we discussed above as part of live ops.

When you're trying to stand out among tens of thousands of competing products, every nuance of how the user interacts with your product and with your company becomes important. Finding every little hiccup in the experience that drives users away becomes critical. Helping new users master the learning curve is critical to retention.

Any app or website that hopes to succeed in the current climate must abandon the narrow objective of building a strong UI.

The only way to move the odds in your favor is to see the chal-

lenge as being one of UX: User Experience. And to do so from the very beginning of your project.

CHAPTER 15

The Power of Part Time (2.4-2.5)

Are you planning to work full time on your Dream Project?

Is anyone else planning to go full time with you?

This topic is most relevant for: Everyone

2.4.1 The Different Kinds of Time

Anyone who's considering building a Dream Project faces an interconnected set of issues surrounding:

- What can and can't be done full time
- What can and can't be done part time
- How to make tradeoffs based on real-world choices instead of perfect-world fantasies, and
- How to always keep making progress

My first objective in asking this question is to get you thinking about these issues and considering all the options based on your personal situation.

If a full-time commitment involves lots of added risks for you at this point in your career and in your life, it's good to review if there's a way to take things more slowly and reduce those risks.

It may turn out that you have only one choice for how you can proceed to build your Dream Project. But it's good to think through all the alternatives just to make sure.

DISCUSSING QUESTION 2.5

Is there a way for you to pursue your Dream Project part-time and still make progress towards your goal?

Do you have potential team members who could work on the project part-time as well?

What parts of your Dream Project could you complete even if you were just working on it part-time?

This topic is most relevant for: Everyone

2.5.1 Part-time Planning

When I say, "I worked on this part-time," I could be referring to a lot of different approaches:

- A passion project I worked on during nights and weekends while I held a full time job
- One of several projects I was working on as part of my regular job
- A summer project done by a teacher who has 10 weeks free each year

Different projects are better suited to the different personal schedules we each have. I've completed and delivered Dream Projects in all three methods described above, including this book.

One secret of building Dream Projects is to identify the time windows you have available. Then you can plan how you'll use that time to advance your Dream Project step-by-step towards completion.

If you have a full-time job the only free time to do project work might be on weekends or occasional late nights, which raises the issue of life balance. Working more hours on a part-time project after long days at work can have negative impacts on family life and relationships, not to mention your health if you shortchange sleep and exercise.

I find that it's best if I plan the time collaboratively with my family, so I maintain a sense of balance between my work and my home life, and between being serious and having fun.

2.5.2 Overcoming Roadblocks

A number of times during my career I've had to put a Dream Project on the shelf and wait. Which scared me, because it meant that I might wait forever and the project might never get done.

Sometimes I see people (including me) stopped by roadblocks on a project when there are other ways they could be making progress.

If I were working on a project and didn't have the time or money to produce a prototype or even a robust demo, a mentor might ask me questions like:

- "Have you thought about building a simpler smartphone app instead of a complex desktop product?" Building a mobile app can take less time and money than projects for PC or Mac.
- "Can you use storyboards to sell the idea instead of building a demo?" Many Dream Projects need prototypes to attract support. Others may only need a well-executed pitch, which we'll discuss in a later chapter.
- "If you don't have the budget to hire a team, what can do by yourself?"

Sometimes we just need someone to ask us the right questions and then we realize what we can do next.

You may face barriers that really can't be avoided or be broken down in this way. Nevertheless, think about alternate approaches while you're in the shower, walking the dog or stuck in traffic.

If your Dream Project is to open a retail store, for example, you can't be open from 9:30 PM to 10:30 PM each night if those are the only times when you can work.

But could you open an online store on eBay, Etsy, Square, WooCommerce or other websites to sell your products?

Is there a local shop where you could sell your products on consignment?

Are there local markets or events where you can rent a booth on the weekend?

Any of these steps would allow you to learn more about customer tastes, how to price your products, etc. And that's meaningful progress!

2.5.3 The Catches in Working Part Time

There are some issues to be aware of when you're doing part-time work:

Laws vary state by state, but in most places you cannot do your own work at the workplace of your employer without their written permission. You can't use even a single pencil or piece of paper from your employer's office either. If you break those rules they could claim under the law that they own the work instead of you. Most firms would never dream of enforcing such a rule over a pencil, but they have the right to do so.

Family life is a priority. No matter how busy I've been in my work life, I never missed watching our kids' weekend soccer and baseball games. If I'm not traveling or at an event I always make it home in time to join my wife for dinner. I've never had a project that was worth ignoring my family.

You can sabotage your mission by sabotaging yourself. Getting enough sleep is critical to staying sharp and using good judgment. Getting enough exercise is vital, both for your health and to keep the right attitude when work gets stressful.

Birds don't fly when they're caged. It's hard to expand your horizons when you're glued to your chair. I go to meetups almost every week to learn new ideas, new technologies and new business models. I meet new professional allies. I can't let my skills or my knowledge atrophy just because I'm on an exciting project.

One person doing all the work themselves can take a long time. I wrote my novel *The Fog Seller* as a personal project in little patches of late-might time, but it took seven years. Nevertheless, I'd gladly do it all again even if I knew ahead of time how much work it would be.

Some jobs do not lend themselves to sharing the space in your head. This can lead to a situation where you do two things badly instead of doing one thing well.

I have friends who are engineers who could easily do one project at work and one project at home.

I've seen other engineers whose work faltered as they were consumed by endless bugs on both projects, with neither code base ever really coming under control.

If your nature is to give your whole focus to one thing at a time, your part-time project may not go well when that attention is divided.

The only real way to find out if this approach can work for you is to try it.

CHAPTER 16

Teaming Up (2.6-2.8)

DISCUSSING QUESTION 2.6

If you have a team, will your group all work together in a big room?

Or will you build a virtual team where you each live in different places and communicate electronically?

If you chose this latter option, how often (if ever) would you want to get together in person to work through issues face to face?

This topic is most relevant for: Dream Projects that involve more than one person.

2.6.1 My Take on the Workplace

I believe that in a perfect world it's ideal to have everyone on the team work side by side in the same office. You'll brainstorm new ideas more effectively and catch problems faster than if the team were scattered in multiple locations.

Of course, we don't live in a perfect world. I've worked on successful projects where the team was split across three continents.

In most major urban centers there are many kinds of short-term shared work environments, with everything from desks in an open setting to a private office or a separate large room for four or more people.

These new shared spaces offer practical options at prices that scale based on your need for space, privacy, and access. They don't require long term lease commitments and you pay only for the space and features you need.

If you choose to work at one of these facilities, be sure to research carefully and negotiate aggressively, since many will offer discounts or deals if asked.

Shared workplaces are often marketed as social cauldrons where great new products are born and where co-founders meet, the product of great minds brought together in an encouraging community. In my experience the operators of many of these facilities over-sell this feature, and the spontaneous winning partnerships they describe are rare.

Sites will offer you the chance to work for free in their office for one or more days as an evaluation period. This is essential, since the noise level, culture, facilities and routines for each facility are very different.

I've been in shared workspaces that were quiet, like a library.

I've been in shared workspaces that were loud, like that bar down the street. In fact, one place had a fully-equipped bar, complete with bartender!

If you need a dedicated office for a team, one cost-saving option is sub-leasing, where you take over a space that another company no longer needs. They may require that you stay for the duration of the original lease, however.

Workplaces don't always have to be offices. The hit game *World of Goo* was created by a two-person team who worked in a coffee shop where they met each day.

If your team is scattered in different locations, you can use regularly-scheduled visits and frequent Skype calls to stay in touch, but monitor the progress and results carefully. Some people thrive in "virtual" companies. Others gradually drift apart, which is often fatal for a project.

Your views about where and how to base your company may differ from mine. What's most important is that you conserve cash, try things and see what works with your personal management style.

DISCUSSING QUESTION 2.7

Of all the people you've worked with in your career, who's the one person with whom you'd most like to work again?

What made them so special to work with?

Would they enjoy working on your Dream Project?

This topic is most relevant for: Dream Projects that involve more than one person.

2.7.1 You Never Know Until You Ask

I have consistently been surprised at the high quality of people who are recruited into small startups when they could enjoy greater job security in large corporations.

Years ago I sat near an engineer whom I especially admired at the game company where I worked. He didn't report to me and the only places our paths crossed were company social events and the weekly schedule-update meeting.

Fast forward several years, and I'm leading my first startup. One day I'm surprised to hear that this engineer is applying to work at our small company. We sat down together, and he told me that he was excited about finally getting to work closely with me.

This was a moment that meant a lot to me. As honored as I felt to hear a guy whom I respected so highly say this, it also made me angry at myself.

I could have hired this strong engineer several years sooner (after he had already left the company where we both had worked), if I'd just had the confidence to reach out and ask if he were interested!

You never know until you ask.

2.7.2 Co-Founders vs. Early Employees

Co-Founders and Early Employees are both critical parts of a startup, but they're very different roles when you're hiring early team members.

I'll discuss the business and legal sides of this issue in more detail in a later chapter, but here's a bullet list of the qualities of each of these vital parts of your team:

Co-Founder:

- Joins the team when the idea is little more than "a glimmer in the founders' eyes"
- Works for less (usually far less) money than they could earn in a job at a mature company
- May be living off of savings, be supported by their partner, live with their parents etc. and take no salary at all
- Earns a larger stock option with special benefits (which we'll discuss later), since they're taking greater risks
- In both actions and words, serves as part of the core strategic thinking that drives the company
- Is passionately committed to the venture and will do whatever it takes to get the product or service completed and launched in the market

Early Employee:

- Joins the team during early stages of the development of the product or service
- Works for somewhat less money than they could earn in a job at

a mature company

- Earns a stock option
- Plays an important role in the early operation of the company
- Is deeply committed to the venture and will work their heart out to get the product or service completed and launched in the market

Later Stage Employee:

- Joins the team after the product or service has had some initial success
- Is compensated within the typical pay range for their job and the relevant industry and geographical area
- May earn a stock option — some companies give them to all employees (as I prefer to do), while others give them only to more senior team members who join at later stages
- Plays a valuable role in the operation of the company
- Is committed to the venture and will work diligently to make the product(s) or service(s) successful

As you look through these lists you'll see that they are very subjective and general, and leave a lot of room for interpretation.

That's intentional. The one rule that trumps all others is, "Listen to the best advisors you can find, and then use your own best judgment."

As you look through these lists you'll see that they are very subjective and general, and leave a lot of room for interpretation.

That's intentional. The one rule that trumps all others is, "Listen to the best advisors you can find, and then use your own best judgment."

2.7.3 Dynamic Duos

Many great startups began with two key players with very different personalities who each played a key role in the company's success.

The most famous recent duo is Steve Jobs and Steve Wozniak of Apple. Wozniak was the engineer who brought the machines to life, and Jobs was the visionary designer and hustler who positioned and promoted them to outperform their big-company rivals.

In tech startups it's common for one person to lead the creation of a complex product, while another has the marketing savvy, connections and chutzpah to sell it.

As we'll discuss in more detail below, most founders need a partner who is very different from themselves. They have to accept that they can't do everything alone.

Note: The "one person invents it and the other sells it" model applies to many startups, but if it doesn't sound right for you, don't get stuck on the idea.

The ideal perfect partnership starts with someone you already know and trust from having worked together before. It's even better if you develop the idea as a team.

That said, it's common to have a great new person join the team later in the process. If they believe in the original vision they can help as effectively as if they were there on the first day.

DISCUSSING QUESTION 2.8

In which past job you held was it the most fun to come to work each day?

Was it the project itself or the people you were working with that made it special?

This topic is most relevant for: Everyone

2.8.1 Can You Analyze Fun?

Ignore the success or failure of the projects you've worked on, and just focus on the most fun project or job you've ever held.

Not "The Best" as judged by someone else, but the project or team you picked simply because you had the biggest smile going to work each day.

Was this a long-ago dream job you're trying to regain? Your most recent project? The first job of your career?

Was the project well run? Was the team productive? Or did all that fun affect the team's productivity and the quality of the product?

It's critical to think about whether it was the work, the people, the environment or all of the above that made the job or project special. Then you can consider what aspects of this favorite experience you want to re-create.

What kind of daily routine did you experience in this favorite job? Did you value the predictability of a job with set hours where you could go home and leave thoughts of work behind?

Founders of startups that grow into teams can have exciting and unique challenges, but the work requires long hours. Issues can demand your attention at any time on any day. If that sounds bad to you now it will only sound worse once you're working in a startup.

It's important to understand what you really want, so you chase the right dreams and find real happiness.

If it was the people you worked with who made this project special, here's one way to apply this to your current project:

1. Make a short list of the best teammates you've ever had in prior companies.
2. List the qualities and characteristics of those favorite co-workers.
3. Use those qualifications to outline the kinds of people whom you want to work with in the future.

2.8.2 My Bullet List for Teammates

Here are the qualities I associate with the best people I've worked with in my career. Remember, though, that many successful CEO's and leaders have their own unique screening criteria for their teams, and there is no single perfect formula.

My bullet points:

Extremely talented at their professional craft (programming, art, marketing, financial analysis, etc.)

Committed to doing high quality work at everything they set out to do.

They do what they say they're going to do, and get it done by the deadline when they said they were going to do it. No drama, no excuses, just results 99.9% of the time (because no one is perfect).

Able to kick around ideas and share thoughts with others and arrive at the best answer to any issue or question without pride getting in the way. They don't worry about whose idea is adopted, just that the best idea is adopted.

Supportive of the people around them. Your child is sick and you have to stay home for a couple of days? They'll help cover for you while you're gone without complaining, and they know you'd do the same for them.

Will argue fiercely over business issues, but it's the ideas and never the people who are attacked in those arguments. They'll say, "I hate that idea," but never say, "You're stupid."

Once the decision on an issue is made, they'll willingly execute the plan, even if they continue to disagree with it. No "I told you so!" Just "Let's make this work."

If they're worried about something they'll come talk to you in private. Great people openly share their concerns with their manager, but they start by doing so one-on-one. This avoids "Reality TV" style drama while making sure problems are identified and addressed.

Someone who's easy to work with, so long as the focus of the work is on quality, but...

If the focus on quality gets lost and things start to get sloppy they stop being easy-going. They get very focused and start looking for ways to push people and processes to get things back on track. They don't go back to being easy-going until the commitment to quality and consistent execution has returned.

2.8.3 No Waiting Around

Good startup teams work hard, but they take breaks and work-home balance is also important. The comments below are not about chaining yourself to a desk. They're about what happens when you're not sure what to do next.

What do strong team members do when they finish something and aren't sure what to do next? They'll immediately ask their manager, co-worker, producer etc. for guidance or suggestions.

If they're waiting for assets from someone else, or if they check off all of their to-do list, they'll ask teammates, "How can I help?"

These rules apply to a company's leaders as well. Strong teams aren't founded by victims of circumstance. A manager never explains, "We couldn't do any important work this afternoon because we never received the documents."

Strong managers always take the initiative: "We never received the information from Acme Inc., so we worked on our proposal for Cloversoft instead."

If people don't display this "I'm free — how can I help?" attitude, don't add them to your team.

CHAPTER 17

The Power of Process (2.9-2.10)

DISCUSSING QUESTION 2.9

What is the best-organized company you've ever worked for? What did they do that made you feel that way?

Where did you work in your career thus far where people got the most done each day, week, month and year? What was it that made the team so productive?

This topic is most relevant for: Everyone

2.9.1 The Magic of Being Well Organized

There are many different ways to organize the day-to-day work of a company. Yet almost all successful companies are organized in a way that has been carefully and consciously chosen by their leaders.

If you've worked on a great team, there's a good chance you want to set up similar systems for your startup. So long as the processes, products and services are similar that's a very good idea.

All of the widely-used project management systems have a handful of things in common. They track:

- Tasks that need to be done
- Who is assigned to do each task
- When that task is due to be completed
- How we can tell that the task has been completed

For example, a home-building company might have broken the process of building a house into 600 separate steps, from grading the lot to handing over the keys.

They would plan these steps in a carefully chosen sequence, and have carpenters, plumbers, electricians, etc. work on each task once the previous steps were done. Electricians and plumbers could work at the same time in different rooms, since neither needs the other's help to finish any task.

Building Inspectors would approve each step in turn, so mistakes are caught before additional work takes place.

In short, the builders know what needs to be done, who is assigned to do it, when it's supposed to be done and how each step is signed off as complete.

There are systems like "Agile Project Management" that are designed for creative projects where it's hard to identify each step on day one. I'll discuss these options in a later chapter.

2.9.2 Flow: What It Is and Why it Matters

In his best-selling book *Flow*, psychologist Mihaly Csikszentmihalyi described how his research identified the ideal conditions for getting work done.

This condition of *"flow"* exists when we:

- Have a clear set of goals
- See that we're making significant progress
- Get consistent, clear feedback so we know we're on track
- Work without lots of interruptions
- Do work that's challenging enough to be interesting, but not so difficult that we fail

As a programmer and as a writer I feel like these rules absolutely apply to me.

A major goal of any organization should be to create an environment where as much of the team as possible can work in that "state of flow" as often as possible.

Of course, organizational design is an imperfect science practiced via trade-offs and the balancing of different priorities and personalities.

We want the programmers and other leaders of our software startup to have the right environment to stay "in flow" as much as possible, so we give them offices with doors and minimize interruptions.

But now everyone who doesn't have an office is upset. There's a perception that "some people are valued and get doors, and some are devalued and stuck on the floor, and it's all about your job title and whether they like you."

Wait, we can fix this. We spend more money and give everyone an office with a door. But now we lose most of the positive effects of spontaneous teamwork. In fact, we start to lose the feeling of being a team, and can start to operate as a group of independent agents on parallel missions. That usually means lots of issues over who-controls-what and increased communication problems.

Wait, we can fix this. We schedule more meetings and add more detailed procedures, so we keep people operating as a team and avoid the loss of communication. But now all the meetings are interrupting everyone, and we're disturbing that productive flow that we gave everyone doors to help them achieve.

I'm exaggerating the issues here, but it's a delicate balance and fixing one problem can exacerbate another. The right trade-offs will be different for every Dream Project.

DISCUSSING QUESTION 2.10

Regardless of how efficiently the team worked, and regardless of how much you enjoyed the process, what is the project you've worked on in your career where you were most proud of the product or service?

What was it that made you feel so proud?

This topic is most relevant for: Everyone

2.10.1 Why Pride Matters

The project that gave you the greatest sense of personal pride is a key beacon in defining your Dream Project. It tells us what you value most in the work you do each day. For example:

If you picked the product or service that made the most money, that may indicate that you derive the most fulfillment from "winning the sales race."

If you picked the project where the team completed the most difficult assignments and overcame the most obstacles, it suggests that you value a challenge instead of looking for easy assignments.

If you picked the project where you liked the people better than on any other assignment or job, that reinforces how much you value great teammates. The people are more important than the specific tasks in your everyday work.

If you picked the product that got the highest Amazon ratings, the best press reviews, or that won the most awards, it suggests that you value producing something of quality very highly, and that you're looking for outside confirmation in addition to your own opinion.

If the product or service you picked did not excel in any of these ways, then there's something else about that project that made you very proud. Whatever it is, consider whether you can include the same qualities in your Dream Project.

Just remember, your Dream Project primarily will be judged on its inherent quality and the personal connection you establish with your customers. Those are the factors that will produce the revenue to make your new venture successful.

2.10.2 What Motivates Top Performers?

How do we build companies where the very best people will feel proud to work? What will make it easy to recruit the best people in our industry?

I've had a lot of theories about this topic over the course of my career, and I continue to evolve my thinking.

It's certainly true that one thing that motivates top people is money. If someone's compensation feels deeply unfair, their morale is headed for the dumpster.

But there are other major motivators that will surpass the value of money for many top performers.

I've come to believe that producing something that is widely respected for its exceptional quality is a deep and powerful motivator. It can command individual commitment even more deeply than cash.

Great products pull in great people, who in turn are far more likely to build something new that's great as well.

So how do you build a team that is focused on producing something of exceptional quality? Here's my checklist:

Look in the mirror and commit to yourself that you're willing to go through all the extra hassle, time, expense and heartache of producing something truly great. When you work your heart out for months or even years just to produce something that's pretty good, it can be tempting to declare you're done and move on. Leaders who are committed to exceptional quality keep pushing.

Hire people who have that built-in commitment to trying to build something great. I can say from experience that once you have a few of them at the core of your team the hiring process starts to work on its own to self-select the same kinds of people.

Compete with yourself. Most companies watch their competitors and try to invent new products to stay one step ahead of the pack.

The great companies ask themselves, "If we had a brilliant, innovative and well-funded competitor, what would they have to do to take our #1 position in the marketplace?"

Then they go out and execute that plan, competing with themselves. In the process they extend their lead over their competitors.

Apple created the massive global smartphone market, and established a big lead over all other manufacturers.

Most big companies would wait three to five years before updating a successful product line.

Apple released a major new version of the iPhone every year, until recently "slowing" to every two years. By upgrading more rapidly than anyone else had ever done, they extended their advantage over all of their competitors.

2.10.3 What Comes First?

So which is the chicken and which is the egg? Do happy teams with strong cultures produce great products? Or do high quality projects inspire happy teams and stronger company cultures?

It's like asking if your heart or your lungs play a more important part in a long and healthy life. If either operates poorly your life goes downhill fast.

If you have either weak products or a toxic company culture, your business goes downhill fast.

Managers of great teams are obsessed with quality. They hire high-quality people who then build high quality products and services. Those products are completed and then shipped to customers who are delighted with what they've bought. When the managers have to make tradeoffs, they err on the side of quality.

If you've worked on teams that were obsessed with quality you've been given a wonderful gift. You know what it feels like to work on a truly great team.

CHAPTER 18

It Keeps You Running (2.11-2.13)

DISCUSSING QUESTION 2.11

How would you feel if you never went back to your current work environment again?

How would you feel if you never saw the people you work with again? Are there some people you'd never miss and others you'd think of constantly?

Are there other perks or activities involved in your current work that you'd be sad to lose?

This topic is most relevant for: Everyone

2.11.1 Ventured, Lost and Gained

Whenever we decide to put time into something new, we have to take time away from something else.

Think about what (if anything) you'd miss if you decided to pursue your Dream Project. If this represents a full-time change, think seriously about this list of people, activities and benefits you value most today.

There have been times over the years when I came home from work and said to my wife, "Today was awful. I just want to tell them to '*&^$%$&#*!' and quit this job."

She'd nod patiently and ask me to tell her what happened. By the time I finished, I usually felt better and my faith in the project had been restored.

If you quit a job and later decide you want it back, there are no magical time machines. Your old boss may have new team members and no longer be interested.

If you're planning a Dream Project to get away from your current one, make sure it's something deeper than an occasional bad day that's driving you to action.

DISCUSSING QUESTION 2.12

What other parts of your life would bring you joy if you could just magically make them go away? Some of these may seem obvious (the IRS?), but writing them down still helps you organize your thoughts.

What other parts of your life would bring you anguish if they were suddenly taken away (e.g. your family, your church, close friends, places you like to go, activities you enjoy etc.)?

Make a short list of things you would and would not like to leave behind, and if you feel especially strongly about any of the people or items on that list, write down why.

This topic is most relevant for: Everyone

2.12.1 The List of Everything Else

What else is driving you to take action right now?

What other realities restrict your choices?

I know that when I start to get excited about even a small, fun project I can lose track of other obligations and consequences. Then I think about it and regain my perspective.

That's what makes answering the questions in this book important. They're here to remind you of everything else that's important to you, not just the Dream Project.

DISCUSSING QUESTION 2.13

Is there anything or anyone in your life now that you need to get away from, so the idea of starting over someplace new sounds especially great?

Is there a bad memory you're trying to escape by moving to a new office or even a new town?

Is there something pushing you towards making a complete, across-the-board clean break and starting over in a different job, a different industry, a different place or with different people around you?

This topic is most relevant for: Everyone

2.13.1 Personal Danger

For most readers this section will not apply, but those cases where it is relevant are incredibly important.

First and foremost, if you are in any situation that represents real personal danger, please get help immediately. I know from experience that these kinds of things happen to good people more often than any of us want to believe.

The issue is not planning the details of what you'll do next. The big issue is finding a way to get you to safety.

It's easy to rationalize someone else's behavior, explain it in an empathetic way and talk yourself out of acting. You convince yourself that a situation is OK, even though you may feel very frightened and threatened all the time.

Whether the help you seek is best offered by a family member, a friend, the local police, someone at your church, a doctor, a counselor or someone else, reach out right now. Whatever situation it is that is threatening you, there is a way to get help to make it better.

Again, if you're starting from a place of personal danger, please act immediately to get help. This book and this process will be waiting to help you plan later steps when you're ready, but for now nothing else matters except getting you somewhere that is safe.

2.13.2 Magnets Can Attract or Repel

Sometimes we can feel like we're stuck in a bad work situation. Continuing in the status quo is unacceptable, but we feel like we have no alternative. I've had times when I hated going to work each day.

I've learned that whenever "getting away from something" becomes my primary motivation I need to stop and think.

If you're running away from a psychotic horror movie villain who happens to be wielding a chainsaw, any direction will do. (But do avoid attics and basements with only one door!)

But when you're planning how to regain the happiness you're seeking, you can't just pick any old direction and run.

No one but you can know how your answers to this series of questions may suggest the next steps in your life and your work. But it's important for you to think about them and about what you really want.

Only then can you fully commit to whatever you choose to do next.

2.13.3 The Power of the New

There's an old joke about a guy who dies after having broken all of the Ten Commandments multiple times, not to mention numerous federal, state and local laws and regulations. He is sent to a dark, foul-smelling corner of Hell, and wanders through its caverns in misery.

Eventually this new arrival comes across a fellow denizen who is smiling and happy, even as a tiny demon appears to be biting him on the leg.

"How can you be smiling?!" the new guy asks. "We're rotting here in Hell! That little monster is biting your leg!"

The happy man looks up at him and smiles. "You don't understand," he says. "This is the Fourth Circle of Hell. I just got reassigned from the Seventh Circle. This place is wonderful!"

Sometimes what is driving us forward is not a specific dream or a thought-out vision, but a deep desire for something new.

But remember, taking the first opportunity that comes along can take you to a worse Circle of Hell than your current one.

PART III

LEADING THE WAY

CHAPTER 19

Leading the Way: The Questions

QUESTION 3.1

When you're working on your Dream Project what will your business card say?

Will it be your only business card or will you still "keep your day job?"

Why did you choose this job title for your card?

Please take your time, write down your responses, and answer fully from your deepest thoughts. Think only about your own opinions, not about what others may want you to think or do. Do not look ahead to other questions until you have finished this one.

QUESTION 3.2

To what kinds of people will you hand your business card? What will you want from them?

What benefit will they expect to gain from knowing you?

What will be the actual benefit they gain from knowing you?

Please take your time, write down your responses, and answer fully from your deepest thoughts. Think only about your own opinions, not about what others may want you to think or do. Do not look ahead to other questions until you have finished this one.

QUESTION 3.3

What will you spend most of your time doing each day when you're working on your Dream Project?

QUESTION 3.4

If there's anyone else working in the office with you, how will they be spending their day?

If there are people working with you who live and do their jobs somewhere else, what will they be doing each day?

How will you monitor their progress?

Please take your time, write down your responses, and answer fully from your deepest thoughts. Think only about your own opinions, not about what others may want you to think or do. Do not look ahead to other questions until you have finished this one.

QUESTION 3.5

If you're planning to take on major leadership duties as the company grows, are you ready to let go of controlling every detail of creating your products or services, and to let other people lead those functions?

If you find yourself hesitating to let go of daily control of the key product or service, why do you think you're feeling that way?

QUESTION 3.6

What's the one small part of the project you most dislike having to delegate to someone else?

What's the one small part of the project where you can't wait for the company to grow, so you can finally delegate that part of the job to someone else and you won't have to do it anymore?

Please take your time, write down your responses, and answer fully from your deepest thoughts. Think only about your own opinions, not about what others may want you to think or do. Do not look ahead to other questions until you have finished this one.

QUESTION 3.7

You and a group of your leading team members are debating how to solve a major problem.

Several team members favor Choice A. Several others prefer Choice B. At times people on both sides start getting angry at each other. Two days later a second meeting ends with the group just as divided as it was before.

This is an important issue that can't be allowed to drag on forever. You're in charge of the team. How will you manage the process, resolve the debate and reach a decision?

Please take your time, write down your responses, and answer fully from your deepest thoughts. Think only about your own opinions, not about what others may want you to think or do. Do not look ahead to other questions until you have finished this one.

QUESTION 3.8

What's the project from your career where teammates and customers or users gave you the most praise for your work?

What were the specific things you did (as best you can remember) that earned that praise?

If your boss praised you for one thing and your peers valued you for something else, and the users valued still a third skill, write down answers for each category.

Please take your time, write down your responses, and answer fully from your deepest thoughts. Think only about your own opinions, not about what others may want you to think or do. Do not look ahead to other questions until you have finished this one.

———————————

QUESTION 3.9

If you've managed people in your work, at which position did the people who reported to you give you the most positive feedback? What specific things did you do to earn that praise?

———————————

QUESTION 3.10

What's the biggest project you've worked on start-to-finish that shipped successfully?

It may be measured in how long it took to complete, in how many people were on the project, or any other common sense measure of "how much human effort was required to ship this product." You decide the right criteria and then list the project name.

Please take your time, write down your responses, and answer fully from your deepest thoughts. Think only about your own opinions, not about what others may want you to think or do. Do not look ahead to other questions until you have finished this one.

QUESTION 3.11

What's the biggest role you personally have ever had on a project that shipped successfully?

Examples: artist, CEO, customer service representative, engineer, executive assistant, GM, industrial designer, product manager, project director, sales manager, technical writer, trainer, writer, etc.

QUESTION 3.12

What's the biggest project or component of a project you've ever led? How many people did you direct on the project?

Please take your time, write down your responses, and answer fully from your deepest thoughts. Think only about your own opinions, not about what others may want you to think or do. Do not look ahead to other questions until you have finished this one.

QUESTION 3.13

Have you ever worked for a startup or very young company that failed? If so, why do you think they failed?

Have you ever worked for a startup or a very young company that became a big success? If so, why do you think they succeeded?

CHAPTER 20

My Story: Two Lessons from a Great Teacher

My boss at my first college job was the late Pomona College Professor of Music Dr. William F. Russell. I enjoyed playing in the band under his (irreverent) direction, and earned money for textbooks working for him as a security guard at the music building.

I didn't recognize it at the time, but he had a gift for making the people who worked for him feel appreciated. My job was simple: open the locked door of the music building for students from 6 PM to 11 PM each Sunday night.

The locked door meant that no strangers could enter the building while music students were scattered, alone and vulnerable, in small rehearsal rooms on three different levels. The security guard's presence each night meant that students could still get in to rehearse after the building closed at 6 PM.

One evening in my freshman year Dr. Russell came into the lobby, looked over at where I was sitting and studying, and waved.

"It's good that you're here," he told me.

Three years later, sitting in that same chair as a senior, I still remembered that he thought it was important I was there, doing my job.

As leaders we don't have to make elaborate speeches to make our people feel appreciated. We just have to tell them that their work is important and that we're glad they're there.

And we have to mean it.

Dr. Russell's greatest gift to us was an idea he shared with the band, and later in a Pomona commencement address. "Be careful what it is that you truly want in your life," he told us, "because you're likely to get it."

You may have heard the similar phrase, "Be careful what you wish for," because the results may not be what you'd intended.

Dr. Russell put a new twist on this idea. His point was that whatever we truly, deeply want most of all – *whether we admit it or are even aware of it* – is likely to come to us in some form.

And, he added, often what we want most of all isn't money or something we can buy with money. But we end up making money from it anyway.

It can actually be harder to make money by chasing it than to make money by chasing our dreams.

Here's another contradiction. Silicon Valley is portrayed as being driven by venture capital and a quest for wealth.

I've been part of a startup that went public, the Silicon Valley equivalent of winning the Super Bowl. Yet as I remember working on that small team, the strongest memory is how much we all loved the products and the work we were doing, even when few people had ever heard of the company.

That's when I remember Dr. Russell's advice: "Be careful what it is that you truly want in your life, because you're likely to get it."

What we all passionately wanted was to build great games, and to be appreciated for the work we did. Because of that passion and focus we got what we really wanted: the fulfillment of having done great work that's still respected many years after the company was founded.

But it also turned out that, because we did great work, the company and the team made a lot of money.

Dr. Russell may have been a great music teacher, but he was even better at teaching us about life.

CHAPTER 21

What to Do with Your Answers (3.1–3.3)

"A DREAMER IS ONE WHO CAN ONLY FIND THEIR WAY
BY MOONLIGHT, AND THEIR PUNISHMENT IS THAT THEY
SEE THE DAWN BEFORE THE REST OF THE WORLD."

— Oscar Wilde

If you have not yet written down your answers, please go back and do so. Writing your thoughts down – even when you're the only one who'll ever read them – will produce far more insights than just answering silently to yourself in your head.

3.0.1 Diving Deeper into the Process

At the start of this book I described what I call the Passion-Process-Product Method:

- We start with our passions
- We experiment to develop a process that allows us to work on our Dream Project, either part-time or as a full-time job
- When we're ready, we launch our product

As we reach Section 3 of this book we are well into the Process stage of the Passion-Process-Product approach. The task may at times feel daunting, but if you keep going the journey can also be a lot of fun.

Most of all, remember the single most important advice I share in this book: only you can discover and decide upon the right path to take to create your Dream Project.

DISCUSSING QUESTION 3.1

When you're working on your Dream Project what will your business card say?

Will it be your only business card or will you still "keep your day job?"

Why did you choose this job title for your card?

This topic is most relevant for: Everyone

3.1.1 Titles and Choices

What title do you put on your business card?

On one-person projects you're doing everything, so the decision about your title is all about marketing. Do you say "Jewelry Designer" to emphasize your craft, "Design Director" to make the business sound larger, or "President" to tell people that you're the founder?

There are only two "wrong answers" when choosing a title:

1. Never sign up for a job you won't do well.
2. Never allow yourself to take a role in your company that doesn't primarily involve doing work you enjoy. Taking a role you hate, even for the best reasons, soon erases your love for the work and for its outcome.

DISCUSSING QUESTION 3.2

To what kinds of people will you hand your business card? What will you want from them?

What benefit will they expect to gain from knowing you?

What will be the actual benefit they gain from knowing you?

This topic is most relevant for: Everyone

3.2.1 That Little Devil on Your Shoulder

How are you feeling as you hand out your card? You're almost certainly feeling proud, because this is your Dream Project.

But what other emotions, in addition to pride, will you be feeling as you pull out that little piece of printed cardboard?

When I founded my first company I was exceptionally proud to hand someone my card. To start with, David Bunnett, our Art Director, had done a fantastic job on the card's design, so I usually got compliments on it. More importantly, I was really confident in the quality of our first products – both turned out to be successful.

Every time I looked at the letters "CEO" on my business card, however, a little voice spoke up inside my head.

"I don't have an MBA," the little voice would tell me. "I've been through management training with three different companies, but that was all at the Director or VP level. I feel comfortable leading the team, but I can't stop worrying. I don't have formal CEO training, and I could be making big rookie mistakes. Next to an Ivy League MBA I look like an amateur. Maybe I'm in over my head."

What I did not know as I endlessly repeated this internal message of self-doubt to myself is that the Ivy League MBA's whom I envied were doing the same thing.

I've talked with friends from top business schools who've shared that a little voice in their head kept telling them, "It's the Stanford MBA (or Yale, or Columbia, etc.) that got me the chance to start this company, and the fact that I was once part of a team on a successful startup. But I was just two years out of school when I became a junior member of that team. I keep meeting CEO's who have years of experience working their way up the ladder in great companies. Next to them I look like an amateur. Maybe I'm in over my head."

This self-sabotaging dialogue is not restricted to CEO's. I've discussed the issue with everyone from Chief Technology Officers to CFO's and from Concept Artists to Advertising Buyers. The majority of them have had that same self-inflicted demotivating experience.

If this "maybe I'm in over my head" dialogue sounds like you, it's good to recognize it. Half the battle is knowing that the self-doubt is normal.

That makes it a lot easier to ignore the discouraging little voice in your head, which is exactly what you need to do.

3.2.2 A Hundred Reasons to Hand Out Your Card

The list you made of people to whom you'll hand your business cards says a lot about what you think you'll be doing on your Dream Project. But sometimes we can miss big opportunities.

Did you list, "people to whom we're selling, pitching, evangelizing, etc.?" In almost all businesses someone has to go out and do the selling. If you didn't list customers as someone to whom you'll be giving your business card, you need to think about:

1. Who will do the selling so all your hard work can generate revenue and results? Or...

2. How will you learn to be great at those selling, pitching and evangelizing duties, since you'll be doing them yourself?

Did you list, "people whom we're recruiting?" First-time CEO's or senior managers often see recruiting and hiring as a secondary part of their job. One of the secrets of Silicon Valley is that it's actually a critical and primary function. If you can't build a great team you can't build a great company.

Did you list "investors?" Although there are other ways to build a business, if you're trying to build something big it's likely you'll be pitching to investors. If you don't have experience, I cover some of the basics later in this book and provide suggestions on other resources.

Did you list "partners and allies?" Many young companies accelerate their progress when their product or service produces a benefit for a much larger company, inspiring an alliance between the two.

For example, if your video editing software shows off the speed and power of Intel's or NVIDIA's computer chips they may be willing to co-develop marketing programs that promote how well your products work together.

If your hand-made stoneware is used at one of the hottest restaurants in the city, you may feature them on your website in return for your company name being listed on their daily menus as their exclusive stoneware providers.

Building these alliances is a key part of a CEO's job.

DISCUSSING QUESTION 3.3

What will you spend most of your time doing each day when you're working on your Dream Project?

This topic is most relevant for: Everyone

3.3.1 Never Enough Hours in a Day

If I'd answered this question back when I founded my first company, my prediction would have been wildly inaccurate.

With just a few people on the team, I found that the coordination of the project and all the extra paperwork that comes with being a CEO conspired to keep me away from the product design work I loved. Being a VP at a large, established company – where much of the admin work is done for you — takes less paperwork time than being CEO of a small, lean startup.

Payroll alone was a twice-a-month exercise in hours of agony, since I had resisted paying for our bank's payroll service to do it for us (which I should have embraced from our first week of operations). Making sure the California and Federal employment taxes and deductions were calculated correctly so we didn't have to pay penalties took an hour all by itself on each cycle.

Not all such distractions are predictable. When you're leading a company all sorts of "unique events" can take your time. Some of the surprises can be wild.

One time the local police issued an arrest warrant for one of our team members. It turned out to be a mistake, but I still lost a full day dealing with the police, other freaked-out team members, and the even more freaked-out team member who was being sought.

Or the day when a key team member's spouse showed up at the office and wanted to help me reorganize our project plan. Right then and there.

Bizarre stuff happens in every group, because we are all unique and human. When you're the leader of a team, everyone's bizarre stuff (at least the public variety) becomes your stuff, too.

So how can you forecast how much time you'll have to work on your product or service?

You can't. In any venture, the more people you have on your team, the more time the CEO and other leaders will spend managing. And that means there will be less time spent selling, researching, creating art, code, or whatever is your personal craft.

CHAPTER 22

Roles and Systems (3.4)

DISCUSSING QUESTION 3.4

If there's anyone else working in the office with you, how will they be spending their day?

If there are people working with you who live and do their jobs somewhere else, what will they be doing each day?

How will you monitor their progress?

This topic is most relevant for: Dream Projects that involve more than one person.

3.4.1 Staying on Track

Your Dream Project may be building fine cabinetry, or importing and distributing Japanese graphic novels, or opening a garden shop that specializes in succulents. If more than one person is involved in the process, by definition, you have a team.

That means that the lessons professionals learn in product development – a team-driven process — can be of help to you.

For example, in mobile app development a small Indie team might have a CEO who is also the designer, along with one programmer and one artist. (They'll need more people after their product ships but I'm keeping this simple as an example.) The three of them sit together in a small room and work with their laptops on a single round table.

The CEO looks across the table at his co-founders and sees them working diligently. But how does he know that they're doing the right tasks? How does he know that they're doing them well? Or that the users in the initial product tests will be able to try out the app by the scheduled deadline?

They're all experienced in this kind of work. The CEO has confidence in their overall abilities. But teams of great people mess up all the time, due to misunderstandings, misplaced priorities and so on.

"Well," you might say, "they'll have agreed on what they're each doing, and the CEO will have a list of features and so on. He knows what they're working on and can see their progress."

That's true. But how do you know that an engineer is half way through completing something?

As one example, I've held the job of Sr. Engineer, and I'll tell you what I learned. When it looks like you're half way there, you're often only 10% of the way to being "done."

You can fool yourself into thinking you're closing in on final code when you're not even close, which means it's easy to mislead your teammates on scheduling.

The same thing happens in other disciplines.

Concept art that's been approved by the Art Director looks like it's ready to drop into the app. But users may think the "Continue" button looks like a toaster. A button may be checked in that takes 32K of memory when the app needs something that fits in 2K.

Changing the color of a button or shaving two millimeters off its size can produce a revenue gain or loss of $200,000 a year. Saving $200K isn't a task you skip past because you don't have a free day in the schedule, which is why completion dates are hard to predict.

You can't run a company just on faith that everyone's work will turn out right on the first try. You can't just assume that all tasks will be completed on time.

3.4.2 The Simple Secrets of Management

There are many excellent books on how to lead teams. Below are a few key points that I've learned working with great managers over the years.

Listen first. When I first met Southwest Airlines Chairman Joel Peterson at a Stanford Graduate School of Business Igniters event, he started our conversation by asking about my background instead of waiting for me to ask a question.

I could tell that he was really listening to me as we talked, not thinking about things he had to do when he got home. Now imagine that your boss always listened intently to you – how good would that feel? What would you need to do to be that kind of boss?

No surprise: Peterson's book, *The 10 Laws of Trust: Building the Bonds That Make a Business Great* is concise and well worth reading.

Weekly 1:1's. I believe that every manager needs to schedule a one-on-one with each of their direct reports each week. When I hear managers say they don't have time, my response is, "what's a higher priority than listening and communicating with your team?"

Most 1:1 meetings are fairly short and review key issues, but occasionally something makes a 1:1 into a very important and thoughtful meeting that runs longer. These can turn out to be some of the most valuable meetings you have all year.

In addition to reviewing key objectives, progress and potential problems, there are two key questions to ask in each one-on-one:

- "How are you feeling?"
- "How can I be of help to you?"

Expect success. Strong performers are motivated by an environment where success is expected of every individual and of the team as a whole. Everyone deserves to start out with your trust and confidence, which motivates them to appreciate and preserve those valuable assets.

Spend more time with your top performers than with less productive team members. Most of us fall into the opposite pattern if we don't consciously alter it. Focusing on the best people is a pattern I've seen in many highly effective managers, because it amplifies the strengths of an organization rather than diverting attention to lingering problems that should already have been resolved.

Don't hire or retain weak performers. It may be a lack of the right skills, or a mismatch of person and job. Either way, continual efforts to turn a weak contributor into a strong one rarely succeed, and distract leaders from higher priorities. Both parties need to find a better fit elsewhere.

Ask before you tell. I discuss "showing respect for everyone on the team" in several different contexts in this book. There's no better way to show respect than to ask for — and seriously consider — someone's opinion.

It won't be feasible on every topic, but whenever it's possible ask your leading team members for their input on tough issues, both 1:1 and in small groups. Then take the time to really listen to their answers and consider them. When time permits, you can broaden these requests for input to more people across the entire team.

With my teams the ideas presented by team members often were better than some – or all – of the solutions I was considering before I asked for input.

Keep making new mistakes. Highly productive teams try lots of initiatives, make lots of mistakes, and then quickly utilize that learning to improve. So long as people don't repeat the same mistake, supporting this "learn by doing" approach motivates and retains top performers.

MBWA ("Management by Walking Around"). You can't lead a group of people if you're stuck in an office. Walk around every day and randomly ask team members, "How are you doing?" Then demonstrate the listening skills mentioned above. People will notice and respond.

Criticize and correct in private. Routine everyday feedback occurs in public, but if I need to deliver a strong negative message I do it calmly in private. "Treat it as a teaching moment" is some of the best advice I ever received.

I had to learn not to soften the message or "beat around the bush." Just wade in, calmly say what needs to be said, then listen to the response and move on.

Celebrate in public. People should be honored in front of the whole team when something was done well. Every Friday we give some small award or recognition for great work that week. If a small group completes a difficult challenge we praise them in front of the whole team.

If a manager praises a team member in our leadership meeting I'll practice "MBWA" and drop by that person's desk to say, "I heard about how you came up with a clever solution for [the problem]. That was great work."

Play by the same rules you declare for others. Do the things you tell people you're going to do and keep your word. Meet your own deadlines. Admit it when you make a mistake. *This single point is some of the most important – and difficult to consistently maintain – advice in this book.*

None of this is new, and most of it isn't easy. People of many cultures, generations and eras appreciate the same things from their leaders.

British Field Marshal Sir William Slim told his officers 75 years ago (and the full text is well worth reading if you search for it online):

"I tell you as officers, that you will not eat, sleep, smoke, sit down, or lie down until your soldiers have had a chance to do these things. If you hold to this, they will follow you to the ends of the earth... Spare no effort to praise and reward soldiers for outstanding performance — it costs nothing and gains everything... Soldiers are smart and can smell a phony a mile away. Get to know the soldiers in your platoon. After three months, you should know their names, names of family members, home towns, and any unique problems with which you can help... If you take good care of your soldiers they will take care of you."

3.4.3 The Most Common Mistakes of New Managers

Steve Jobs, Warren Buffett and Jeff Bezos all were first-time managers at some point in their careers. It's a rite of passage we all go through.

In this section I'll share the most common mistakes that I see managers make early in their careers, and some basic ways to avoid each trap. We'll also cover these issues in greater depth below.

Oh, and one more thing: I made each of these mistakes myself as I was learning how to lead teams.

Problem 1: Being buddies instead of being a manager with a team. This is one of the most common problems I see in my advisory work. The manager has worked for bad leaders who disrespected team members, and they're determined to act like a friend instead of a boss.

The solution: It's important to demonstrate respect for everyone on the team, but someone has to be in charge. If that's you, strong performers *want* you to lead the team and direct the work that's being done.

If the team isn't getting things done or isn't making money (or achieving some other critical goal), people won't go home each night feeling proud of the company. And they won't get the promotions, the raises or the bonuses they hope for.

Leaders who respect everyone around them and are focused on producing strong results are far more popular than the managers who try to be liked.

Respect and results are the two most important things a manager has to demonstrate, and the former is critical to producing the latter.

This "buddy" issue can also take the form of trying too hard to run the business like a family, something I did earlier in my career. Consider the following list of leadership attitudes:

- Sincerely liking the people on the team
- Wanting to do right by them
- Respecting them and showing that respect
- Helping people develop new skills and advance their careers
- Compensating people fairly
- Showing consideration for individuals with families or other obligations that may require flexibility in work times

This list represents things that good managers do, regardless of whether they think of their company as a business, a family or anything else.

But there are places where those business and family models diverge. If our young children continually failed to do things they needed to do, didn't pay attention at school, etc. we would have taken action to get them back on track.

First we'd talk with them. If that didn't work we'd try turning off the video game system, cutting back on TV time, suspending a favorite activity until they corrected the problem.

But we couldn't fire them and kick them out of the house, because they're family.

Sometimes team members who have been valuable and productive will start to have performance problems. Our senior managers and I would sit and talk with them, try to figure out what was wrong, try to help them correct the problems.

But if they couldn't fix those performance problems after we worked with them and gave them opportunities to improve, they'd be fired.

Managers who get too preoccupied with the idea of "family" take too long to challenge, discipline and terminate poor performers. By doing so they lose the respect of their top performers instead of winning the loyalty they feel their "family" attitude deserves.

A related problem is...

Problem 2: Responsibility without accountability. You may have heard of "Responsibility without authority." This means assigning someone a goal without giving them enough control or resources to achieve it. Picture someone who's directed to complete all arrangements for a team's air travel, but who's given no authority to spend money to book the flights.

Responsibility without accountability is the opposite problem: a manager has the authority and the resources to do a job, but doesn't take action to ensure that the team achieves the desired results. The same individual creates problems, doesn't get things done, produces less than their peers, but nothing ever happens.

People wonder, "Doesn't the manager see what's going on?"

Let's say that Anne, Barbara and Carlos each oversee a department in a local clothing store. They schedule staff time, and ensure that shelves and dressing rooms are straightened as time allows.

If you walk through the store you'd see that Barbara and Carlos have their areas staffed and that everything looks inviting and fresh. But it can be hard to find help in Anne's department. Some areas look more like a dorm room than a stylish display. Anne's sales totals are just as disappointing.

Inexperienced leaders may hesitate to discipline Anne for her poor performance. It's not fun to tell people that their work needs to improve, and sometimes those people get angry. It feels awful to fire people.

If he does nothing but admonish Anne, the store owner is practicing responsibility without accountability. He's not insisting that managers achieve results. The weak and the strong managers get the same treatment.

After a few months Barbara gets tired of reading bad Yelp reviews about the business where she works – based on Anne's department — and she quits. Strong performers want to feel proud of the company and everything it does.

Problem 3: Not setting clear goals, objectives and ground rules in advance, and putting them in writing. I'm often hired to help young (and not so young) companies when projects start to fall behind schedule. The most common cause for these problems is that the team started doing its work without first having agreed upon the most basic aspects of a plan for the collaborative work they were about to do.

I'm not talking about writing a 50-page plan packed with details. What's often missing is a set of answers to the most basic questions of how the project will be completed, answers that can be worked out in a few hours of meetings at the beginning of the project.

Let's say you're one of eight teachers who are collaborating to write a textbook. As you start out, the leader and the team would sit down together and agree on:

- **Who** as editor would direct the team and approve the final version of each chapter (usually the project leader)

- **What** subjects would be covered, and what unifying threads run through the chapters.

- **How**: Guidelines for chapter length, fonts, formats, footnotes, illustrations etc.

- **Who** would write each chapter

- **When** the first draft, second draft and final copy of each chapter would be due

- **When and where** you'd meet to review issues, resolve questions, share feedback on each other's work, etc.

- **How much** you'd each be paid (often discussed individually in private)

- **When** payments would be made

If a plan meets these "who-what-when-where-why-how much" objectives for each step in a project and has a realistic budget and schedule, it's probably a good starting point for the team.

Passion and excitement are wonderful components of creating a Dream Project.

Starting without a basic plan – even if it just covers the initial experiments to develop a new idea – makes everything much harder to complete.

Problem 4: Under-delegating and Over-delegating. There is no such thing as a perfect level of delegation. It's like driving a car on a narrow, twisting road: you have to continually watch what's going on and adjust accordingly.

Under-delegating is a fancy term for micro-managing the team and not letting go of the details. All decisions are made by the leader, instead of being distributed to the right people at the right levels of the team, and reviewed via the right processes.

Your strongest contributors will resent micro-managing the most, and I've found that it's useful to regularly ask those top people for their feedback on the issue.

Over-delegating is often a side effect of managers trying to be popular with the team. They relinquish control of day-to-day processes, allowing team members to make important decisions without the manager's review, feedback or approval. The manager doesn't ask tough questions, doesn't review and adjust where time and money are being spent, doesn't intervene until problems become big, and tries to be a people-pleaser when it's time to make tough decisions.

Team members resent micro-managers.

They develop contempt for over-delegators.

Neither extreme produces results for the teams these people lead.

Problem 5: Managing deadlines with hope instead of action. It can be very hard to predict how long any project will take unless you've already done the same job several times. So what happens when a project – as so often happens – starts to run late?

The roots of the delay can be a combination of many different factors. The project could:

- Have been started without a clear plan, so many people are unclear on what to do
- Be larger than planned and take longer to complete
- Have too few people on the team
- Have one element that is very difficult to complete
- Have lots of components that are 20% done, but nothing that's completed
- Be discarding lots of work because it doesn't fit the project's requirements
- Any of a wide range of other issues

What should a manager do? First of all, keep careful track of progress, week by week or (for shorter projects) day by day, starting at the very beginning of the effort. I discuss methods for doing this below.

The moment you see that something is running late, investigate the reasons and then ask yourself and the team, "What do we have to do to keep this problem from continuing?"

The potential answers are diverse: cut features, add people, get different people, increase the budget, redesign things, reorganize things, cancel the project altogether, or do something else.

A steady stream of small changes and revisions can help keep a project on time. If these adjustments aren't made continually, eventually the dramatic actions needed to put the project back on schedule later on will cost lots of money, lower the product's quality, and/or further delay the completion date.

The leader's job is to work with the team to identify problems quickly, develop potential solutions... and then act decisively to do what's needed to get back on schedule.

3.4.4 "If Only We Had Known..." Project Management

Here's one example of "Managing deadlines with hope instead of action."

One month into a project the team leader knows that they're running behind, and so do his team members. Even with lots of experience, they fall far short of what they had hoped to accomplish in the first month.

They're already working their hearts out, but they have to catch up with the schedule so they work even harder. Nobody's getting much sleep, but it feels like they're operating in slow motion, even as they race ahead.

They may suffer from "feature creep," where great ideas keep being added to the project but corresponding cuts in lower priority features are not made. Since the project can only become larger, never smaller, it's guaranteed that the team will miss its deadline.

The schedule continues to slip, and everyone works harder and harder and harder. They cut some small features but refuse to cut anything big and important.

With only ten days left to go before the big deadline, it's clear that disaster is imminent. The only way to make the date is to cut two of the five big features planned for the product, something they have steadfastly refused to do.

They have no choice, so they make those cuts. But even this leaves little time to polish the remaining three key items. The initial product is good, but it looks and feels rough instead of polished.

Everyone says, "If only we'd known at the start that we were going to have to make those cuts! We could have put all that time into just three features, and they would have been elegant and solid instead of sketchy."

3.4.5 Picking a System

The only way to prevent this scenario is to use some kind of a detailed project management system.

I'm a fan of the Agile project management approach (which I summarize below). I learned the basics in one night by reading the first 70 pages of *Agile Project Management with Scrum*, by Ken Schwaber.

Agile is not owned by any company and was developed by a multiple-industry consortium, although there are many different books, software systems and apps that can help you use it.

If you're working as a solo entrepreneur an understanding of Agile systems is useful, but most of its rewards come with teams.

The initial time investment in a process like this can save you weeks or even months of wasted work down the road.

3.4.6 How I Learned Agile Development and Scrum

Why did I become so strongly committed to using this system?

We tried using Agile on a project that ran for eleven months, with a team that peaked at about 60 people and a budget of close to $8 million. The game shipped on time, but our team already had a perfect record for meeting the carved-in-stone deadlines of big games.

Here's the consensus we heard from our team members at the post-completion review meeting:

- Using Agile and "Scrum" processes gave us about a 10% increase in how much we produced, without feeling like we had to work harder than before
- We worked late less often and had fewer times when people felt they had to come in over the weekend to make sure we met key deadlines
- People said they felt less stress than on our prior game, even though this one on paper looked like a tougher schedule
- We wasted less time and threw away less work that was done by mistake, or that had to be cut from the game (which may explain some of the benefits above)
- Over 90% of the team voted to use Agile on all of our projects going forward

As you can imagine, when I saw how strongly our team supported the idea I adopted it without hesitation.

When teams fully commit to an Agile system they acquire natural defenses against over-optimistic scheduling and "feature creep," the two factors that most often damage projects. It's based on simple everyday processes that keep projects on schedule and focused on the highest priority work.

Implementing Agile on an established team does require a transition process. I'm not excited about changing my habits or routine, and neither is the typical team member. Nevertheless, it's worth working through the issues.

3.4.7 Summary of Agile Project Management Terms

Please remember that the summary below is a super-simplified "cheat sheet" for a system that is relatively easy to learn, but where all the details don't fit on two or three pages.

I've organized the information by defining key terms, and listing them in order as they'd come up on a project:

Product Owner. The term for the person who leads the team and directs its work.

Sprints. At the start of a project the team leaders decide how long the chunks of time into which the project is to be broken should be. Each of these blocks of time is called a "sprint." A long project may have sprints that last a month each, others may go for two weeks. Projects that need very short cycles use a related system called "Kanban," which you can learn online or via guidebooks.

Sprint requirements. Every sprint has the goal of completing a planned set of features that can be demonstrated and tested, even if it's in a very basic manner. This keeps teams focused on finishing the highest priority elements of the product on each sprint. It also prevents teams from starting work on too many features at the same time and never finishing anything.

Sprint Planning. At the start of each sprint the team meets to decide what features they'll complete on that cycle. They then break those features down into tasks and people volunteer to be the ones who will complete each task and estimate how long it will take.

User Stories. Each feature is called a "User Story" or simply a Story. This comes from the idea that every product feature can be described by a sentence that starts out with, "The user will be able to..." This is part of the Agile focus on finishing something useful in every sprint.

Scrum Master. The Scrum Master organizes the lists of planned features, tasks and time estimates from the Sprint Planning process. Each task is then printed on a card with its volunteer's name and its projected duration. This may be done by a software package or completed manually by the Scrum Master.

Scrum Team. The typical Scrum Team size in Agile is about five to eight people, so in a large project the team would split into sub-groups.

Scrum Task Board. At the start of each sprint the Scrum Master prepares a bulletin board or wall in a dedicated space or room. They create columns of index cards that are tacked or taped to the wall. This is called a Scrum Task Board. Tasks for the current sprint are sorted into columns for:

- Not yet started
- Started
- In Test (or "To Verify")
- Completed

Scrum Meeting and Scrum Room. Each morning each scrum team meets in an unoccupied office or a reserved area called a Scrum Room for a maximum of 15 minutes. Everyone is expected to arrive on time, and if you're late the team will start without you.

There are no chairs in the Scrum Room and no one will sit down (apart from the requirements of a physical disability). This makes everyone want to wrap up fast and get to work.

During each Scrum Meeting each team member:

- Shares what they completed the prior day
- Describes in a sentence or two what they plan to complete today
- Moves their task cards to the correct column for "Started," "In Test" etc.

If the team realizes that a task is missing from the plan they write it down, assign it and add it to the board. Over the course of a sprint all the task cards will gradually march across the board from left to right as they are started, tested and completed.

Blockers. If anything is keeping someone from completing a task it's called a "blocker." A blocker can be as simple as "my computer's not working" or as complex as "I can't complete the website until we get all of the photos." Blockers are called out in the meeting and passed along to the Scrum Master, but any discussion of solutions is postponed until after the Scrum Meeting to save everyone else's time.

Burndown Chart. After the Scrum Meetings for each team the Scrum Master checks on the status of each task for this sprint and where it sits on the board. They then use their chosen Agile software system to prepare a "burndown chart," which keeps track of how much work for this sprint has been completed and how much is yet to be finished. This allows teams to recognize it immediately if they start to run behind so they can decide what to cut, what to keep and how to prioritize resources.

Sprint Review. At the end of each sprint the teams demonstrate their tested and functional work and earn applause from the project team. If all of the sprint goals are not met the meeting is not as happy, and the lessons learned are carried over into the next sprint.

Product Backlog. Any tasks that were cut from the plan during this sprint are automatically added to a "Product Backlog," which is a list of tasks that have not yet been completed. These are then considered for inclusion in the following sprint.

The Sprint Retrospective Meeting. At the end of each sprint the entire group discusses three questions in an open meeting:

- What worked well during the last sprint?
- What did not work well?
- How could we do better on the next sprint?

At the end of every project a final Sprint Retrospective is held, which covers the lessons from the project as a whole.

On the first couple of Agile projects you undertake, I recommend that you follow the standard rules in the guidebooks. It's hard to customize a recipe to your own tastes until you've made the meal a couple of times and tasted the results.

3.4.8 The Simplest System: Weekly Objectives

If you're hesitant to jump into using Agile, I've used the very basic system described below in a variety of settings. It does two things extremely well:

- It keeps everyone on the team – including the CEO – focused on the highest priority tasks that need to get done each week.
- It tracks whether those tasks are being completed.

Note that this system does not by itself keep complex projects on schedule.

Once a team gets used to the process it takes about 20 minutes a week unless an unusual issue comes up.

Step 1: Definition. Each week the leader and the team sit down together. We go around the room and each team member answers the following question:

"What are the two most important things I absolutely positively have to get done in the next seven days?"

They don't list things they hope to get done. They don't everything they plan to do. They only list the two most important things that they absolutely positively guarantee they are going to get done in this week.

The group also discusses and agrees on the two most important objectives for the company as a whole.

Completion Criteria. Objectives always have to be worded in such a way that the question, "Did you complete it?" can be answered with a yes or no. "I'll make the presentation look nicer," is an unclear objective. What I think makes it nicer might, in your eyes, make it worse.

"I'll add at least eight new images to the presentation" is very clear: either there are eight new images in the deck one week from now or there aren't.

Review and Discussion. If anyone in the meeting sees that a key task is being missed, they can raise it.

Step 2: Writing It Down. The objectives are written down during the meeting, and afterwards they are sent out as an email, printed and taped to a door etc.

Step 3: Follow Up. The following week the team meets again. Everyone, including the leader, takes a turn answering "yes" or "no" about whether they completed each objective according to its criteria.

When everyone has answered the group then sets objectives for the coming week.

Everyone will miss an objective once in a while. If a team member has a regular pattern of not meeting two reasonable objectives in a week, it suggests that:

• They may not understand how the system works

- They may be unclear on what they should be doing that week
- They may be receiving contradictory direction or input about what needs to be done
- They may have a performance issue that needs to be addressed

Changes. Sometimes something happens during the week that changes priorities. Maybe there's a big storm and the building loses power for a day, so several people cannot complete some of the work they'd planned.

If I'm an artist, I could send a note to my manager, and say I'd like to change my objective from "complete redesign of home page of website" to "diagram on paper the menus we'll implement in phase two" since we have no power today. The manager approves it, and the next Monday I confirm that I completed this revised objective.

If you don't have a system of your own, give this one a try. I believe you'll find it makes communication more clear and reduces wasted time. After the first couple of iterations it will take very little time each week.

CHAPTER 23

Making Tradeoffs (3.5-3.6)

DISCUSSING QUESTION 3.5

If you're planning to take on major leadership duties as the company grows, are you ready to let go of controlling every detail of creating your products or services, and to let other people lead those functions?

If you find yourself hesitating to let go of daily control of the key product or service, why do you think you're feeling that way?

This topic is most relevant for: Dream Projects that will grow to employ a team.

3.5.1 Cutting the Rope

Occasionally I'll be mentoring at an accelerator when a startup team member – not the CEO – will ask to talk in private. The discussion will go something like this.

"Thanks for talking with me," she'll start out. "I've got a problem with the UX design for our product."

"What's wrong?" I ask her.

"It's Jeff. The spec he wrote teaches kids reading in a whole new way using a tablet. He's a brilliant guy."

"I agree," I tell her.

"But he keeps giving me new suggestions, and we've got a deadline to meet. He's the Founder so I don't want to tell him to stop, but..."

"You're afraid you'll miss your ship date," I suggest.

She nods. "I think he's just trying to make the screens feel alive with animations. That's... I like that approach and I think it's good that he keeps reminding me."

"Uh-huh," I say.

"The thing is, I get emails from him every day," she tells me. "He wants me to discuss everything in detail. I think he misses doing the design himself and he just can't let go."

It happens all the time. I'm sure that my team members said the same thing about me when I first delegated my design role.

As an organization grows the leaders have to delegate more and more of the details. The CEO can retain control through the approvals and signoff process, but we can't be supervising every team member every minute.

And if we could do so, they'd all get mad and quit!

DISCUSSING QUESTION 3.6

What's the one small part of the project you most dislike having to delegate to someone else?

What's the one small part of the project where you can't wait for the company to grow, so you can finally delegate that part of the job to someone else and you won't have to do it anymore?

This topic is most relevant for: Dream Projects that will grow to employ a team.

3.6.1 Bouquets and Boredom

Whatever you chose as your favorite small thing you hate to delegate, watch this issue, because it's the place where you might find yourself "saying you're delegating but not really doing so."

Your least favorite thing? Every job has parts of the work day or work week that are less fun, and if you hate some small aspect of the job it's no big deal.

If what you dislike is at the core of building your Dream Project and your company, however, then your plan needs to be revised. Remember, the goal here is that much of the time you're doing work you love, not work that you think you ought to do.

CHAPTER 24

Deciding to Decide (3.7)

DISCUSSING QUESTION 3.7

You and a group of your leading team members are debating how to solve a major problem.

Several team members favor Choice A. Several others prefer Choice B. At times people on both sides start getting angry at each other. Two days later a second meeting ends with the group just as divided as it was before.

This is an important issue that can't be allowed to drag on forever. You're in charge of the team. How will you manage the process, resolve the debate and reach a decision?

This topic is most relevant for: Dream Projects that will grow to employ a team.

3.7.1 Decisions, Decisions, Decisions

In this question I'm not picturing petty rivals fighting over who gets the corner office. The topic may be something like this, where two reasonable people are deeply committed to very different and credible strategies:

Person A: We have to put more money into online marketing. The people who buy our app love it, but awareness is still way too low and if we want to get into the top 50 in the app stores then we have to increase sales.

Person B: You know that Acme and the other big players are bidding up the prices on our keywords. If we increase our bids to get more impressions and clickthroughs we're throwing away money. We should do a flash sale and cut prices for two weeks so we get more installs. That's how to make the Top 50.

Person A: That will just make things worse, because when we revert to higher prices users will be angry and we'll lose more sales than we gained. We have to spend on product awareness, which means online display ads.

Person B: Users know about us, they just don't like the pricing. Maybe we should just do a price cut across the board, do it once and take our medicine. Then we'll start to climb the charts.

Person A: We can't do that! If we take our price point out of the premium category there's very little to keep it from being forced all the way down to 99 cents. We'd undermine the perceived value of the whole brand, which means we'd undermine the valuation of the whole company!

Which of our two debaters is right?

It could be either of them. It all depends on the product and its market position, and even if you had all that data at your fingertips the answer might not be obvious.

Neither of the debaters is driven by selfish motives. Both are trying to make the company successful. Yet as they argue they're getting more and more angry at each other.

Bob Wallace is a highly-respected software industry advisor based in Silicon Valley, and an ally from whom I have learned many valuable lessons. He has a saying that I always think about when I hear teams arguing: "Consensus is great... when you can get it."

There are many different ways to settle things when the leaders of a project, a function or a team don't readily find consensus. Some are useful, others destructive.

3.7.2 The Worst Possible Answer

If you drive north from Silicon Valley towards San Francisco, you have to decide which of the two parallel routes you'll take, Highway 101 or Highway 280.

Which one is faster? It depends on the time and the weather and whether schools are in session and...

When teams have a hard time deciding on major issues, I always remind them about that high-speed driving decision.

"If you can't decide whether to steer towards 280 or 101," I tell them, "you'll hit the concrete divider between the freeways at 70 miles an hour. Freeways remind us that on major business decisions either choice is usually better than no decision at all."

3.7.3 The Leader Decides

If you as CEO simply make a decision and tell everyone what to do, there is no danger of Death by Indecision.

But if you employ high-quality people who show initiative and think independently, making decisions solely based on rank and authority will undermine your support.

It's a strategy you can use occasionally when necessary, but there are usually better options.

3.7.4 Consensus Or Else

Here's the method I like to use on tough decisions. Note that I only handle issues this way if I'm willing to support the premise of any of the choices under discussion.

Step 1: The Leader Questions. I'll ask questions like, "What would you do if sales in our category started to slip for one or both of the big app stores, rather than growing as we think they will?"

A logical series of questions, asked without prejudice or emotion, can create a more collaborative brainstorming mood in the room.

If this discussion does not produce a consensus answer that allows us to proceed, we move on to...

Step 2: The Leader Provides a Deadline. I'll share with the team, "It sounds like we're stuck. Let's break for now and think on it. If you guys can come up with a consensus answer to recommend to me by noon Friday I'd love to see it. If we're still stuck at that point I'll make a final call and we'll move on."

The benefits of this approach are:

> **The team has time to try to brainstorm and collaborate to arrive at their own solution**. They have the chance to make a decision on their own.

> **People are motivated to keep looking for agreement** because they prefer solving their own problems to being told what to do.

> **There is a clear, pre-announced deadline**, so when that moment comes no one is surprised.

> **Everyone knows that, one way or another, a decision will be made** by Friday.

Step 3: The Decision. In my experience even angry debaters will often work out a compromise to avoid being told what to do by the CEO!

If I'm given a recommendation I'll review it with the team members, ask questions, and sometimes I'll adjust some details. Most often the decision they are recommending is a good one and is approved.

If we still don't have agreement by noon on Friday, I'll make a final decision based on the arguments from all sides.

My decision may or may not be popular. But everyone on the team will recognize that I gave them a chance to solve it on their own, and that we're never hobbled by indecision.

3.7.5 Parkinson was Right

Many years ago an economist named C. N. Parkinson came up with "Parkinson's Law" as both a serious and a humorous commentary on our nature as human beings. It states:

"Work expands to fill the time available for its completion."

I am a great example of how this law works.

When I'm getting ready for work in the morning I try to shave, brush my teeth, shower and get dressed at an efficient pace. I don't want to waste time because I'm usually excited about something I want to work on.

Even with all that motivation, on days when I don't have an early call or meeting I may pause to hear the weather forecast on the radio, or get lost in thought as I brush my teeth.

On days when I have a deadline my behavior is different. I shave and shower more quickly. I keep moving when an interesting story comes on the radio. I throw on my clothes in no time.

As Parkinson would put it, on non-deadline days my work expands to fill the time available for its completion.

I teach CEO's how important it is to understand Parkinson's Law, because it applies to every team.

I also teach them that trying to have "perfect" efficiency under Parkinson's Law is a recipe for disaster:

Each task has its own reasonable minimum time. You could not say, "Hey Don, if you'd focused more you could have written this book in eight hours!"

Perfect efficiency squeezes all the joy out of work. In the early and mid-1900's companies engaged in "time and motion studies" to determine the fastest possible time that any task in a factory could be done. They would then push every employee to execute at that speed. Needless to say, the executives doing the pushing were not having their workdays scrutinized in the same way!

Good teams will operate effectively even if they're not being pushed. Strong project management can increase teams' effectiveness without making work feel like hard labor.

I believe that good leaders are aware of Parkinson's Law and work to minimize its negative impact... without over-doing it.

3.7.6 The Concept of Timeboxing

When we develop new products, parts of the project are purely creative. How long does it take to design the next great breakthrough product?

It depends on whether you ask the question before the product is invented or after your face appears on the cover of Forbes or Fortune.

So how do we schedule things when we can't predict exactly how long everything will take?

Part of the answer is "timeboxing," and I used it with the teams that couldn't settle their argument above. By giving them two days to try to solve a problem on their own before I made a decision for them I defined a "time box" within which they had to complete their work.

This works well for resolving debates, but it also has uses in projects where teams are trying to come up with new ideas, designs, concepts, etc.

Let's say that you are CEO of a fruit juice company and you assemble a team to create a new blend of flavors. You could give your team:

- Two weeks to do research on current fruit juice blends
- Three weeks to formulate three potential new blends that meet higher nutritional standards and have a pleasing taste
- Three weeks to test the new blends with consumers, note their reactions and adjust the recipes based on the feedback they receive

At the end of two months, as CEO you'll try the final blends, study the research results and decide which new blends – if any – will be added to your product line.

Why is exactly one or two or three weeks the right timeline for each step? There is no magic answer, and managers will experiment to produce the best results.

When using time boxes, remember Parkinson's Law. Always look for the smallest time period that still produces good results without forcing the team into working at an unreasonable pace.

CHAPTER 25

Playing to Your Strengths (3.8-3.13)

DISCUSSING QUESTIONS 3.8 AND 3.9

Question 3.8: What's the project from your career where teammates and customers or users gave you the most praise for your work?

What were the specific things you did (as best you can remember) that earned that praise?

If your boss praised you for one thing and your peers valued you for something else, and the users valued still a third skill, write down answers for each category.

Question 3.9: If you've managed people in your work, at which position did the people who reported to you give you the most positive feedback? What specific things did you do to earn that praise?

Question 3.8 is most relevant for: Everyone

Question 3.9 is most relevant for: People who have previously managed teams or businesses

3.8.1 What Position Do You Play?

Early in my career I worked at a company that sent managers to a week-long leadership training program. Their goal was to prepare us for more senior roles.

As part of the exercise we received detailed "360-degree" reviews that the consultants conducted, gathering feedback from our bosses, peers and direct reports.

There were eight managers in our little group, from different departments across the company. We each faced different challenges.

When they handed out the reviews we all got very different feedback. But there was one pattern all eight of us had in common.

Every single one of us thought we delegated responsibility to our teams and that we did it well.

Every single one of our teams disagreed.

After a long career of leading companies and advising clients, I've learned that relying solely on self-perception doesn't work. We have to get real and honest feedback from other people.

That's why I asked about when the people around you gave you the most compliments. That praise is an independent sign of where your greatest natural strengths may be found.

So long as those strengths align with your personal passions, they're a great place to start planning your personal role in building your Dream Project.

(Question 3.9 is also covered by the text above.)

DISCUSSING QUESTIONS 3.10, 3.11 AND 3.12

Question 3.10: What's the biggest project you've worked on start-to-finish that shipped successfully?

Question 3.11: What's the biggest role you personally have ever had on a project that shipped successfully?

Question 3.12: What's the biggest project or component of a project you've ever led? How many people did you direct on the project?

These topics are most relevant for: Everyone

3.10.1 The Biggest Job You Ever Mastered

When you start a company you're hiring yourself to do a job. In fact, you're hiring yourself to do several different jobs, and to do them simultaneously!

If the projects where you have gotten the most praise have been ones where you were an individual contributor rather than a leader, it doesn't mean that you're not cut out to manage people. All it means is that you haven't had the chance to lead yet, or haven't yet succeeded at doing so.

If your Dream Project involves leading a team for the first time, is there a way to move towards a leadership position in your current company? Can you hone those skills serving your present manager before you start out on your own?

Do you enjoy being a leader? Are you always on the organizing committee for the company party?

Or does being a manager feel like having to go to the dentist and get a tooth drilled five days a week?

I once worked with a really talented engineer who was also very good with people. He was a natural leader, very well-organized, and he was good at listening to people and giving them useful feedback. He earned great reviews as a leader. There was just one problem.

He hated being a manager.

This engineer wanted nothing more than to be programming on a really challenging assignment for our company. We paid managers and top non-managers similar salaries to avoid forcing them to go into management to earn more money, so there was no penalty for his decision. When he requested the change I approved it, with regrets.

If you hate managing, find a different person to do that job. Then you can focus on the work you love that will make your Dream Project special.

3.10.2 Learning on the Job

Or maybe it's just that you've never managed a business before and you're worried about it. It's rare that the leaders of small companies have experience in every aspect of their project.

My Master's Degree is in Education, not Business. My internship was spent teaching in barrio classrooms, not pitching in elegant board rooms. There are a lot of lessons about running a company that I learned by making mistakes. Lots of mistakes.

When I founded my first company many of the questions in this and the following sections of this book would have stumped me. My goal here is to make sure that in the future none of these questions stump you.

In a perfect world, the size of your team and your role within it should not dramatically exceed the size of your role in the largest project you've done while working for someone else.

Even if you have experience leading large teams, remember the K.I.S.S. principle: it's good to keep things a simple as possible.

Building something at a similar or smaller scale than projects you've experienced means:

- You've seen one way that people successfully tracked deadlines and managed schedules

- You understand the emotional ups and downs of working on deadline-driven teams with people who (like all of us) aren't perfect

- You've experienced what it's like to complete something and ship it

- You've lived through (and survived!) the 80-20 Rule (also called the Pareto Principle), which states: "The last 20% of the work takes 80% of the time"

- You have the necessary experience to provide a foundation for growing the company, if that's part of your plans

(Questions 3.11 and 3.12 are also covered by the text above.)

DISCUSSING QUESTION 3.13

Have you ever worked for a startup or very young company that failed? If so, why do you think they failed?

Have you ever worked for a startup or a very young company that became a big success? If so, why do you think they succeeded?

This topic is most relevant for: Everyone

3.13.1 The Other Kind of Equity

If you've only worked for successful companies, you're working at a disadvantage compared to your less-successful peers.

As human beings we learn fastest and absorb knowledge more deeply when we fail.

In my career I've had a number of big projects that were successful, and I enjoy talking about what I learned on them.

But if you ask me, "Don, what are the most important lessons you've learned as a long-time tech executive?" something different happens.

I'll reel off a series of bullet points, and I can hear myself getting emotionally revved up. That's because many of the lessons I'll share come from when we as a team – and often I as an individual — made decisions that led to failure.

I'm really determined not to make those same mistakes again.

If you've been part of an organization that failed, think about what you learned. Are there lessons that you can use on your Dream Project?

Sometimes when I ask this question I'll get a flip answer like, "I learned not to take a job working for an idiot."

That's missing the point. A failed business is a trove of potential learning, but you have to get past the blame (and the avoidance of blame) in order to learn from it.

I was discussing this issue recently with Bob Wallace, the veteran Silicon Valley advisor.

"That's the difference between entrepreneurs and other people," he told me. "Non-entrepreneurs see the failure of a product or a company as rejection. Entrepreneurs see it as experience, and a milestone on the road to getting things right."

PART IV

WHERE AND HOW

CHAPTER 26

Where and How: The Questions

QUESTION 4.1

What are the five single words that best represent your most important principles and values, the five words that tell people what you stand for?

In what order would your prioritize those five values, with the *most important* one, the one that takes precedence over everything else, listed first?

Since the words "values" and "principles" mean different things to different people, I'm going to start you off with 50 options from which to choose.

Please feel free to use your own words if you don't find the right concepts below. If my "placeholder" definition feels wrong, ignore it and write down your own meaning.

The hard part is picking the five most important values and principles for your Dream Project and ranking them from #1 to #5.

Note: I use "we" in the definitions below, but most of these priorities could just as easily apply to a one-person project.

Our initial 50 options, in alphabetical order, are:

Accountability – When things go right people are praised and rewarded. When things go wrong we look to teach and correct, and if problems persist people are disciplined.

Adaptive – Our world and our market change rapidly, and we change ourselves and what we do to adapt with it. (cf. Classic.)

Aggressiveness – This can take many forms: our sales team contacts lots of potential clients and makes lots of proposals; our pricing doesn't match the competition, it crushes them; our ads are bold, proud and loud, etc.

Classic – In a world where "the fastest way" and "the cheapest way" have taken over, we create exceptional value for customers by doing it "the quality way." (cf. Adaptive.)

Collaboration – We value people and teams working together to produce the best results. (cf. Competition.)

Commitment – We're not doing one thing, then traipsing off to do something else. We're committed to our product, to our customers and to our team.

Community – We are part of communities (neighborhood, industry groups, users, etc.) and derive benefits from them, so we seek to give back to those communities as well.

Competency – We only do things we believe we can do well.

Competition – We compete in everything we do to bring out the best in everyone and everything. Our internal teams and individuals compete with each other in order to better compete with outside rivals. (cf. Collaboration.)

Courage – We aren't afraid to try things, even if they seem hard, risky or unpopular.

Data-Driven – We generate and gather data and then leverage the learning we gain from it.

Decisiveness – We investigate, discuss and evaluate complex issues, but we make fast decisions. If a decision turns out to be wrong, we fix it.

Discipline – Once decisions are made and instructions are given, everyone does what they've been told to do.

Diversity – We want to build a team that is made up of a wide range of kinds of people.

Earth-Friendly – We don't harm the environment in any material way as we carry out our work.

Efficiency – We make the most out of every minute and every dollar, and we do it every time.

Empathy – We "walk in the shoes of the users" and focus on the quality of their experience, not on our own perspectives.

Equality – We treat all of our team members and everyone with whom we deal in a consistent and fair manner.

Experimentation – We constantly try out new ideas.

Fair Trade – We pay our partners a fair amount in all transactions so that they can meet their basic economic needs, even if we could negotiate lower prices.

Faith – Our personal religious beliefs and values also govern our business (e.g. we don't have anyone work on a Sabbath, even if the day falls in the middle of a major conference or trade show).

Fast Learning – We learn fast from our experiments and continually use that learning to try new things.

Focus – Throughout the organization, we prioritize one clearly-defined goal at a time and do whatever it takes to achieve it.

Growth – In order to prosper, the business has to grow.

Honesty, Integrity, Truth – We don't lie, we do what we say we're going to do, and we say what we really think even if it's unpopular. When we say something that turns out to be wrong we acknowledge and correct it.

Initiative – Our people come up with their own ideas and use their own best judgment. They don't always wait for someone else to tell them what to do.

Innovation – We create new products or new ways to do things.

Internal Growth – Whenever possible, we look to promote people from within rather than bring in experienced people from outside the company.

Intuition – It's hard to explain, but ideas just come to us. We vet them and then we implement the best ones.

Investor Focused – We place a very high priority on creating value for investors.

Knowledge – We seek to learn from everything we do.

Loyalty – We show loyalty to our customers, partners and team members, and work to earn their loyalty in return.

Market-Driven – We see needs in the market and then we fill them. (cf. Passion-Driven.)

Passion-Driven – We envision products or services that we are passionate about bringing to life and that we believe will inspire passion in customers. Then we create and sell them. (cf. Market-Driven.)

Persistence – We don't give up just because something is difficult or discouraging when we first try to do it.

Personal Development – We support everyone on the team as they work to steadily improve on current skills and to acquire new ones. We try to be better at what we do every single day.

Philanthropy – We give money, time or both to causes and charities in which we believe.

Price Leaders – We produce the same products with equal or better quality than our competitors at lower prices.

Professionalism – We take our work seriously and we don't mess around when it's time to get things done.

Profitability – We're here to make money. (cf. Revenue and Users.)

Quality – Every product we ship, every service we offer is of exceptional quality. If something doesn't meet that goal we'll improve it till it does or discontinue it.

Reliability – We keep our promises, whether they be about products, services, or how we work inside the company.

Respect – We'll disagree with people all the time, both inside and outside the company, but we always treat everyone with respect.

Results Focused – Other things don't matter if we don't get the results we need from the work we've done.

Revenue – We have to generate revenue. (cf. Profitability and Users.)

Scale – We don't want a small customer base. We want our product or service to be used by millions of people or businesses.

Shipping – You haven't achieved anything until you ship the first usable version of your product or the first trial run of your service. We focus on shipping things, not just talking about them.

Transparency – We do our work "in the light of day" and don't secretly do things that violate our values or that mislead communities, customers or team members.

Uniqueness – We're not like everyone else. You see our product and you instantly know it's ours. You look at our website or a video or a magazine ad and you'd know who it's from even if our name weren't on it.

User Growth – We're out to build a large user base. (cf. Profitability, Revenue.)

Please take your time, write down your responses, and answer fully from your deepest thoughts. Think only about your own opinions, not about what others may want you to think or do. Do not look ahead to other questions until you have finished this one.

QUESTION 4.2

Think of someone you've worked with where things didn't go smoothly. The reasons don't matter, and we can't work perfectly with everyone.

What are the five words that this person would say best represent your values if they're asked to describe you?

How do you feel about the words they would choose?

Please take your time, write down your responses, and answer fully from your deepest thoughts. Think only about your own opinions, not about what others may want you to think or do. Do not look ahead to other questions until you have finished this one.

_____

QUESTION 4.3

We all struggle with being perfect in living our values. You may value being on time but may arrive late when traffic is bad.

Which of your five key values presents you with the greatest struggle? In what ways?

_____

QUESTION 4.4

If you could pick any place to work on your Dream Project, where would it be?

Is it just down the street, or a dream destination like Hawaii or Southern France?

Is it your dream to work from your home office?

Please take your time, write down your responses, and answer fully from your deepest thoughts. Think only about your own opinions, not about what others may want you to think or do. Do not look ahead to other questions until you have finished this one.

QUESTION 4.5

Will your office be one big open room? Cubicles with high or low walls? Offices with doors? Will there be windows?

If you'll work at home, what furniture and equipment will you need?

QUESTION 4.6

If you plan to hire people to work with you on your Dream Project, how many will you hire in the first year? In the second year?

What skills or professions will you be looking for? Which kinds of people will be easier to find, and which will be especially hard?

Please take your time, write down your responses, and answer fully from your deepest thoughts. Think only about your own opinions, not about what others may want you to think or do. Do not look ahead to other questions until you have finished this one.

QUESTION 4.7

When you're hiring new people for your team, how will you identify great people in a sea of applicants who are "pretty good?"

What process will you use to interview people who apply to work on your team? How will you make final decisions on who to hire?

QUESTION 4.8

Are you planning to set up a new company for your Dream Project?

Or is it something small where (at least initially) you won't have large payments coming in and you can report it as personal income on your taxes?

If you're forming a company, do you know what legal classification of company you want to organize?

Please take your time, write down your responses, and answer fully from your deepest thoughts. Think only about your own opinions, not about what others may want you to think or do. Do not look ahead to other questions until you have finished this one.

_____

QUESTION 4.9

If your company grows, how will you organize things? Will you have departments (e.g. an engineering department) or will you arrange people so project teams work together?

_____

QUESTION 4.10

Are you planning to outsource any manufacturing as part of your Dream Project? How many different items, pieces, components, molds etc. will you need to create?

Please take your time, write down your responses, and answer fully from your deepest thoughts. Think only about your own opinions, not about what others may want you to think or do. Do not look ahead to other questions until you have finished this one.

QUESTION 4.11

Are you planning to outsource any software development, hardware engineering, web development etc. as part of your Dream Project?

QUESTION 4.12

Are there any other regulatory approvals you'll need in order to start up your business, or to manufacture, import or offer your product for sale?

What kinds of licenses will you need (if any)?

Is anything about your place of business subject to inspections, signoffs, etc.?

Please take your time, write down your responses, and answer fully from your deepest thoughts. Think only about your own opinions, not about what others may want you to think or do. Do not look ahead to other questions until you have finished this one.

QUESTION 4.13

If you're going to have employees, are there any special employment laws in your city and/or your state that add additional costs, paperwork or operating rules to your planned business?

CHAPTER 27

My Story: Clarity Inspires Commitment

My wife and I were married very early in my career. I was finishing my master's degree in Education and was working as a bilingual middle school teacher in a barrio school in Southern California.

The games industry did not yet exist. We thought I would have a career as a teacher and (I hoped) as a professional writer.

Then fate intervened. My hobby of writing computer games on the university mainframe computer had prepared me for the emerging video games industry, and my path veered from Education into high-tech startups.

My wife has ridden all of the wild ups and downs of the Silicon Valley rollercoaster at my side, as well as all of the booms and busts of the video games industry. We've experienced success, failure, and everything else, and we've always stuck together through it all.

I have told every team that I have ever led that I have very clear priorities. "I am completely committed to the company and to the project," I'll say, "but there's something you should know. There is no company, no project and no job that is more important to me than my marriage and my kids. And I'm completely cool with it if you feel the same way about your family as a member of our team."

I say the same thing at conference sessions that I give around the world on the topics of leadership, management and game development.

I've had people come up to me after those speeches and disagree strongly with my position. "There are times when everyone has to just drop everything and work their butts off as many hours a day as they can," they tell me. "You can't just give people a 'get out of jail free' card because of their families, because that just makes more work for everyone else who has to cover for them and breeds resentment."

Here are my responses to this argument:

The fact that my wife and family *know* that they come first does not make it harder for me to work long hours when there's a big deadline. It actually makes it easier. When there's no doubt about your partner's priorities it's more comfortable for families to support these bursts of effort.

Our sons are both grown men. As I mentioned in an earlier chapter, I have absolutely no regrets that I attended every weekend game the boys ever had as they were growing up (with rare exceptions if I was out of town at a conference or trade show), from kindergarten soccer through high school baseball. I made it to many of their weekday games as well.

I lost no business opportunity by doing so, though I know many companies pressure team members to skip kids' soccer games when a major deadline looms.

Even in the toughest times, when I've worked 90-plus hour weeks, I usually took time out to have dinner with my family and help put the kids to bed. I've followed the same guideline for having dinner with my wife after our children were grown and on their own.

Being part of a startup means you have lots of long days. Startup teams usually have less money than usual, fewer people than usual, and the potential for much greater rewards than usual. You know that you're not signing on for a nine-to-five lifestyle when you join this kind of team. It's a lot more work than a typical job.

If super-long hours that block out the sun of family time go on too long and too often, however, it's destructive to the goals of the company. In fact, I think that treating such long-term "crunch time" schedules as acceptable invites self-fulfilling bad planning by leaders.

It all comes back to the words that I use so often in this book: balance and common sense.

I have friends who believe that startups have to crunch continually for months or even years, and others who think that you can have a winning "nine to five" startup where extra time is discouraged.

I disagree with both of those opinions.

Whether you agree or disagree with my ideas, the most important thing is that you think consciously about your own opinion and your priorities. Then you need to honestly and openly share and discuss those values with the people who love you.

Finally, you then need to discuss them with the people who join your Dream Project.

CHAPTER 28

What to Do With Your Answers (4.1-4.3)

"AS YOU GET OLDER YOU BECOME THE PERSON YOU
ALWAYS SHOULD HAVE BEEN."

— David Bowie, 2012

If you have not yet written down your answers, please go back and do so. Writing your thoughts down – even when you're the only one who'll ever read them – will produce far more insights than just answering silently to yourself in your head.

DISCUSSING QUESTION 4.1

What are the five single words that best represent your most important principles and values, the five words that tell people what you stand for?

In what order would your prioritize those five values, with the most important one, the one that takes precedence over everything else, listed first?

This topic is most relevant for: Everyone

4.1.1 (Almost) No Wrong Answers

This exercise is designed to get you thinking about your management style, and especially about the priorities and trade-offs that inevitably come with leading real-world teams on Dream Projects. If you've seriously considered these 50 potential concepts – and perhaps more – you'll know a lot more about your priorities and values from the process of selecting the five ranked choices you wrote down.

If you have co-founders or collaborators, it can be fulfilling and constructive to discuss these issues with them as well.

There are very few "wrong" choices on the list, although they vary based on the goals of your new business. In that context, here are some choices that would raise red flags for me if I were advising your team:

If you did not list Profitability — If you're hoping to take home any money from your Dream Project, or if you're hoping for it to support itself financially for more than a few months, this goal needs to be high on your list.

As every first-time entrepreneur discovers, running even a small business involves more costs than we predict when we start out. Our first-year revenues are often lower than we expected. Even if making money is not the primary goal of your Dream Project, if you don't make a profit you won't be able to do the work you love for very long.

The news headlines often equate "Profit is our Goal" with ruthless magnates who pillage the world of business.

If you're running your business responsibly there is nothing wrong with making money. In fact, if you're doing great work you deserve to be rewarded in this way.

But you have to recognize the need for profit, then actually prioritize it. You have to be willing to say to yourself and the people you work with, "We're here to make money because this is work we love, we're proud of what we do, and we have to make money in order to keep doing it."

For some people this comes naturally. For others – especially those in creative or artistic fields — it requires a deliberate change of attitude. If you want to do work you love, it's a road you'll almost certainly need to travel.

If you listed Profitability as your top priority — Listing profitability as #1 implies that Honesty is to be sacrificed in the quest for money. In one recent example, Wells Fargo Bank encouraged such a results-driven culture that employees created over two million fictional new accounts in an effort to meet targets and earn bonuses. The ultimate result: millions of dollars in fines, multiple lawsuits and the resignation of the CEO.

If you did not list Quality – I discuss the issue of prioritizing Quality repeatedly in this book. I have seen very few teams succeed in business – or in anything else – without this value being inscribed near the top position on their list.

If you did not list Honesty, Integrity, Truth or similar values – Would you want to work with someone who didn't treat these values as important? Would you want to do business with them?

Diversity – The most effective way to reach a broad, diverse audience is to build a diverse team. If photographs of your team and of your intended audience feature the same kinds of people your chances of success grow dramatically.

Historically many businesses have employed fewer women and fewer ethnic minorities than the population at large, and done so at lower salaries. Improving these ratios is a matter of fairness. The teams who follow those inclusive principles, however, will be rewarded with larger audiences and increased sales as well.

4.1.2 Nought May Endure but Mutability

The famous English poet Percy Bysshe Shelley (whose wife Mary wrote the original *Frankenstein* novel 200 years ago) concludes one of his most famous poems with the line, "Nought may endure but mutability."

In modern language, we might (less poetically) rephrase that line as "Nothing lasts very long except the fact that nothing lasts very long."

Even though your principles may not change, the world around you is morphing constantly. Sometimes you have to find new ways to conduct business based on your principles.

A core value of mine is "loyalty." At one time I lived that value by keeping all of the work at our studio in-house rather than outsourcing.

My objective was to retain a stable cross-disciplinary team, rather than building and then disbanding all but the core group for every project. I reasoned that keeping complete teams together would produce higher quality work, and talented people were more likely to return my loyalty by staying at the studio.

Years later the business environment had changed. Publishers, anxious to hold back rising production costs, had lowered their budgets.

We had to cut our pricing by 25% to stay in step with these new rules, and could no longer employ complete teams year-round on every project. We had to work with outside studios who had lower production costs to meet new project budget restrictions.

I still value commitment and loyalty very highly, both as something that I owe to others and as something I look for in return.

But market changes forced me to alter how I turn my values into action. I still try to build as much long-term stability as I can at the heart of a project, but I have to accept that I cannot manage the same way I did 20 years ago.

4.1.3 Team Values and Living What You Preach

Knowing and sharing your core values gives you a place to start with your team on any tough issue.

We once hired a team member who got off to a good start on his first day. The next day his wife called to say that he was in the hospital in critical condition with an infection, and would be away from work indefinitely.

I had a decision to make. This was an important job, one we'd hate to leave open for very long. After just one day we could easily terminate him and hire someone else.

At our management meeting that week we discussed what we

should do. Most of the leaders in the room had worked with me for years, so they knew what was coming.

"We always start from our values," I told them, for what was probably the hundredth time. "We expect commitment from our team, so we have to live the same values. Termination is not an option. We have to find a way to hold things together until he's back."

I didn't actually need to say anything at all. Each of our senior managers would have made the same call on their own if they were the CEO . Sharing values is part of what holds teams together.

In fact, if I'd suggested termination our Directors would have revolted. because it would have compromised values they held before they ever joined our team.

We cobbled together a plan to cover for the missing team member. He was unable to return to work for several months but we got through it.

When another manager and I went to visit him in the hospital, he apologized for missing work and thanked us for the support.

All I could think of to tell him were the four words, "You're one of us."

P.S.: The rest of this story is happy. The team member recovered and worked for our company for several years. We remain friends, he and his wife now have a growing family, and he continues to have a successful career.

DISCUSSING QUESTION 4.2

Think of someone you've worked with where things didn't go smoothly. The reasons don't matter, and we can't work perfectly with everyone.

What are the three words that this person would say best represent your values if they're asked to describe you?

How do you feel about the words they would choose?

This topic is most relevant for: Everyone

4.2.1 Harsh Critics Can Be Our Best Teachers

The story above about following our values when a team member was in the hospital is one that makes me proud.

But we all have memories that make us anything but proud.

One time I got caught up in my own ego and confronted a combative manager in another group at the company where I was working, creating a cross-team feud. I wasn't standing up for an important value – the issue we were fighting over was trivial. What I saw as his condescending attitude had made me angry, and I publicly accused him of being petty and political.

Of course, by saying so in front of our peers I was being petty and political myself. Not to mention making it harder for both groups to work together.

This manager (or anyone else looking at my behavior) might have written these five "values" as what they saw in my behavior:

1. Aggression

2. Competition
3. Intuition
4. Passion-Driven
5. Initiative

I'm not proud of that behavior. Those five values can be very positive in some contexts, but as a summary of the attitudes I projected that day I'm embarrassed to list them.

I've thought back many times to the moment when I picked that fight unnecessarily out of impatience and ego, and reminded myself not to make the same mistake again.

This process of reflection mirrors the two self-review questions recommended by Dr. Vijay Sathe of The Drucker School at Claremont Graduate University in his book, *Manage Your Career*:

When you do well, consider who else helped you... instead of losing perspective and becoming overconfident.

When you do poorly, consider what you can learn from the experience... instead of losing perspective, beating yourself up and losing your confidence.

DISCUSSING QUESTION 4.3

We all struggle with being perfect in living our values. You may value being on time but may arrive late when traffic is bad.

Which of your five key values presents you with the greatest struggle? In what ways?

This topic is most relevant for: Everyone

4.3.1 What I Learned from a Parenting Class

When our sons were young we went to a parenting class at one of their schools. That class taught me something that I realized was just as true for businesses as it is for families:

Your kids don't judge you by the rules and values and rules you tell them they ought to follow.

They judge you by the values they see you live and the rules you follow in front of them. Even when you think they're too young to understand, they start to know you as you really are.

The clerk at the store gives you a ten-dollar bill as change when it should have been one dollar, and you say nothing. Your child knows your advice to "never cheat" can be ignored, because you ignore it.

You want to get home to watch the big game on TV so you drive the wrong way on a one-way alley for a block to escape a traffic jam. Your child knows your advice to "always obey the law" can be ignored, because you ignore it.

The hardest part of having kids isn't being awakened in the middle of the night or getting them to do their chores and homework.

The hardest part of having kids is having to live the values we tell them to embody, instead of merely reciting those principles and then ignoring them.

This principle applies at work as well. If you always start meetings a few minutes late you'll notice that your team stops arriving on time, even if you remind everyone to come at 2:00 o'clock sharp.

I'd known this in principle, of course, but the parenting class really drove it home. I had kept extra change I was given by mistake when we were at the store. I had exited through a parking lot's "entrance only" driveway onto a different street to avoid traffic.

Ever since that class, I've done a much better (albeit not perfect) job of living by the rules we taught our kids.

CHAPTER 29

The Home Team (4.4-4.7)

DISCUSSING QUESTION 4.4

If you could pick any place to work on your Dream Project, where would it be?

Is it just down the street, or a dream destination like Hawaii or Southern France?

Is it your dream to work from your home office?

These topics are most appropriate for: Everyone

4.4.1 Fun Spots

In this book the person whose feelings matter is you. In that context, here are some factors to consider.

Are you picturing a favorite vacation spot? I've dreamed about what it would be like to run a company in Europe or in some tropical location. I throw away the idea each time because I love where I live, and I know the romance would wear off of other places once I moved there and started missing friends and family.

Businesses in popular vacation spots often have higher costs because of their location. In the United States, residents of Hawaii and Alaska pay more for just about everything because of higher than usual shipping costs. Real estate is more expensive in popular destinations

If your business is travel or hospitality related, it may benefit from a location in a popular area.

I live less than an hour from the heart of Northern California's Wine Country. Many entrepreneurs whose passions relate to wine and wine production have been drawn there by the volume of vintners and wine-loving travelers.

If you're doing a wine-related startup Northern California is both more expensive and more efficient than other potential places to call home.

Ask yourself, "Is it the project itself that gets me excited, or is it just the prospect of being in such a great place?"

Doing work that you hate in a wonderful location will, in time, wear you down and make you miserable just as certainly as doing work you hate in a boring office.

4.4.2 Local Spots

Is the location for your Dream Project someplace close to home that also works well for other reasons?

I established each of my companies within a twenty-minute drive of my home. This is both convenient and practical, since I live in the San Francisco Bay Area, a hotbed for top tech talent.

Is your ideal spot a leading business hub for the industry that includes your Dream Project? For example:

- A mobile game company might want to be in San Francisco or

Silicon Valley, where many of the leading professionals in the space work and live.

- A clothing designer's workshop could prosper most easily in New York, London, Paris, Milan, Shanghai, Tokyo or other world fashion centers.
- An American automotive metals research company might build its business most readily in Detroit.

Are you looking to tap the talent at a particular university known for strong professional specialties? For example, if your idea is tied to filmmaking, you might want to be close to USC or UCLA. For technology it might be MIT, Cal Tech, Carnegie Mellon or Harvey Mudd.

4.4.3 Within Four Walls

Maybe it wasn't the location that got you excited, but the work environment for you and your team. Just the right light, the right equipment, or the right environment.

The cost of offices, however, can be substantial. For some businesses it remains essential, but consider whether you can use a smaller space or shared office (with no long-term financial commitments) to help keep your costs down. I'll cover this issue in more depth below.

DISCUSSING QUESTION 4.5

Will your office be one big open room? Cubicles with high or low walls? Offices with doors? Will there be windows?

If you'll work at home, what furniture and equipment will you need?

This topic is most relevant for: Everyone.

4.5.1 Natural and Artificial Turf

When companies are just starting out the founders may all work in someone's dining room.

When that no longer works they often move to small, short-term offices. Everyone sits at desks in a single room. Everyone understands it's a startup and money is tight.

If a team grows larger and you need more space, however, issues of territory can become a distraction. Who gets the window? Who gets a door?

When I worked as an executive in a traditional American corporation I loved having my private office with a door.

I then went to work on a startup team where the CEO, CFO and everyone else lived in cubicles in a single large room. Conference rooms were located nearby when a private conversation was necessary.

As much as I loved the door and traditional office, the team I joined had better communication, less politics and fewer distractions.

Of course, earlier in this book we discussed psychologist Mihaly

Csikszentmihalyi and his definition of "the state of being in flow." It's that place where we're both happy and highly productive, and if your team can spend lots of time there it's a good thing. Not being interrupted while we work is part of how we attain "flow."

One way to allow people to work without being interrupted is to give them offices with doors... the very system I criticized above.

Managing is complicated and there are no one-size-fits-all answers. You need to experiment and figure out what works best for you, your team and your Dream Project.

4.5.2 Who Goes Where

As we've discussed, the option for team members to be working in different cities presents new opportunities and new challenges to the managers leading projects.

In my experience there is no one right answer, and you have to experiment to figure out what will work for you. I've seen teams that were split between Scandinavia and San Francisco who collaborate effectively with just occasional in-person visits.

I've also seen teams that were split between the east and west side of the same building who couldn't meet for more than 20 minutes without bickering!

Here are my guidelines for considering these long distance partnerships or contracted services relationships:

Don't Do It Just It to Save Money. If you buy a cheap used car it will break down all the time. If you buy cheap wine glasses they'll chip the third time you use them. If you pick partners just because they're cheap you'll be the one having the breakdown.

If you work with remote teams in search of price advantages:

- Look for strong, quality-focused groups who will save you some money and execute well, rather than just accepting the cheapest bid. The principle of "you get what you pay for" still applies.

- Look for teams that have finished projects of similar size, style and complexity.
- Talk to references in your home country who've partnered with the potential team.

Count the time zones between the teams. The greater the difference in the hours you're in the office, the harder it is to collaborate

The exception: if the gap is between five and eight hours or so, meetings can happen early in the day at one end and late in the day at the other. The team members who are at the beginning of their day can then do a full day of work based on the feedback they received from the team that would soon be going home.

Every team member, every subcontractor should be on a project solely because they're the right people for the task at hand and you're confident they can collaborate well. That applies to someone six feet away as well as someone six time zones away.

If both teams are employees of your company, work as peers. Teams in non-HQ offices sometimes feel like they are treated as second-class citizens by the staff from the home office.

Sharing a Language Matters. I'd be an inefficient member of a project team where everyone only spoke French, because I only know about 20 words. A company from France should consider that if they consider hiring me.

In some countries of the world English is taught as a mandatory subject in schools starting at an early age. Professional conferences may be held in English, which sometimes works as a *lingua franca* when divergent groups of people share that one language in common.

Visit before you commit, and consider more than one vendor in more than one place. It is valuable beyond words to do a personal visit to the offices of potential contractors. Talking with several team members, even if some need translation, gives you a far better feel for what they'll be like to work with than just talking to the smiling face that leads the sales team.

In software development, animation, engineering and other disciplines, teams have been known to show the work of one very talented employee to every client. But once the contract is signed that's not the person who is actually leading your project. Meeting people in person and getting specific names whose participation can then be required in a contract can help.

Visiting more than one potential partner in person lets you compare and contrast the teams and facilities. You can visit one who is nearby and another who is very far away, and get an idea of how it would be to work with each.

I've seen teams choose a distant partner solely based on quality, not price, when a visit went especially well. I've seen teams that were planning to use overseas partners change their mind when they realized the real costs of travel and lost efficiency.

Know the Employment Laws if You're Hiring Employees. Different U.S. States and different countries have very different laws about how companies have to pay employees, what benefits must be offered, working conditions etc. If you're hiring people in any jurisdiction other than the one you already understand, make sure to check out all these variables first.

Invest in Tools. A good Skype video setup and a fast Internet connection are essential. So is a screen-sharing system.

Keep Showing Up. Don't stop visiting a distant partner after a project has begun. Regular visits are part of good communication, as well as keeping their focus on you instead of on other clients.

Budget for the Travel and Tools Costs Before You Start. Sometimes the excitement over finding a great partner at a bargain price makes teams lose track of the extra travel costs, the spending for video links etc.

Is the team in a country where citizens of your country routinely travel? There are areas where Americans or other nationalities rarely travel or where they can be prohibited from traveling. These are not places where you can partner effectively with a remote team.

DISCUSSING QUESTION 4.6

If you plan to hire people to work with you on your Dream Project, how many will you hire in the first year? In the second year?

What skills or professions will you be looking for? Which kinds of people will be easier to find, and which will be especially hard?

This topic is most relevant for: Dream Projects that will grow to employ more than a small team.

4.6.1 What Size is Right?

Many entrepreneurs deliberately keep their Dream Projects small. In many cases small is the ideal size for the mission they're looking to accomplish.

Growth sometimes happens by accident. A product turns out to be in high demand. Word of mouth brings more and more new clients. You blink, and a team of three has turned into a team of thirty.

Some companies — especially those backed by outside investors – build a plan that will require that their brand-new startup grows their headcount rapidly. Their backers won't give them time to evolve the business slowly "like running a marathon."

These investor-backed startups are required to make an all-out sprint to create a product, blitz the market and scale the company into a large business.

Here's what's most important: pick the size of your company, don't let it pick you. But remember that some Dream Projects only work out if they stay small, and others will only work if they are allowed to grow. It's your job as a founder to make sure you understand where in that spectrum your Dream Project falls.

I've seen cases where a business that made sense as a small company sabotaged its own best interests by trying to go big. Sometimes the trigger is as simple as the CEO getting a lecture from Uncle Jimmy at Thanksgiving dinner about "what it really means to succeed in business."

The following Monday the CEO stops using common sense and starts using Uncle Jimmy sense, which leads to lots of new hiring or new advertising or other expensive new things. Disaster ensues.

I've also seen the opposite problem: a startup has a runaway success, but they turn down business "so we don't have to bring in lots of people and ruin the great feel on this team." Copycats or rivals fill the vacuum and grow dramatically. After a few years the one-time success story closes its doors.

Sometimes the world of business isn't fair.

A Silicon Valley veteran told me long ago, "If you're generating cash and you've built up some reserves, start the next phase of growth with one small initiative. Let it prove it's worth the time and money before you add more resources and take greater risks."

4.6.2 Why Growth Isn't a Dirty Word

In business school, however, managers are taught the principle that "a company that isn't growing is dying."

I rejected this idea at first, but then realized that it's a matter of mathematics and probability. Here's how that math works:

The "status quo" for any company and for any category of business rarely lasts for long.

New products may have unpredictable ups and downs, but

older products almost always have declining sales. You eventually reach the point where everyone who wants your polka dot toasters has already bought one. Your iconic umbrella colors may go out of style. A competitor may come out with a great new rival product.

New product revenues can be very hard to predict. The new self-opening umbrella isn't the big hit everyone expected. Stuff happens.

Managers who are focused on not growing their companies arbitrarily resist responding to larger opportunities. But they *can't* control random downturns in revenue.

If you refuse to grow, the only other options are staying at the same size or shrinking. The random nature of business means that eventually something will go wrong and that downturn will happen.

It's a matter of math, and once you understand it you'll always be looking for at least some growth in your company to counteract the natural downdraft of aging products.

4.6.3 Looking at the Status Quo Instead of the Future

There's a strategic issue here as well. If your guiding strategy is to avoid growth, it means that:

- You're *not* looking for the next successful product
- You're *not* constantly thinking about how to improve your business with new ideas
- You're *not* looking to be the innovative force driving the next stage of development
- You're *not* thinking about how your company has to operate five years from now

You may not be thinking about all these things, but your competitors have no such restrictions.

They're out there trying to be leaders in the introduction of new kinds of products, and taking advantage of new technology to serve their customers better next year than they're serving them today.

I know it's hard enough to deal with today's issues, but part of leading a company is also being able to think about the opportunities and obstacles that face us in the future.

DISCUSSING QUESTION 4.7

When you're hiring new people for your team, how will you identify great people in a sea of applicants who are "pretty good?"

What process will you use to interview people who apply to work on your team? How will you make final decisions on who to hire?

This topic is most relevant for: Dream Projects that will grow to employ a team.

4.7.1 Making the First People the Right People

Regardless of the size of your Dream Project, the choices you make when you hire people are some of your most important business decisions.

Your first three people, all by themselves, establish the core culture of your team, and if you're the leader your impact is the greatest of all.

It's critical that those first three people use the next seven hires to refine and reinforce the culture that governs how the three of you get things done. They in turn will model it for the next ten hires, who will model it for the next twenty, and so on. I've seen this approach work up to and beyond 200 people at a company.

If there are parts of the culture you don't like when you grow larger, look back at the first ten people, including yourself. Often you'll see that the roots of the large company problems were already present in those early hires.

Or you may recognize the moment when you didn't stick to your values and began to hire people who changed the culture in ways you didn't want.

4.7.2 My Law of Company Culture

I made up my Law of Company Culture as part of a conference keynote speech a few years ago. Here's how I defined it:

A Company's culture consists of:

1. How things really get done, regardless of official systems or policies, and...
2. How the people in the company feel when they come to work each day.

If you bring in top performers, avoid hiring destructive people and show respect for team members you'll have quality teams.

If you truly commit to building great products and you have processes and procedures that work well, those productive people are likely to be happy. Continually work to improve your processes and they'll be even happier.

Learning how to play the company culture game really well – in a way where everybody on the team wins — takes years of study. But it's one of the most interesting challenges I've ever taken on.

4.7.3 The Power of Terminology

You may have noticed that I rarely refer to "employees" in this book. I prefer to use the term "team members."

Disney calls all their employees "Cast Members." Many companies call them "Associates."

I think that what you call people as a group or a class says a lot about what you think of them.

I personally don't care for the terms "Employer" and "Employee" (outside of formal documents). The Employer has all the control and the Employee is under control. It implies that one of them is supposed to do the thinking and the other is supposed to do as they are told.

"Teams" work together under the guidance and direction of a coach or manager. But soccer, baseball or basketball players don't stop in the middle of the action to ask their boss what to do.

They operate by planning, discussing and taking direction from their manager, and then using their best judgment about what to do.

Team Members who emulate that system at work will be far more effective and productive than their counterparts who wait to be told what to do. That's why I call the people I hire "Team Members."

4.7.4 The Myth of the Warm Body

As a CEO and as an advisor to startups I have often heard people say, "We haven't been able to find anyone good to fill this job, and the backlog of work just keeps piling up. If we don't find someone soon we're just going to have to get a warm body in here so we can finish this project."

People who've worked on our teams know what happens if someone starts to talk about "warm bodies" in front of me.

I know it's tough. If there are major tasks that aren't being completed you can feel like you're watching the long fuse on a stick of dynamite slowly burn down. When you run out of time the explosives will blow up your team.

These are some examples of the times when you'll be tempted *not* to stick to your values:

When you're trying to find a strong software engineer to code a critical part of your product. These are rare engineers, and everyone is looking for them. Hiring a good one is both very important and very hard to do.

You interview a guy who's clearly capable of doing the work, but he's obnoxious, condescending and rude. He looks at a code sample from your CTO and says, "This must have been written by an 8th grader." People would hate to be around him, but he'd solve a huge problem your team is facing.

Will you hire him or stick to your values of only hiring great people?

When you need an experienced sales executive who knows your segment, the key accounts and their buyers. The team interviews a man who can name them all off the top of his head.

But his cologne smells worse than last night's trash. He tells one interviewer that she'd look good if she wore certain kinds of clothes. He's repulsive, but he could reach a lot of accounts that won't return your calls.

Will you hire him or stick to your values?

When you need a controller to clean up the tangled mess of two different accounting software packages so your fast-growing company stays on top of cash management. You interview a woman who has all the skills necessary for doing the job.

But she tells each interviewer that she graduated *cum laude* from Vassar. Her resume includes the fact that her 7th great uncle served with George Washington at Valley Forge. When she hears that the Marketing Director got his B.A. at Oregon State she wrinkles her nose in contempt of his non-Ivy-League status.

She's disrespectful, egotistical and inconsiderate, but she could save you $50,000 on your next corporate tax return.

Will you hire her or stick to your values?

Many managers would disagree with me, but here's how I handle these situations.

I say no.

I would rather endure whatever consequences we'd suffer from an open position than knowingly hire someone who will be a bad fit and undermine our culture. Being consistent on this "no jerks" policy has actually made it easier for me to recruit great people.

The current problems will come and go. But a bad hire keeps doing damage as long as he or she is there, until you finally fire them. Firing them is a time-consuming process that reminds you and everyone else on the team that you never should have hired them in the first place.

Worse yet, once you hire the toxic team member you stop considering alternative solutions for the problem:

- Outsourcing a portion of your programming with a company that matches your culture
- Using a distributor for the first year to reach additional buyers
- Having a temp agency accountant clean up your accounting systems

None of these are risk-free options. But when you stick to your guns on only hiring quality people you're proving your team that you're committed to your values.

Your team will notice your actions, not just your words.

4.7.5 Planning and Recruiting Under Pressure

Full disclosure: I am married to a successful recruiter who has been working with tech companies for many years. All opinions I express about recruiting should be considered in this context.

The traditional method of recruiting is that you put an ad on a huge online website and a steady stream of resumes from qualified people piles up on your desk. That will still work for some jobs.

But for many positions you could easily get a hundred resumes without a single strong candidate. That's really frustrating when you paid a lot of money for an ad.

The best way to recruit is to have current team members recommend former co-workers whom they know and respect. These pre-screened candidates will have a much higher success rate than strangers. Many companies pay a bonus for referring successful candidates to motivate people to call up their friends.

The first place prospective hires will go to learn about your company is your website. With so many demands on your time, building a great company website early in the recruiting process is a priority that's easy to postpone, but if you are recruiting it's a necessity.

If the position is one that a recent graduate can fill successfully? Local schools have placement offices where counselors will spend time working with students interested in applying for your jobs. This can save you significant time and money on recruiting fees.

Any schedule that assumes that several people will be hired for tech-based jobs in a short period of time is almost certainly overoptimistic and unrealistic. If any of them are especially tough hires they need to be spaced out with long lead times before they're needed. Be sure to budget in "padding" time for their training and for them to come up to speed, because even the best people don't learn the ropes overnight.

Interviewing someone for a job is not just a matter of blocking off a half hour of one manager's schedule and the candidate strolling in for a chat. Developing the right questions, preparing the team and planning who will be in on the interview all require time and thought.

If you have several positions open there may be a significant number of interviews before you fill them, which in the aggregate can take a lot of time from people on the team. That time needs to be budgeted to avoid the process being rushed and careless, and to not impact important project deadlines.

Not everyone you hire is going to work out, and this risk has to be recognized in your plans and schedules if you're experiencing a lot of growth. In California and in many other states in the U.S. employers can establish policies saying that they have 90 days in which to evaluate a new hire and make sure they're settling in successfully.

After those 90 days separating them from the company can be more complex and expensive. Check the requirements in your state, province or country to make sure you understand the relevant laws.

If your team gets to be twenty or more people, it can be helpful to have an outside attorney who specializes in HR law review your employment documents and procedures. The regulations are often complex, individual cities may have their own local rules, and it can be easy to try to do the right thing and still be hit with a significant fine.

Recruiters' services are often expensive, so it's worthwhile to use them only for difficult-to-find professions and specialties.

Some recruiters charge by the hour for their services. "Contingency Recruiters" charge a fee only if they bring you a candidate whom you hire, and their fee will be a percentage of the new employee's annual compensation. More experienced and better-connected recruiters charge a higher percentage than less experienced people, but are more likely to bring you high quality candidates.

"Retained Search" recruiters are paid the same kinds of salary-based commissions as contingency recruiters, and are paid in installments as they start and carry out the search, regardless of whether you hire someone or not.

4.7.6 The Art of the Interview

Many of the founders of Electronic Arts came from Apple, and they brought some of Apple's processes to EA. One of those Silicon Valley traditions was the extended personal interview, which has become standard practice at many tech companies.

Here's a summary of how that system works:

Resumes are screened by a recruiter, by the hiring manager for the job, or by both.

The hiring manager calls the top few candidates and has a short (30 minutes, give or take) interview called a "phone screen." He or she approves a short list of candidates to pass to the next round.

In the case of some technical positions the manager may also ask the candidate to fill out a test of their technical knowledge. Engineers, for example, might be asked to write a short program to achieve a simple goal, or they may be given existing code and asked to identify problems within it.

Some companies have expanded these required tests for different disciplines into extended, complex mini-projects. In my experience this pushes away the best candidates and is often counter-productive.

Note: Some states of the U.S., as well as other nations, have very specific laws about how these tests can be used in hiring. If you're going to do candidate testing, get legal guidance from an HR attorney.

The candidate is asked to come in for a series of interviews, and told the process will take several hours.

The key decision makers pick people to do interviews with each of the candidates.

When we were a small company we involved everyone on the relevant project. When we grew larger we selected the relevant managers and a mix of peers and (for a new manager) potential reports to the position. We'd usually end up with six to nine people, some who interviewed as individuals, some who talked to the candidate in groups of two or three.

If the team was serious about a candidate, I would interview him or her last. This avoided having my comments as CEO color the answers that the candidate gave to other interviewers.

On the day of the interview the recruiter or hiring manager greets the person when they come in, has them fill out an employment application form (if they haven't already done so), and gives them a schedule of the planned interviews.

It is important that every interviewer walk in to meet the candidate not knowing if the prior interview(s) have gone well or badly, so every discussion starts from a clean slate.

After the last interview the candidate is thanked for their time by the hiring manager and released to go home.

4.7.7 Making Decisions

If you're the CEO, it's critical to make clear to teams that their role in this process is one of being advisors, not of controlling the decision.

That said, in years of using this interview system I don't remember ever hiring someone on whom the team's consensus was clearly negative.

Once every few years (yes, that's *years*) I would veto a hire that a majority of the team members wanted to make. The fact that such vetoes are so rare tells you how well you can trust the judgment of good teams... if you start with the right people.

In interview debrief meetings we always go around the table and have everyone give their input before I speak. When CEO's speak first – even those who encourage open debate – it discourages contradictory opinions.

If the team is split in their opinions I do not act as a tiebreaker. Instead I ask questions to help reinforce the key skills we're looking for in this job, which often helps produce a consensus as people talk.

If that consensus does not emerge the CEO then makes the final decision and the meeting is complete.

CHAPTER 30

Setting It Up (4.8-4.9)

DISCUSSING QUESTION 4.8

Are you planning to set up a new company for your Dream Project?

Or is it something small where (at least initially) you won't have large payments coming in and you can report it as personal income on your taxes?

If you're forming a company, do you know what legal classification of company you want to organize?

This topic is most relevant for: Everyone

Note: This is a topic on which I can share my own experiences, but before you make any major decisions I'd advise contacting your attorney and your accountant. The relevant laws are different in many countries, and vary highly just among the different states in the U.S., so there are no "one size fits all" answers. There are taxation risks and other issues involved regardless of which choices you make, so understanding the individual factors and options is important.

4.8.1 Forming a Company

In many jurisdictions, if you're doing a small, part-time venture you don't need to go through the trouble and expense of setting up a separate business entity. If you're just taking in a small amount of money, you can report that revenue for taxes as personal income.

You can also inexpensively set up a very simple form of business if the amounts of money involved are not large. Be sure to research laws in your region to confirm the regulations that apply in your personal case.

If you are planning to ask for money from investors, you're unsure or there is anything else complex about your company I'd recommend a face-to-face attorney meeting to get advice before you file any paperwork.

4.8.2 When do I Need to Set Up an LLC or Corporation?

Depending on local, state and national law, you may want to take this formal step:

When your revenues reach a threshold defined by laws or regulations. In some jurisdictions there are formal requirements that apply.

When the deals you're doing involve sizable amounts of money. If you're doing work that involves larger payments, or if you use a car, truck or equipment in your work, you may want to have a company engaging in the business rather than accepting payment personally.

Let's say you're a contractor renovating a home for a client. The plumber you hire backs up his van into a neighbor's house, damaging the structure and breaking a window. The neighbor then sues you for the very expensive repairs, since you're the general contractor.

In many jurisdictions, if you are working as an individual rather than as a company the neighbor is suing you personally. If he gets a judgment against you, he can force you personally to pay him what he's owed, potentially with additional penalties.

If the neighbor were injured in the accident the results could be catastrophic. In the United States individuals injured in accidents can be awarded millions of dollars as settlement from the person who is deemed to have caused the accident and their employer. Any activity that exposes you to these risks is best done from within a formally organized entity.

4.8.3 The Curse of Co-Equal Partners

There are some company structures that can dramatically lower the chances of success for a startup.

When a company has three (or four or five) equal owners and no pre-arranged formula for who controls the final decisions, "Who's In Charge?" is always a negotiation.

When the partners agree, the business proceeds normally. But the moment that one partner disagrees and a discussion does not resolve the issue, there is a two-to-one vote and one partner "loses."

This tends to tear down the personal relationships that hold the company together. If one partner is always on the losing end of the debates he or she may leave. If, for example, that person is the CTO that may doom an early-stage business.

On any decision where two partners split, they may each curry the favor of the undecided partner. Partners may spend more time trying to outmaneuver each other than they spend running the company. Such teams rarely succeed.

To be fair, this arrangement is not always dysfunctional, and one of my long-time clients has three co-equal founders. One night at a dinner with their management team I asked their CFO how they made it work.

"We were aware of the problems that can arise without one final decision maker," she told me. "We'd worked together before, and we wrote down rules so we wouldn't be haggling with each other all the time."

I share this story to illustrate that equal partners is not an impossible structure for a business. But it does take the right people who share the right values in order to make it work.

4.8.4 Trademarks

You'll want to protect the name of your company and the names of your unique products or services with trademarks, which protect you from someone else using the same name and creating confusion in the marketplace.

If you have a slogan or tag line you can also seek trademark protection for that phrase. For example, Geico's famous "15 minutes could save you 15% or more on car insurance" line was registered as a trademark back in 2008.

If a name is already trademarked by someone else in your category you'll generally need to pick a different, word, phrase etc. If you're manufacturing vacuum cleaners and the term is trademarked only by a greeting card company, there's a good chance you can use the word or words.

As with so many legal issues, to lock down your protection you'll need at least a short interaction with an attorney. Depending upon the complexity of the issues you may be able to save money by using a service like LegalZoom, but if your entire business is based on getting a certain trademark it's better to work with a trademark attorney. (Note: I have no business relationship with LegalZoom.)

As a ;preliminary check, you can do a free online simple trademark search via the United States Government Trademark Office site (do a Google search for "us trademark search tess" to find links to the TESS trademark search page). This system will identify existing and expired trademarks, but may miss valid ones that have not yet been filed or finalized, so the results are not conclusive.

4.8.5 Copyrights

Copyrights are somewhat simpler than trademarks to secure, but like any kind of legal protection they can get complicated.

You can copyright your package design, website, app, book, game, painting etc. just by placing a copyright notice on the item, the packaging or (where possible) the title page or landing page. Many people don't realize, however, that this does not protect your ideas, concepts, algorithms (if you have a website or app) etc. It doesn't even protect the product's name or title, for which you need a trademark.

What it does protect is the product's text, code (if software is involved), visual design and audio (if relevant). The copyright in your packaging or to computer code is easy to define, but how different does the look and feel of a copycat product have to be to avoid being sued for copyright infringement? Clear and outright copies are easy to spot, but if there are differences in the items then the issue is open to interpretation by the courts.

Many basic questions about copyright in the United States are answered at the government copyright office website at https://www.copyright.gov/help/faq/index.html.

For those dream projects where you expect to make a significant amount of money, copyright is another one of those issues where you'll want to consult with an attorney. This is best done when your project is approaching completion, so you have a clear idea of what you'll want to protect.

4.8.6 Patents: From the Ridiculous to the Sublime

A patent attorney once told me, "Most patents are sizzle, not steak – especially software patents. Startups get them to make themselves look good, not because they'll protect them from a well-funded competitor. Occasionally a startup's patents will fill a gap in a big company's portfolio and they'll get acquired. But a patent is usually like a tuxedo: you buy it thinking you'll get a lot of use from it, and then it just sits there in the closet."

I've heard this opinion many times in Silicon Valley, though never so eloquently as this quote. Yet the allure of patents is so strong – and the value of the few broad and enforceable patents is so high – that The Valley keeps generating them at a record rate.

That's because investors like companies that have already proven themselves, so the VC's are making less risky bets. One of the formulas for defining a company's progress is "Prototype, Patents and Partners."

I'll discuss prototypes and partners in later chapters. Let's break down the patents comment above into several pieces to explain each point.

Most patents are sizzle, not steak – especially software patents. The sizzling sound of a steak will put a smile on your face (at least if you eat red meat!) but it won't fill you up or nourish you. Only eating the steak will do that, which is why in marketing parlance "sizzle" refers to perceived benefits from a product or service, and "steak" refers to the real benefits.

The patent systems around the world were built to protect physical inventions: machines, chemical processes, metallurgy and so on.

The relatively recent phenomenon of patenting software has overwhelmed these systems, producing confusion and a lot of lawsuits.

If your dream project is a physical product, your path to gain and to defend a patent is easier than if you're looking for a software patent. Silicon chip and computer patents tend to fall somewhere in the middle. Software patents are possible, but they are a comparatively difficult and less rewarding process.

In recent years the American courts have worked to clarify software patents and to defeat the most egregious strategies of "patent trolls." These are individuals and companies which exploit gaps in the patent system to blackmail legitimate businesses with lawsuits based on irrelevant but confusing patents.

Startups get patents to make themselves look good, not because they'll protect them from a well-funded competitor. A patent shows investors and key potential hires that the company's product meets a minimum standard of uniqueness. It also shows that the team is capable of following the arcane process of going through the necessary steps to file a complete application. With so many half-baked startups looking for money and for people, patents do help a company stand out.

So why doesn't a patent provide strong protection for a new company?

Filing patent infringement cases costs a lot of money. If a big company infringes a small company's patent, they know it can cost the little guy hundreds of thousands of dollars — or even millions — to sue the infringers.

Aggressive competitors will not do direct copies that are no-brainer infringements, but they'll look for ways to "muddy the waters" and create questions about whether their new product infringes on a small company's patent. With so many details to argue, the case and the legal bills can drag out for years. Most small companies don't have the resources to do so and they don't sue.

Occasionally a startup's patents will fill a gap in a big com-

pany's portfolio and they'll get acquired. As one example, many of the big tech companies compete in multiple markets. Apple, eBay, Facebook, Google, Intel, LinkedIn, Microsoft, PayPal, Samsung, Sony and others all have large patent portfolios. They all know that if they decide to sue one of their giant brethren over a patent, they are probably equally vulnerable to being sued by the other company over a patent that the target company owns.

This bizarre balance of power means that there are far fewer such lawsuits between the tech giants than you might expect. It's not worth it to start a patent war with a big rival when you're as likely to lose as to win.

This standoff also motivates these companies to keep track of where they or their competitors are vulnerable to patent suits. They will work to either invent new technology to broaden their patent portfolio, or they will find and acquire patents to improve their competitive position. Small companies that own a patent that a big tech company deems useful may be acquired or have a big payday from the patent sale.

But a patent is usually like a tuxedo: you buy it thinking you'll get a lot of use from it, and then it just sits there in the closet. The patent impresses investors and potential key hires, but startups are unlikely to ever sue an infringer or sell their patents. Hence the comparison to tuxedos.

Knowing these liabilities full well, I have still pursued patents on behalf of startups. If you elect to do so, you'll need to work through a patent attorney. Experienced attorneys will give you advice on whether an idea is worth pursuing, and will do so before you make the big up-front financial investment that a patent requires.

DISCUSSING QUESTION 4.9

If your company grows, how will you organize things? Will you have departments (e.g. an engineering department) or will you arrange people so project teams work together?

This topic is most relevant for: Dream Projects that will grow to employ more than a small team.

4.9.1 The Internal Services Model

To explain this concept I'll use a silly example: Acme Enterprises has a website that sells three product lines: cosmetics, motor oil and baseball cards.

They could have all of their graphic designers work in a single department, and do the same for the copy writers and for the engineers. A manager would head each department and ensure that each project gets what it needs.

This is sometimes called an "internal services" model, because each group treats the Cosmetics team, the Motor Oil team and the Baseball Cards team as clients. These internal "clients" submit requests for services, and the departments respond to them.

4.9.2 Cross-Functional Teams

Alternatively, Acme Enterprises could assign to the Cosmetics team the necessary designers, copy writers, engineers etc. to support all their activity on the website. Staff members would likewise be integrated into the units that sell motor oil and baseball cards. A manager would coordinate all the work for each product category.

These self-sufficient groups are often called "cross-functional teams," because they don't need to request services from any other department. All the different professionals who would perform those services already work within their team.

4.9.3 The Patterns I've Seen

My first three years in business were spent at a large, traditional corporation. Every product line was split into marketing and product development teams, each reporting to a marketing or product development executive.

There were times when it seemed that the departments spent more time on internal politics than they spent trying to build and sell great products.

Later in my career I joined small startups where the focus was on surviving and succeeding. Engineers, artists, designers and other professions all reported to a single manager, so everyone in the group had a shared goal. In many companies Marketing has been integrated into these teams as well.

These experiences gave me a strong opinion: having everyone assigned to a project team reporting to the same manager usually produces far better results than teams divided into traditional departments.

CHAPTER 31

Playing by the Rules (4.10-4.13)

DISCUSSING QUESTION 4.10

Are you planning to outsource any manufacturing as part of your Dream Project? How many different items, pieces, components, molds etc. will you need to create?

This topic is most relevant for: Dream Projects that will manufacture at least one item.

4.10.1 The Mana of Manufacturing

If you are planning to enter any business arrangement where you will be manufacturing items overseas, it is critical that you secure the help of highly experienced professionals.

If someone who speaks the language and knows the ropes is part of the team you can get a good result. If you try to do it by yourself, even extensive preparation may not protect you from disaster.

I recently served as one of three volunteer mentors talking with the CEO of a startup company at an event. They were creating new kinds of educational construction toys, with interlocking plastic parts. It was our job to prepare them to pitch to VC's by asking questions that might come up in such meetings.

I come from the software business, so most of what I know about manufacturing comes from advising other businesses and from friends. The young CEO of this startup sat down with the three of us and ran through his preparation for signing a deal with an overseas manufacturer. He sounded well-prepared.

One of the other mentors was an experienced consumer goods executive. She smiled and said, "You've prepared well, but you'll still need to hire someone experienced to work with you. If I were the person sitting across the table from you in Asia... let's just say I'd be thinking that this is going to be a very profitable deal for my firm."

The CEO hung his head, and I felt badly for him. But sometimes we need to bring in experts.

In addition to manufacturing expertise, you are also going to want to engage lawyers who have expertise in these deals. There are separate risks in the contract with the manufacturer and in the contract with the shipper. Specialized attorneys may be able to introduce you to the right overseas consultant. They can also give you a checklist of required steps and pitfalls to avoid.

4.10.2 Manufacturing Domestically or Overseas

Below is a series of items to think through if you are planning to manufacture anything as part of your Dream Project.

Will the manufacturer be located close to your offices? In China? Somewhere else? Will all of your products be made in the same region, or will you have to utilize manufacturers from a variety of locales? Will one manufacturer have to ship components to another for final assembly?

Some overseas manufacturers offer workers a clean and healthy work environment. Others are abusive to their people. In the U.S.

and Europe there are laws about required minimum working conditions inside the source factories of imported goods.

Every time that raw materials, components or finished goods are
shipped across international borders there may be taxes or duties
to pay, as well as permissions or other issues that you'll need to
research early in the process.

The problems aren't always with the receiving country. The customs agents in the country of origin can and do hold up shipments
for weeks because a permission form or regulatory step was not
followed in the procurement of a single component.

Do you already know high-quality manufacturers? The sophisticated turnkey manufacturers are working with big partners like
Amazon, Wal-Mart, Costco and Target. They're filling huge orders.
As a startup or a small business you may not have access to these
skilled high-volume companies.

**Will you have to ship any sample units to a manufacturer over-
seas** that you or your team build yourself from off the shelf parts?
Is the export of any of the required parts restricted by the U.S. or
other government? Will you ever bring back a single sample product in your luggage to test inside your company?

Companies are sometimes surprised when a routine shipment of a
single sample from the U.S. to a manufacturer turns out to require
several different approvals, forms and fees, with potential delays
attached.

You can even have to pay a high fee (over $1,000) for bringing back
to your home country a single manufactured prototype in your luggage for specific kinds of items that governments may want to reg-
ulate. Again, research this early in your process.

Will you have to pay import duties, taxes and other charges?
Many countries, including the U.S., charge import duties if you're
bringing products here from abroad, and those duties may range
from zero to an exorbitant amount based on the kind of item. Dif-

ferent ports and airports within the same country may have differ-ent rules in the case of "Free Trade Zones."

These laws and charges change all the time as nations joust with each other over trade balances.

On top of import fees, levies and duties, different states in the U.S. and different countries (and even cities) of the world tax differ-ent kinds of merchandise in an incredibly diverse range of ways. Tobacco and alcohol, for example, routinely face extra taxes and fees, but there are many other less well-known special cases.

Don't just assume that there are no relevant taxes that affect your product that you'll have to pay when shipping to retail. Research the issue as it applies to the factory location, your industry, ship-ping method and your local jurisdiction.

Are there EPA (in the U.S.) or other environmental agency reg-ulations that you'll need to comply with that may not align with the manufacturing methods of the lowest-price external manufac-turer? Some chemicals that are prohibited for use in manufactur-ing in the United States are legal elsewhere in the world, so you need to double check all these details.

You could have three different factories working on your product, all of them in the same foreign country. Everything goes perfectly until you discover that one of the three factories used known car-cinogens on their printed circuit boards. Your entire product can be refused for entry into the United States, recalled and/or expose you to legal liability.

Are lithium batteries included in any of your products being manufactured overseas? Are you compliant with the shipping requirements for those batteries, which can catch fire in transit if not handled properly?

Will your product be painted or coated with any other chemical or material? Paint ingredients that have been outlawed in the United States are still used some places in the world. If your product were painted in this way it could be refused entry to the U.S. or you might have to recall it from stores.

Will you have to create any injection molds for plastic pieces, electronic device cases etc. apart from what may be included in a master manufacturing contract?

Some kinds of items cost less to manufacture overseas than they would in the United States, but have expensive set-up costs. Anything made out of plastic – sometimes even the packaging your item comes in – has to be made in an injection molding machine, which means you have to pay for a steel mold into which that plastic can be injected. Complex toys with multiple parts and custom packaging, for example, may require additional molds.

The more complex the item, the more cavities the plastic has to fill, the higher the required precision, the higher the price will climb. You also have to decide whether to pay more to have the mold made locally, or to pay less and have the mold made (for example) in China, where you'll do the final manufacturing.

New 3D printing technology may someday make this process much cheaper, but for right now that option only works for small manufacturing runs.

Apart from the costs involved, some entrepreneurs don't read the contracts carefully and discover that when they do a combined "build the mold and make the plastic parts for one all-inclusive price deal," they don't own the molds when all is said and done. The manufacturer does, and if the startup plans to re-use the molds they'll have to buy them first at a price set arbitrarily by the supplier!

Will other parts like printed instructions, power cords etc. have to be included? Where will they be made, and by whom? Many small companies have horror stories of having products arrive in the U.S. ready for distribution, only to find that one small item was never ordered and is not in the beautifully printed – and sealed – boxes.

These additional items are often called "pack-ins." Legally-required warning labels, coupons with discounts for add-on sales ("Get 20% off a custom weatherproof cover for your new BBQ!"), registration cards, power cords, instruction manuals or secret decoder rings all have to be thought of early in your planning process. Adding something to the "bill of materials" (the complete list of what is shipped as part of the product) after the manufacturing contract is signed can be very expensive.

Will you be designing a package for your Dream Project? Some product creators are so preoccupied with making sure their Dream Project is of the highest quality that they pay too little attention to the details of the package design (like required warning notices), start the package design process late, or both.

Many manufacturers will integrate package design with the assembly of the product in a one-stop operation. This can be very efficient for the packing and shipping of the items, but the design may suffer if the manufacturer's graphic designers don't know your segment well, or if they don't have a good feel for your market's culture, competitors and consumer tastes.

For items that will be sold at retail, package design can be a make-or-break decision, which calls for involving experienced professional designers and marketers in the process. Once you sign off on the design, the drawings and digital files can then easily be sent anywhere in the world for printing and assembly.

If you use a "print and pack" option, ask your manufacturer how much lead time they need after they receive final graphics designs for the package in order to complete your units on schedule. Then add time for the package design itself, and start the process as early as possible to give yourself some scheduling safety margin in case the first round of designs doesn't satisfy you.

How will you ship the product? Companies that sell physical products have to pay to ship their goods from the factory to their warehouse, either directly or via an "all-included" price where shipping cost is included in the manufacturing.

The concept of "drop shipping" saves money for companies by shipping directly from the factory to the retailer or even to the customer. However, drop shipping small quantities and single orders can be very expensive.

When the manufacturing of a product is running late, the CEO of the company that ordered the goods is asked the most famous question in shipping: "Is it worth it to you to ship by air?"

Always plan ahead so you never hear that question. Air shipment compares to ocean container shipping in the same way that Gucci and Louboutin designer shoes compare to rubber flip-flops. Air cargo is many times more expensive, and has many additional content restrictions (like those lithium batteries). For heavy or bulky items it's simply not an option.

Even ocean shipping can have its problems. There are many different types and sizes of containers, and the shipper needs to have the right kind in the right place in order for your shipment to go out on time. Weather can affect navigation and schedules, and cause damage to cargo.

Bills of Lading (not to mention customs, tariffs and other taxes) can be as complex as the most intricate business contract, and the wrong contract definition of the term "package" can cost you hundreds of thousands of dollars.

If the labor contracts at the port of entry for your products are about to expire, your products could sit offshore for weeks while ships wait to unload. This happened at American west coast ports in 2015, and it's not a rare occurrence.

Be sure to have any deal reviewed by an experienced attorney and evaluate relevant insurance, since under the Law of the Sea there are many cases where the shipping company pays you nothing if cargo is lost at sea.

After the product is manufactured, where will it be stored or warehoused before it is shipped to retailers or direct to consumers?

Most companies marketing new products to retailers or consumers try to order larger quantities in order to get lower per-unit pricing. That can turn warehousing from a secondary cost into a major expense, as you need more space and you need it longer than you'd expected.

Having a truckload of unsold product sent off to a landfill because it's too expensive to keep in storage is a tragic event that happens far too often.

By the same token, trying to follow the "just in time" principles to get product in hand at the precise perfect time to avoid warehousing costs can often backfire.

During certain times of year (especially leading into the Christmas season) retailers may have early deadlines for receipt of products they order. If you miss the deadline for that early delivery to their warehouse by as little as one day, you can lose an order for millions of dollars of goods.

4.10.3 Getting Off to a Good Start

Here are still more problems of doing overseas manufacturing without specialized advisors:

Inexperienced clients often start the process without a clear, detailed specification for what they're trying to build. You'll want detailed drawings by experienced engineers, designers, draftsmen or whoever would be appropriate for the task. You could go to the best manufacturer in the world and have problems if you have contradictory requests or ambiguous specifications.

Inexperienced clients can sign a contract with an overseas manufacturer, only to have it turn out that the contract has loopholes or doesn't require the manufacturer to maintain quality standards or meet deadlines. The client has no way to use the courts or the laws of the country involved to force compliance, because the manufacturer is in fact obeying the badly-written contract. This can also happen when the manufacturing is being done in the U.S. or Europe.

If you have any hesitation about hiring an experienced attorney in this space or buying comprehensive business insurance, think about the liability issues. One of your electric teapots could catch fire while no one is home and the consumer's house burns down. The problem may lie with the manufacturer, but if you haven't been careful in your contract language you're the one who could be found liable.

Inexperienced companies often neglect to research potential manufacturers on key topics like:

Technical Experience and Equipment: Have they made similar items before? Do they already have all the necessary equipment not only to manufacture the items, but to safely move and pack them? Do they have experienced people to use and operate that equipment?

Volume: Can they make as many as you need before the shipment deadline and still do comprehensive quality control? Do they require a minimum order that is much larger than what you plan to build, making your costs skyrocket? Do they require an exorbitant up-front payment for tooling etc. that leaves you vulnerable if they fail to follow through? What is their guarantee on making good for defective units?

Materials Management: Can they reliably get the raw materials or components required to manufacture your product? If they're missing one shipment of $1.45 LED's they might be unable to complete $1,450,000 worth of work on your item and your deadlines won't be met.

Quality Control and "Fit and Finish": Do they do exhaustive tests on every part of every product before it's packed and shipped? If not, you could get 5,000 desk lamps in your order and discover that only 1,654 of them look nice and can actually be sold. Two thirds of your order didn't work or looked so splotchy that no one would ever buy them.

"Change Management:" It's routine to make small changes in a product during the specification and planning phase of its development. Experienced manufacturers have a set process for how to handle these changes and the associated costs. Lower quality companies can produce surprising additional charges you might be forced to pay.

Financial Health: What if your manufacturer runs out of money half way through the run of your product and shuts their doors forever? You could lose all the money you've given them and have nothing to show for it. Research the companies' financial health, and investigate insurance that can protect you against some risks.

Add this all together and (unless you already have relevant experience) for small manufacturing runs it is often actually cheaper in the end to pay higher per-unit costs of a local manufacturer.

DISCUSSING QUESTION 4.11

Are you planning to outsource any software development, hardware engineering, web development etc. as part of your Dream Project?

This topic is most relevant for: Dream Projects that involve technology.

4.11.1 External Technical Teams

Is there any electrical engineering work or other hardware design you're expecting to commission externally?

Is there any software that you'll be selling (or firmware that you'll be embedding) in your product that will be produced by an individual or team outside your company?

If your product is an app or website, who will design it? Who will create the art? Who will create the sound effects and music? Who will do the programming?

The good news about these topics is that outsourcing technical design and engineering – where delivery can be done via the Internet – avoids many of the potential fabrication, shipping, delivery and warehousing hazards of manufacturing.

The bad news is that outsourcing any kind of engineering work requires even more planning and research than manufacturing. The work is far more ephemeral, the challenges are even more complex, and there is more opportunity to be cheated by unethical partners.

4.11.2 Having the Right People on Your Team

For tech companies, if you aren't an engineer yourself it's critical that you have a strong and knowledgeable tech leader. Ideally he or she will be a co-founder, with a deep commitment to and passion for your Dream Project.

Many years ago I was working on a highly specialized game project using tech with which I had no personal experience. I knew an external team with the right specialized skills. I thought that the fit was so perfect that I made an exception to this rule of having a great internal technology leader on my team.

The "perfect" team struggled and could not keep up with the demands of the project. The product went through extensive delays before it finally shipped.

A tech leader inside your team can:

- Help evaluate what parts of your product (if any) can responsibly be outsourced
- Play a key role in hiring and contract decisions relating to technology
- Review the technical capabilities of outside partners with whom you may do contract work, where they can spot issues that non-technical managers will miss
- Validate the schedules and budgets proposed by internal and external engineers
- Monitor performance on all tech projects
- "Call BS" if an engineer or consultant ever uses tech talk to deceive non-tech people in the room

4.11.3 Start at the Source

Every app, website and program has "source code," the code written by a programmer. Typically source code is then "compiled" or "interpreted" so that it works on the user's phone, computer, etc. The compiled or interpreted version is called "object code."

When the product is completed you have "final source code." If you have a copy of the source code, a programmer who knows the same computer language can read through the pages and figure out how to fix most problems with your product, even if the original programmer has moved on.

If you have "object code" or anything else that's not source code, a new programmer has little to go on when trying to figure out why a program isn't working properly and how to fix it. If you print object code on the page it looks like gibberish, and even tools that show its underlying machine code leave it difficult to understand.

If you're working with programmers, make sure that you get regular deliveries of the source code to your project, and that each version of the source you receive can be "compiled" into a working version of the program or (in the case of web-based code) runs properly when dropped into the browser. This protects you from many dangers inherent in software development and allows your tech leader to review the work.

Contractors will want to ensure that you don't use this source code delivery requirement to not pay them for their work — and the potential for clients to do so is real. An experienced attorney can help you build a deal that is fair to both parties.

If you develop software for third parties as part of your business, you will likewise want legal help with contracts in order to ensure that you're still paid after you have delivered source code to a client.

DISCUSSING QUESTION 4.12

Are there any other regulatory approvals you'll need in order to start up your business, or to manufacture, import or offer your product for sale?

What kinds of licenses will you need (if any)?

Is anything about your place of business subject to inspections, signoffs, etc.?

This topic is most relevant for: Everyone

4.12.1 Looking for Approval

One of the most frustrating parts of running any business is getting governmental and organizational approvals. For example, in the United States:

- Some technologies cannot be sold overseas without special certificates, or sales are prohibited to countries like North Korea

- Anything powered by electricity needs to be certified for fire and electrical safety by UL (Underwriters Laboratories)

- Hardware that includes any kind of radio transmittal (RC) capability has to be approved by the FCC before it can be sold, both for signal and for shielding

- Any business that sells food is subject to some form of safety inspection

- Films must receive a rating such as PG-13 etc. from the MPAA under an internal industry requirement

- Video games go through a parallel process of ratings to identify which titles are and are not suitable for kids, and to specify required packaging and online labels

The key guideline here is, "Never assume." Follow up on every possible issue, check out every potential problem.

**If you are planning to open any kind of retail operation your
exterior signs are critical to your success**, but they are also
closely regulated.

Most cities in the U.S. require you to have a business license
in order to operate, even if you're just one person working from
home. These rules are enforced aggressively in some jurisdictions,
while in others small home-based businesses are largely ignored.

**Environmental restrictions on some businesses may require
special approvals** and certifications if chemicals of any kind are
involved. Common paints and dyes, fuel for small gas-powered
equipment, etc. can trigger these requirements in some cities. Storage of any kind of flammable material will require inspections by
the fire department.

**If the business is adjacent to a waterway, a lake or the ocean,
special rules may apply.** A car wash located where storm drains
lead to a local stream may have to filter and re-use water and to
not allow runoff into the public drain system.

DISCUSSING QUESTION 4.13

If you're going to have employees, are there any special employment laws in your city and/or your state that add additional costs, paperwork or operating rules to your planned business?

This topic is most relevant for: Dream Projects that will grow to employ a team.

4.13.1 Letter of the Law

This is another area that requires research. Some rules will apply to all employers, while others may kick in when you reach 20, 50 or more people on your team.

In the United States, the employment laws in California and Washington are dramatically different from those in Texas or Kansas.

Cities can have their own rules. San Francisco has employment laws that apply to businesses based there, but not to those in any of the surrounding communities.

Areas where surprises might be waiting include:

- Minimum wage requirements
- Local rules about what constitutes overtime, and formulas for overtime pay
- Required personal leave and parental leave
- Rules for who is considered an employee and who can be hired as a contractor
- Special taxes and assessments on payroll, revenues and (in rare cases) stock sales

- Rules for which job holders can be paid with a salary and who must be paid on an hourly rate
- Minimum required levels of benefits
- Rules for break and meal times
- Expense reimbursement policy regulations

If you're moving to a new city, state or country, assume that there will be lots of local employment rules you'll need to learn and follow. If you have more than a few employees, it may be worthwhile to consult a local HR attorney.

PART V

THE BUSINESS OF DREAMS

CHAPTER 32

The Business of Dreams: The Questions

QUESTION 5.1

How are you feeling about your Dream Project right now?

Excited? Optimistic? Worried? Disappointed?

Something else?

Write down all the feelings you can identify.

What about your Dream Project do you think is inspiring each of those feelings?

Please take your time, write down your responses, and answer fully from your deepest thoughts. Think only about your own opinions, not about what others may want you to think or do. Do not look ahead to other questions until you have finished this one.

_____

QUESTION 5.2

Earlier I asked the question, "What is your Dream Project?"

Let's refine the question as you start to hone your thinking: What product or service will be created and offered to people as a result of you building your Dream Project?

Please take your time, write down your responses, and answer fully from your deepest thoughts. Think only about your own opinions, not about what others may want you to think or do. Do not look ahead to other questions until you have finished this one.

QUESTION 5.3

What is the best way to share your vision of your Dream Product? How do you get investors, potential partners or key team members interested?

If you're an engineer, can you code a simple prototype so you can demonstrate it?

If you're an industrial designer, can you craft a model of the product that someone can hold in their hands?

If you're an artist, can you create concept sketches?

Can you create a video trailer like those used to promote movies?

If your Dream Project is a website, can you create the top-level screens to demonstrate its value?

If your business is a service, can you offer it to a few test customers, so they give you feedback and write online recommendations?

With your personal experience and skills, what would be the right approach for you?

Please take your time, write down your responses, and answer fully from your deepest thoughts. Think only about your own opinions, not about what others may want you to think or do. Do not look ahead to other questions until you have finished this one.

QUESTION 5.4

What problem is solved or what need is met by your product or service that has not yet been solved or met by existing competitors?

Please take your time, write down your responses, and answer fully from your deepest thoughts. Think only about your own opinions, not about what others may want you to think or do. Do not look ahead to other questions until you have finished this one.

QUESTION 5.5

How will you make money on your product or service?

What will you charge for?

Will you sell directly to consumers, or work through retailers or distributors?

QUESTION 5.6

If you're the passionate creator, who will market and sell the product of your Dream Project?

If you are driven by the financial potential of your Dream Project, how will you create a product or service that inspires passionate customers?

Please take your time, write down your responses, and answer fully from your deepest thoughts. Think only about your own opinions, not about what others may want you to think or do. Do not look ahead to other questions until you have finished this one.

QUESTION 5.7

How will you test your product with real customers to see if it works as well and will sell as well as you expect?

If your Dream Project is a software product, how will you test it to make sure it works as designed, operates in a stable manner and has no significant bugs?

QUESTION 5.8

Exactly when and by whom will you be paid?

If you receive money from someone other than consumers, how will those payments be calculated, and by whom?

How far in advance will you know approximately how much money will come in each week or each month?

Will there be any cases where you refund people's money after they've paid for your product or service?

Please take your time, write down your responses, and answer fully from your deepest thoughts. Think only about your own opinions, not about what others may want you to think or do. Do not look ahead to other questions until you have finished this one.

QUESTION 5.9

Pretend that your business has been operating for a year and you're having some success.

If someone asked you to estimate how much money your business would have in the bank in 30 days from that moment, what would you add and subtract from your company's then-current bank balance to calculate the answer?

Please take your time, write down your responses, and answer fully from your deepest thoughts. Think only about your own opinions, not about what others may want you to think or do. Do not look ahead to other questions until you have finished this one.

_____

QUESTION 5.10

How much cash will you need to start with in order to cover all of your Dream Project's expenses until it starts producing positive cash flow and pays for itself?

_____

QUESTION 5.11

What will you do if you complete your Dream Project, offer your product or service to the world... and it doesn't sell?

Please take your time, write down your responses, and answer fully from your deepest thoughts. Think only about your own opinions, not about what others may want you to think or do. Do not look ahead to other questions until you have finished this one.

QUESTION 5.12

What will you do if you sell something to someone or provide them with services, but then they refuse to pay or ignore you?

QUESTION 5.13

Have you ever written a Business Plan?

Do you already have one for this Dream Project?

Please take your time, write down your responses, and answer fully from your deepest thoughts. Think only about your own opinions, not about what others may want you to think or do. Do not look ahead to other questions until you have finished this one.

QUESTION 5.14

What would the best possible financial result be from your Dream Project?

Is your ideal to sell the company for millions within three years and walk away wealthy?

Or do you picture success as building a company that will pay you the salary you need to live comfortably while doing work you love, so selling the company isn't a big goal?

Is there some other ideal financial goal you're picturing?

CHAPTER 33

My Story: The Chess Game

Note: The story below comes from the experiences of my larger clients in the games industry, but the lessons apply to all categories and sizes of businesses. The dollars at risk in your Dream Project may be smaller, but most of the issues are the same. Use this example to always remember that bad things can happen when you're dealing with "good" companies.

For many years of my career I worked as a studio GM or CEO, and much of what I've written in this book comes from those personal experiences.

When I started advising other companies, however, something interesting happened.

I didn't just see a few deals a year, I saw many contracts and business relationships. I learned many more best practices. And I saw more kinds of unethical behavior.

The tale that follows is inspired by a handful of client stories I've encountered over the last ten years. Unlike the other "My Story" segments in this book, the specifics I've written below are fiction, so I can give you a simplified example to cover an important topic. This also allows me to share very real business risks without violating NDA's (Non-Disclosure Agreements) on any one specific deal.

In our archetypal story the game development studio, which I'll call "Acme," has a deal with a large corporate publisher that is headquartered far away. The budget is about $10 million, and Acme wants the payments to come in at an even pace.

During the contract negotiations the publisher wants to hold back a sizable amount until after the project is finished, a common strategy to ensure that the developer finishes every detail of its work. But they want to hold back much more than normal.

Acme worried about this arrangement, because once you hand over your final product you no longer have the leverage of withholding delivery until you're paid

As an Advisor I can raise these kinds of concerns when I'm working with indie teams, but if a studio doesn't have another potential deal at that moment they still have salaries to pay. It might take three months or more to find and sign another deal, which could consume all of the company's cash and destroy the team.

As you've read in these pages, I always advise the leaders with whom I work to conserve cash. It's a prime directive.

Acme's team weighs the pro's and con's. They decide to sign the contract.

The final compromise they strike is that all but $362,000 of the money would come to Acme in regular intervals. The last $362,000 would be paid after the game is selling in stores.

Fast forward to the shipping deadline. Acme finishes the game on time and the publisher ships it to all the major retail chains and offers it for download. The date for the $362,000 payment arrives.

But the check does not arrive with it.

Acme's producer calls her contact at the big publisher, who is surprised and concerned. He tells the producer he'll investigate and call her back.

The next morning the producer's phone rings. Her contact has been told to direct any questions from Acme to the Finance Department. He apologizes to her, clearly embarrassed, and they hang up.

The publisher has just made the first move in a familiar game of chess, one played with cash and lawyers instead of knights and pawns. Here's how the script works:

Step 1 of the Chess Game: The publisher refuses to pay the money specified in the signed contract. Acme can complain all they want, but the publisher is already selling the game in stores and online so the studio has little leverage.

Step 2 of the Chess Game: Acme has to decide to fold or fight. Folding means giving up on the $362,000. Fighting costs money, because you have to use sophisticated lawyers to take on a big company.

Big corporations have their own attorneys on the payroll, so legal disputes with small adversaries don't cost a lot of extra cash. A comparatively small company like Acme, which might have $5-$10 million in annual sales, would not have an attorney on staff.

Just writing a letter demanding payment requires Acme to pay their attorney to spend the time to check the full 35-page contract, at a cost of well over $1,000.

If Acme sues the publisher and the big company plays a delaying game, Acme might have to spend $200,000 to collect $362,000. If the publisher were really good at stalling it might cost Acme $400,000 to collect $362,000. Obviously, not a good strategy.

Some courts have a habit of splitting everything 50-50, so if Acme sues they could easily "win" the case but only get $181,000 after spending $200,000 or more.

To make things worse, all of the time that Acme's team leaders would spend on a lawsuit would be time taken away from working on new projects to cover the loss of the $362,000. This distraction factor, combined with the costs of a lawsuit, has destroyed more than one talented software developer.

The unnamed executive who is stepping in to take Acme's money knows about all these costs. He's betting that Acme will complain, then take a small consolation payment and go away.

Step 3 of the Chess Game: Acme calls their lawyer, spends the money and has her send a "demand letter" to the publisher.

The publisher ignores it. This is standard practice when big companies try to bully small ones.

Step 4 of the Chess Game: Now Acme faces a key decision. If they file a lawsuit they'll spend tens of thousands of dollars to try to get their $362,000, and they might not ever see a penny.

They confer with their Board of Directors, and discover that an associate of one of the Board Members has a close professional relationship with a senior executive at the publisher.

At Acme's request, the associate calls his friend and says, "This is all 'off the record,' but I wanted you to know. Acme's contract is really clear. Your company is about to get served with a lawsuit for Breach of Contract, and there may be other charges as well. I don't know how much your CEO knows about what's been happening. Maybe this guy is being a cowboy and is acting on his own. I didn't want you to be surprised."

The friend listens and makes no comment, though Acme's representative thinks he hears empathy in his friend's tone of voice. They exchange best wishes and say good-bye.

Step 5 of the Chess Game: Acme hears from an attorney inside the publisher. The attorney makes up a story about something being wrong with the game, which everyone knows is a hastily-conceived tall tale. He offers Acme $35,000 in settlement for the $362,000.

Yes, they offer less than 10% of the money they owed Acme under the contract.

Over several days and a series of phone calls between the lawyers, numbers go back and forth.

Acme ends up settling for about $215,000, and they only get that much because they have enough money in the bank to be able to afford to file and publicize a lawsuit that would make the publisher look bad. That $215,000 is more than Acme ever would have gotten after legal fees from following through on any legal action, and both sides knew it.

I don't share this story to discourage you from pursuing your Dream Project. In fact, I have seen few such terrible experiences in my long career.

I share this story so you'll know that such people do exist, and that they can hold important positions in large companies.

If you know that such things can happen, you're prepared to read any contract with a careful – and cynical – eye. And that's what I want to motivate you to do *every* time you receive the draft contract for a potential deal..

CHAPTER 34

What to Do With Your Answers (5.1)

"ANYBODY WHO THINKS MONEY WILL MAKE YOU HAPPY
HASN'T GOT MONEY."

— David Geffen

If you have not yet written down your answers, please go back and do so. Writing your thoughts down – even when you're the only one who'll ever read them – will produce far more insights than just answering silently to yourself in your head.

5.0.1 The Third Link in the Chain

We have discussed the Passion-Process-Product Method that forms the basis for this book:

- We start with our passions
- We experiment to develop a process that allows us to work on our Dream Project, either part-time or as a full-time job
- When we're ready, we launch our product

In Section 5 we start diving into the Product stage, with extensive discussions about starting and running a business.

Before we begin, however, we're going to go back to the foundation of this approach and review our passions.

DISCUSSING QUESTION 5.1

How are you feeling about your Dream Project right now?

Excited? Optimistic? Worried? Disappointed?

Something else?

Write down all the feelings you can identify.

What about your Dream Project do you think is inspiring each of those feelings?

This topic is most relevant for: Everyone

5.1.1 Pausing for a Moment

So, which if these three general cases best describes how you're feeling right now?

1. Excitement. By discussing your Dream Project you've gotten more and more excited about it.
2. Worry. You're still very interested in the idea, but you're also aware of problems or obstacles and you've lost some of your momentum.
3. Disappointment. You're coming to believe that your Dream Project is not a good idea after all. Or the fear of the "rocket launch" may have you stalled.

If it's #1, excitement, then keep reading! That excitement will help carry you through the highs and lows of building that dream.

If you're worried, that's fine, too. Most initial ideas have strengths and weaknesses, and startup CEO's will tell you that discouraging moments are always part of the process. I'll help you find ways to work through them.

If you're considering abandoning your Dream Project, first I'd like to ask you to brainstorm ways to solve the problems you've identified. Give yourself a few days, take some quiet time by yourself on a few occasions.

If you don't come up with a way you'd like to proceed, then it may be time to put this particular Dream Project on the back burner.

You'll notice that I didn't say "discard it," or "toss it in the trash." I said, "put it on the back burner." I've had ideas I thought about for years before I ever built the product. Sometimes setting something aside and coming back to it later helps you take a good idea and turn it into a great one.

I have more good news if you're deciding to make a change: there's another great benefit to setting your current Dream Project aside.

Once you stop obsessing over a Dream Project that isn't right for you at the moment, your mind becomes free to come up with another idea which may turn out to be a better Dream Project to pursue.

5.1.2 Yellow Lights, Not Green or Red

There are books that tell you that being an entrepreneur requires you to "always give yourself a green light."

"Don't be discouraged! Don't be afraid! Just blindly keep rushing ahead and everything will be OK!" they tell you.

Those books are lying to you. Some ideas are good and some are not. If you over-commit to a badly-timed or mis-targeted idea you can financially damage yourself and your family.

On the flip side, some "experts" are full of doom and gloom about how individuals can never accomplish anything.

"Investment has collapsed for your sector!" they proclaim. "Entrepreneurs should realize there's nothing but red lights everywhere! Only big companies can produce great products," they tell you.

Those pessimists are just as misguided as the "Rush ahead blindly!" guys.

The principle you'll keep hearing from me is the concept of the yellow light. Proceed carefully, look in all directions each time you make a decision to proceed, but don't be paralyzed by fear.

If your Dream Project is worth doing there's always something positive you can accomplish on the road to chasing your dreams.

CHAPTER 35

The What and the How (5.2-5.3)

DISCUSSING QUESTION 5.2

Earlier I asked the question, "What is your Dream Project?"

Let's refine the question as you start to hone your thinking: What product or service will be created and offered to people as a result of you building your Dream Project?

This topic is most relevant for: Everyone

5.2.1 But You Haven't Told Me How You'll Do it!

When I ask startup CEO's the question above I may get an answer like, "We're making it as easy to buy a car as it is to buy a deli sandwich!"

That's a great line, and it does describe the problem they're trying to solve: the historically frustrating and aggravating experience of buying a car.

But what don't we know yet? We don't know *how* the new company is going to do this. Many startups have tried to make buying a car as easy as buying everyday items. They've all failed.

Would you join or invest in a startup if you didn't know how they planned to succeed where so many others have failed?

Look back at your answer to question 1.1 at the start of this book and at your answer to the question above.

If a stranger reads the description of your product or service, would they understand what you planned to do well enough to decide if they're interested?

If not, please go back and add a few words (remembering that this is still just one sentence) about the "how" behind your great idea.

5.2.2 So Exactly How Do You Define Success?

Not all projects have to be about making a profit, or even about making money. Some Dream Projects are built just for fun, or to gain experience, or as artistic expression.

All projects do need clear and well-defined goals, however. Look back at the criteria for success that you wrote in for this question.

Does the goal feel realistic?

Can you afford to do this project if it earns this much revenue? If revenue isn't the goal, can you afford to build it?

Will you and any team members be OK if it doesn't earn this much revenue?

We're getting to the part of this process where we'll be talking in more and more detail about money, and this is a key moment for you to revisit these issues.

DISCUSSING QUESTION 5.3

What is the best way to share your vision of your Dream Product? How do you get investors, potential partners or key team members interested?

If you're an engineer, can you code a simple prototype so you can demonstrate it?

If you're an industrial designer, can you craft a model of the product that someone can hold in their hands?

If you're an artist, can you create concept sketches?

Can you create a video trailer like those used to promote movies?

If your Dream Project is a website, can you create the top-level screens to demonstrate its value?

If your business is a service, can you offer it to a few test customers, so they give you feedback and write online recommendations?

With your personal experience and skills, what would be the right approach for you?

This topic is most relevant for: Everyone

5.3.1 How Should You Pitch Your Idea?

I'll be covering how to craft a pitch in a later chapter, but you'll always do better if you have something impressive to show (or to let people try out) instead of just talking over a slide deck.

In the last twenty years the entire approach to how new companies demonstrate their potential value to investors has changed in Silicon Valley. The sections below will summarize those changes, and how you'll be expected to develop, test and perfect your new product or service.

Remember, pitches, demos and prototypes are not just critical for winning support from investors. They can also be used to impress:

• Potential partners, such as a company with whom you could cross-promote your products

• Team members whom you'd like to recruit

• Retailers who may carry your product

• Journalists who may write about your company

5.3.2 What You Need to Know About "Lean Startups"

The term "Lean Startup" has come into wide use in Silicon Valley – and around the world — over the last few years. It describes a series of steps that has become "standard procedure for entrepreneurs."

These concepts began to develop in the mid-1990's, and eventually produced books by entrepreneurs and engineers like Steve Blank (*3 Steps to the Epiphany*, 2003) and Mary and Tom Poppendieck (*Lean Software Development*, 2003).

Many of these ideas were pioneered in the games business. In 2002 Mark Cerny was working with Sony when he introduced a version called "The Cerny Method," and I had the privilege of leading one of the early teams that adopted his approach.

Eric Ries studied with lean business pioneer Steve Blank in the early 2000's. In 2011 he extended Blank's ideas about launching new businesses in a book titled *The Lean Startup*. Although I give an overview below, I strongly recommend reading the book for your-self.

As defined by Steve Blank, startups are different from estab-lished companies because they are operating on a theory of how their business will work, not repeating and refining systems that they already know work well.

Startups have to experiment, gather feedback and then mod-ify their ideas in a race to make them successful. These steps have to be repeated rapidly and efficiently in order to prove the company's value to investors with only a small amount of money placed at risk. This process is called "Rapid Iteration," and mimics an important part of the process of Lean Software Development as described by Mary and Tom Poppendieck.

In 2001 SyncDev's Frank Robinson coined the term "Minimum Viable Product" (MVP) to describe the first, most basic version of a startup's product. Customers can buy and use this MVP and then report on their experience. Their feedback and their spending pat-terns help the team quickly modify and re-test the product.

After many of these rapid iteration cycles the company hopes to steadily improve their MVP and ultimately demonstrate "traction." To do this they need to build a small but growing base of customers who are spending money on the product and generating revenue for the company.

If the product doesn't gain traction after a reasonable period of experimentation, the project is closed down. As painful as this is, it's far less damaging than continuing on the wrong path and losing far more money.

Learning quickly that an idea isn't working represents a big win for small part-time businesses as well as big ones. Writing off an experiment after a few hundred or a few thousand dollars – as I've done on some small projects -- is a lot easier than losing $40,000 or $400,000 on an idea that was two years ahead of its time.

5.3.3 The "Standard Requirements" for Startups

If a startup is pitching to investors in Silicon Valley today, they know before they walk into the room that there are three major requirements they'll have to meet. You'll recognize them from the Lean Startup principles above.

Your goal as an entrepreneur is to be able to say, "Yes!" when asked if you've met each of those three requirements, while spending the least possible amount of money in doing so. (That's where the "Lean" in Lean Startup comes in.)

Requirement #1: A Basic Form of Your Product or Service. That will be your Minimum Viable Product, or MVP, as discussed above.

For example:

You're designing a great new line of luggage with wheels that roll more smoothly on carpet than existing products. For an MVP you'd start with just the one most popular size of suitcase. You'd make sure your great new wheels are really working better than the competition – that's the unique selling point part – and that the bag is attractive. You'd use quality off-the-shelf materials for everything except your unique wheels to save time and money.

You can order a relatively small number of your suitcases from your supplier, and test your MVP by placing them in a handful of retailers in your home city. You can train store associates in the best ways to demonstrate your superior bag wheels.

If you have an attractive and well-designed bag that rolls better than anyone else's product, those units will sell quickly when customers try them out in the store.

Two years from now you may have six models, but we want to start with just one to get feedback and implement improvements.

You're selling a pizza oven that fits into the back of a pickup truck and looks like a camper. You'd start with just one hand-built example as your MVP. Your key benefit is that a pizza parlor that uses your traveling oven can get pizzas to the user twice as fast, since they'll be baking while the driver is on his way to the consumer's home or office.

Your prototype truck can have a standard pizza oven inside rather than the custom-designed one in the production version. The attention-grabbing exterior can be ordered as custom decals. The unit will have to pass all relevant DMV and Fire Department and Health Department inspections.

To test your MVP you partner with a single high-volume local pizza shop. If they report that delivery speed jumped 60% and sales jumped 25% you'll be in great shape.

Two years down the road you may have 397 mobile ovens instead of one, but this is how you get things started.

You have a great new app that sends greeting cards printed on high quality paper with a computer-generated message in your own handwriting, so you can never miss another important event.

For your MVP you'd start out with a handful of card designs — if the idea works you'll be able to add lots of designer cards and varieties later. The quality of the paper, however, will be the same high standard you plan to use in your final products.

To get your initial group of users you could partner with several local flower shops that will display counter cards offering users free downloads of your app, and you'll give those shops free ads on your app and website. Bartering promotions with other companies is an inexpensive way to get test customers.

If consumers are thrilled that you've made cards look like you wrote them by hand, your business will grow. The six designs you offer today will be 600 varieties in a few years.

You'll notice that in each of these three examples we did not just test the products in a lab. Our fictional startups sold the suitcases, the mobile-pizza-oven's pizzas and the machine-handwriting birthday cards to real consumers who paid real money.

Testing how people behave when they're spending real money for real products will always give you far better data than anything you can get from a free giveaway, focus group, interview etc.

Each of these companies might discover unexpected problems:

The innovative luggage wheels might trigger airport security scanners. They'd have to be redesigned.

The mobile pizza ovens might arrive before the pizzas were fully baked. An app would have to route the driver to correctly time each delivery's arrival.

The computer-generated handwriting system might be unreliable for left-handed customers. A second scanning algorithm would have to be created.

Requirement #2: Traction. Picture that you're driving your car uphill on a road and it's snowing. If the snow gets too deep you'll start to slip, then stop in your tracks, then start to slide backward.

Introducing a new product can be like driving that car up the hill. Your first version may not sell, and may have problems. You tinker with it, make it work more efficiently. You start to get more sales.

You make more and more tweaks and changes, practicing rapid iteration. A few of these adjustments make sales worse, but most of them are improvements.

You're still a relatively small business, but you've now tuned your Minimum Viable Product so it doesn't feel quite so minimal. You may just be selling in one city or targeting one demographic, but you have a list of cash-paying customers who are happy and are telling their friends. Sales are getting better every month.

That's what Silicon Valley calls "traction." You're not stuck or sliding backwards. You're moving forward, going faster and you're going up.

When a prospective partner or investor asks, "Do you have traction?" this is the story they're asking you to tell them. It can feature one piece of luggage, one pizza oven, or one set of consumers. But the direction of your revenue curve has to be going up.

Requirement #3: Team. Chronologically, of course, this requirement comes first, especially for tech companies who need engineers to build their MVP.

If you ask any investor what's more important, the team or the new product, they'll almost always answer, "The team." Bad teams can ruin good products, but great teams can take an OK concept and turn it into a hit.

5.3.4 MVP's and Traction for a Small Solo Dream Project

This all sounds lovely for a team that's trying to start a big company, but what if you're a solo entrepreneur?

You're not trying to raise money from investors. In fact, you may just want to prove to yourself and your family that your Dream Project can bring in some extra dollars along with the dreams.

Here are two examples of how you might inexpensively get a Minimum Viable Product, test your idea and achieve traction.

The Part-time Pottery Maker:

Don't spend any extra money buying equipment you don't already own. Use or rent time at the same wheel, kiln etc. that you have been using up till now. In Lean Startups you spend as little money as possible until you know how well your product sells.

Make two of each of your favorite bowls, plates, vases or other pieces. Or make fewer kinds of pieces and glaze items in different colors. This "product mix" is your Minimum Viable Product. You'll recognize this approach from the story of Jane Hernandez, the fictional flower seller we discussed in Section 1.

Take the pieces to the Farmer's Market or other event for a few weeks and see which ones sell. This is how you test your MVP.

Put up a sign that says "We do one-of-a-kind custom pieces!" Charge a premium for these based on how much time they take you to make, since people will pay more for custom work. This is another step in listening to your customers, not to mention a more profitable line of business.

Make and bring more pieces to replace those that sell each week. If you get new design ideas based on the sales patterns you're seeing, that's great, too. This is how you practice rapid iteration.

If any pieces are not selling, play with the prices each week to see what price point makes each item sell.

Don't make more of items that don't move well at the right price. Culling the weak products so you can focus on the strong ones is a key part of the process.

For your most popular item(s), experiment with color and size to see which variations sell best.

After a few weeks in which you have invested time (but not a lot of money) you'll know what sells, and does so at the best prices. You'll have a rough estimate of how many you could sell each week.

You'll know how your prices relate to how long it takes for you to make the items. If you made enough profit on your work to feel happy, you have traction.

Using a spreadsheet or a calculator, you'll be able to predict how much money you'd make each month if you continue these experiments in search of the ideal product mix. Marketers call this "finding product-market fit" but it's really just figuring out what sells and what doesn't.

You'll also have a good guess for how much clay and glaze you'd have to buy, how much space and time you'd need on the potter's wheel and in the kiln, the farmer's market fees, and any unexpected extra costs that turned up.

With that forecast and that list of costs you can make an informed decision about whether this is a Dream Project you want to pursue. And you will have followed the basic tenets of a Lean Startup!

The After-School Tutor:

First of all, if our sample entrepreneur can pursue other paying work during school hours it will create more financial freedom to experiment with this initiative.

Tutoring is a service business, and your success is based on a) whether kids like you, and b) whether parents like how their kids do in school after they've spent time with you. Treat every session as your MVP, and work for a 5-star review from every client.

To succeed you'll need word-of-mouth referrals, Yelp reviews etc. To prove you have traction, however, you need an initial round of kids and parents to try your service and pay you for it.

Check with your local school and with your City Hall to make sure you understand any and all relevant laws regarding adults who work with kids in your area. These laws are there to protect children and need to be taken seriously.

Do you have a child at a local school? Attend PTA meetings, Cub Scout meetings etc., and hand out certificates for discounted tutoring. If you add a blank that says, "I was referred by..." you can give additional discounts to satisfied parents who bring in new customers, so they become your sales team. This lets you build the small test audience for your MVP.

Local community groups like Rotary, Lions, and other service organizations are often looking for speakers for their meetings. If you can deliver a strong 15 minute talk on "how parents can help kids succeed in school," you can then hand out your discount certificates to members.

Try different hourly rates, certificate discounts and referral rewards to see what mix works best. This is how you practice rapid iteration.

You're excited about driving a brightly painted van to visit students' homes, but that's a very expensive experiment. Resist the temptation to buy the van and fancy paintjob until the business has proven you can afford it.

Magnetic car signs, however, are relatively inexpensive. A small investment could make the vehicle you already drive more eye-catching. Better yet, the signs can be removed and thrown in the trunk if you go out for a romantic evening. Now that's Lean Startup thinking!

After two or three months of effort you'll know if you've got traction. You'll know whether the amount of money you're making for this work feels like something you want to continue.

You may not make pottery or tutor kids for a living, but let these two examples spur your thinking if you want to leverage the Lean Startup approach.

CHAPTER 36

The Why (5.4-5.5)

DISCUSSING QUESTION 5.4

What problem is solved or what need is met by your product or service that has not yet been solved or met by existing competitors?

This topic is most relevant for: Everyone

5.4.1 Defining the Problem

Defining the problem you're going to solve or identifying the "pain point" you're trying to relieve is another of the new standard terms for Silicon Valley startups.

Whether they're funded by VC's or building the next great smartphone app in Mom and Dad's spare bedroom, entrepreneurs know that they'll be asked about this issue and that they need a good answer.

Not every "problem" feels like an inefficient process that needs to be improved. In the games business the problem we solve is boredom and loneliness, and our solution is to (at least temporarily) give people fun.

If you're starting a new cupcake shop, what's the problem you're trying to solve?

If there are no bakeries that make really good cupcakes in your area. there's a cupcake vacuum. Given society's affection for cupcakes, it's likely that some people see this as a problem.

If – and only if – you offer great cupcakes at a reasonable price you could fill that need, solve that "problem" and build a successful business.

But many problems aren't as simple as finding a neighborhood without a cupcake shop.

5.4.2 "Kind of" Problems

Many entrepreneurs search for a "pain point" by talking to friends and watching strangers, looking for a moment where someone is frustrated because there isn't a convenient way to get something done.

Of course, all the really obvious ideas get addressed quickly, so what's left are more subtle problems. It's much harder to thrill people with a breakthrough solution if the problem wasn't a big deal in the first place.

When I judge pitch competitions I hear a lot of these "it's kind of a problem and we have a solution!" ideas like the ones below, which I just made up (and whose signature products don't appear to exist in real life as of this writing):

Waiting too long for your Chinese take-out delivery to arrive? At Famous Dragon we use a network of restaurants to guarantee any of 30 popular Chinese menu items reach your door in 30 minutes or less!

Don't trust a stranger with your dog or cat? BondedDog-Groomers.com does full background checks on Fido's caregiver and insures you for $100,000 per pet!

Are your kids picky eaters? With KaleKookies they think they're eating dessert but they're really eating vegetables!

These ideas aren't bad. But it's hard to see any of them ever becoming large-scale businesses.

Famous Dragon Chinese Food Delivery might pick the closest Chinese restaurant to your home and use computer models to track drivers' routes. But if you're getting food that's not from your favorite place just to have it arrive 15 minutes sooner is that a win? If an idea only works in big cities, how would you grow the business?

Bonded Dog Groomers.com: I'd certainly like anyone to whom I gave our house key to be bonded, but am I willing to pay more to have the person who clips our dog's claws be bonded when we drop her off and pick her up at their shop?

KaleKookies: How much sugar and how many chocolate chips do you have to put in a cookie made with kale before kids will eat it? If they do start to catch on, Nabisco can develop a kale-based cookie that they roll out nationally while you're still struggling to serve five big cities.

That's why I call these examples "kind of" problems. They're pretty good ideas, but they aren't good enough to build a big business. And they might not be good enough to build a profitable business at all.

5.4.3 Write What You Know

When we were back in middle school the teacher assigned us the task of writing a short story. Lots of kids asked, "What should I write about?"

The teacher would say, "Write about something you know. If you've been to a rodeo but not to the ballet, write a story about the kind of event you've actually attended."

That's still good advice. Stop looking for problems other people are having in the world, problems that haven't dramatically affected *you*.

Stop looking for "the next iPhone" or "the next Facebook" or "the next Starbucks."

Now go back and practice the work you currently do. Play the sports you play, engage in the hobbies you love. Do the things you love to do with your family and friends.

Once you're not distracted by everyone else's problems you'll start to notice processes that are so slow or confusing that you get *really* irritated. Not just mildly annoyed, because mildly annoyed is not a real problem. But you'll experience something that just irritates the heck out of you.

If it isn't a function of local, state or national government, you may be on to something that will reward a Dream Project.

5.4.4 Start from the Heart

Your boss wants you to design tall, slim coffee pots, but your mind keeps coming back to short, stout teapots.

You just love 'em. You can't stop drawing little pictures of them. Your sofa, your bedspread and your shower curtain are all decorated with short, round teapots.

Is there a teapot "problem" in the world? No.

Is there a teapot "problem" in your head? Yes, and the way to deal with it is to start exploring how you could design uniquely shaped teapots. Maybe you can start as a part-time hobby and then see if you want to graduate to making it a profession.

The world does not owe you a career of designing teapots just because you love to do so. But if it's what you love and you can pursue it in a common-sense way, do you want to look back at age 80 and regret that you never tried?

I can't guarantee your success, but I do know that people who love a product category will design and invent far better products than people who are just doing routine work. Some of those better products will sell, and will make money for their creators.

After all, Steve Wozniak, co-founder of Apple and a member of our Board at Electronic Arts, didn't design computers because he thought it was a hot category. He designed computers because that's what he felt like he was born to do.

DISCUSSING QUESTION 5.5

How will you make money on your product or service?

What will you charge for?

Will you sell directly to consumers, or work through retailers or distributors?

This topic is most relevant for: Everyone

5.5.1 Ways to Make a Buck

In recent years we've seen explosive growth in the kinds of products and services available to consumers and businesses. And we've seen even more innovation in the variety of business models being used to sell them:

Software companies like Adobe sell "licenses" to their software, so consumers and businesses pay to use it for one year. In recent years they have been migrating this model from boxed packages to the cloud.

For decades the video game business sold games in boxes on consignment to toy stores, so the publishers had to take back any product that didn't sell. With the advent of the Internet and online games, new business models emerged, such as allowing people to play a game for free but charging money for add-on content.

The inventors of a great new kind of consumer item (like those "wheelie" suitcases) have a choice of business models. They could manufacture and sell the product themselves, or charge a license fee from other manufacturers that want to add the exciting new feature to their products.

Don't just default to using the standard or common business model for your category. If you come up with a better value-for-money or a more convenient way to pay, that alone can drive success for a great product or service.

5.5.2 Don't Stop at the Traditional

There are lots of ways that companies try to be the top company in a category:

Create the best product or service. This is the gold standard that gives you big advantages, but doesn't guarantee success.

Lower your prices. Usually a bad idea, because the resulting "race to the bottom" of price competition is suicidal unless lower costs are built into your business.

Out-market and out-support your rivals. If you understand every nuance of your business and communicate more clearly to customers, you're the one who gets the sale. Your customer service is outstanding, so unhappy users become loyal fans who promote your company to their friends.

Invent a new business model. Solar panels were too expensive for most people to buy, and banks charged too much to finance them. Millions of families wanted solar panels, so new companies installed them for free, then "leased" the panels to the homeowners in return for monthly payments.

Create a more efficient way to do something without sacrificing quality. Uber and Lyft succeeded because people were frustrated with an overpriced, inefficient and (often) unpleasant taxi system that exploited its own drivers.

Create a service that is open to everyone instead of just "the big guys." Square did this by allowing small merchants to process credit card transactions on their mobile phones, bypassing the expensive banks.

Create a tool that helps people do high-value tasks better. Wall Street has repeatedly embraced new technologies that allow stock trades to be processed faster and with greater accuracy.

Modernize a process that industry leaders would never modernize themselves. Health Care lagged far behind in adopting computerized records. New laws that required strict privacy controls opened the door to new software sold to hospitals and doctors.

5.5.3 Pricing Your Product or Service

The psychology of how we decide to buy things is complex. There are no simple answers on how to price products and services, and the right price today may be the wrong price three weeks from now.

You'll have to experiment. Start by doing research on the competitors that you believe are the most similar to your company. Set your prices to match theirs, then experiment with trying slightly higher or lower prices for a few days at a time (or longer, if you have a long lead-time product or service) to see what effect the changes have.

Experiments that are too short may be like visiting the desert on a rainy day: the data is accurate but not representative. Over time you can zero in on the best price points, though they'll continue to evolve.

If you have a service or sell high price-point products, this process can be more complex. Customers who realize they have a $50 (or $50 per hour) price difference will be a lot more upset than those who paid $1 more for smaller purchases. If you're concerned about price confidentiality you can experiment in smaller increments over time.

In open markets the "race to the bottom" drives prices down

to almost nothing. Inexperienced marketers keep trying to undercut each other one penny at a time until they reach the minimum allowed price. This is why so many products in the mobile app stores dropped to 99 cents so quickly after the launch of the original iPhone.

Don't get caught in this race to failure. Set prices in a reasonable range and stick to that range, or use an alternate business model to make money in a different way.

Established customers who value your product or service will describe it as being worth a higher price than people who have never done business with you. This is why so many businesses offer ways for people to easily sample their product. Service businesses like attorneys often offer a free initial hour of consultation to make clients feel more secure once they have to pay high hourly fees.

Pricing your product or service too low makes people assume it's lower in quality. This is why it's better to start out matching the price range of competitors, not undercutting them.

If your product or service is popular, you can raise your price. One games team that I advise moved their price for an online title from $2.99 to $4.99 once their title became successful, without losing sales volume.

In service businesses, if you have more work than you can handle it's traditional to raise prices if you're not already near the top of an acceptable range. The better customers will stick with you, and you'll make more money for the same work.

Don't feel guilty about making money. If your price is too high people won't buy and you'll know you have to lower it. If your price point is working well, it means you're offering good value for the money and you deserve to be paid for it.

5.5.4 Key Performance Indicators

For many years our primary KPI's (Key Performance Indicators) for packaged goods were:

- Average wholesale price per unit
- Manufactured cost per unit
- Sell-in (how many units were sold to stores, wholesalers, distributors etc.)
- Sell-through (how many units were sold to end users)
- Returns

If your Dream Project is based on an app or website, however, it will be programmed to collect and data for your team. That data can then be analyzed in search of issues that are lowering results and opportunities that might give sales and revenue a boost.

If your project is built around an app or website it's critical that you become comfortable with calculating, interpreting and using the relevant KPI's for your segment.

Once you understand the relevant KPI's, you'll know the right kinds of experiments to undertake to move those numbers in the right direction.

The critical KPI's include:

DAU and MAU: Daily and Monthly Average Users. This describes the average of how many people enter your website or app each day, and the average per month.

DAU is a better indicator of how active your customer community is, since it only measures users who signed in today. Someone only has to log in once every 30 days to be counted as MAU, so the higher the ratio of DAU/MAU the better the product is doing at growing user commitment.

CPI: Cost per Install. Cost to acquire each new user (all marketing expenses divided by the number of product downloads). Online advertising costs are the big variable that can inflate this number.

LTV: LifeTime Value. Average revenue received per user who downloads the app, whether all at once in an initial sale or gradually over a period of months or even years. LTV must exceed Cost per Install to be profitable.

Conversion Rate. The percentage of people who pay money to upgrade, add extra features, eliminate ads etc. A user who pays even a few cents for something is counted as being "monetized."

Cohorts. Cohorts are not a KPI, but a way that users are sorted in order to better study the numbers. Users may be broken up into different groups called cohorts so that the data on their activities can reveal more detailed patterns:

• Users who respond to one ad may be placed in one cohort and those from a different ad placed in a different cohort, to test if one ad or the other attracted users with a higher LTV, etc.

• Users who download your app or visit the website after a major upgrade may be tracked in one large cohort, while those who joined earlier are tracked separately so their retention rates and LTV can be compared

ARPU (Average Revenue Per User) and ARPPU (Average Revenue Per Paying User). These calculations may be described by the day, month or lifetime value.

ARPU is total revenue for the period divided by either DAU (for the daily rate, called ARPDAU) or MAU (for the monthly rate).

ARPPU counts only those users who have been converted to paying customers, so total revenue is divided not by all users, but by the count of how many have been monetized.

Minnows, Dolphins and Whales. Companies that offer tiers of participation and spending often use ARPPU to sort users into these categories, which are borrowed (unfortunately) from the gambling industry. Minnows spend very small amounts, and dolphins are the more committed users.

I absolutely hate the term "whales," which refers to people who spend larger amounts. All the teams with whom I work are familiar with my insistence on the term "Most Valuable Players," so our best customers are honored instead of being derided.

Average Session Length (or Average Session Duration). How long the typical user stays logged in after they arrive. In general, mobile apps do best with short session lengths and desktop users support much longer sessions.

User Progress. There isn't one set term for this, but we always want to measure how far into an app or website a user has gotten. Any event that drives people away is a high priority for tuning, since they rarely return.

D1, D7, D30: Retention Rate. The percentage of users who are still entering the app or site a set number of days after the initial download. D1 is the next day, D7 is after a week, and so on.

The opposite of retention is "Churn," the percentage of people whom you don't retain. The sum of the percentages of retained and churned users always equals 1. Different apps use different formulas, but "no sessions for 30 days" or "for 45 days" are common definitions of a churned user.

One secret of making these business models work is to start with the retention rate when you're trying to improve financial results. Retention (along with its mirror image, reducing churn) is the gatekeeper to success with any app.

People leave if they can't figure out how to use the app or software, or if it doesn't deliver the benefit they were expecting to receive. We need to get them to stay long enough to get into the meat of the product so they'll fall in love with the experience. When retention grows then Conversion and LTV will improve as well.

5.5.5 KPI's for Online Advertising

Note: If you experiment with online advertising, start with tiny budgets and short experiments. On some dashboards new users have misunderstood forms and spent thousands of dollars on useless ads in just a few hours without realizing they were doing so. Proceed with caution.

If you're buying online ads and trying to figure out if an ad increases revenue or wastes money, remember the rule of "mobile first." More people consume content and surf the web on cell phones than on desktop computers.

Sophisticated "responsive" websites attempt to address this by having one arrangement of content and ads when displayed on phones, and another when displayed on a PC or Mac.

If you review your ad placement on a desktop monitor it might look like you have a great spot, but when the ad is displayed to the larger smartphone audience it might be far, far down the page and thus invisible.

For ad performance measurement additional KPI's are relevant:

Impressions. This measures how many times an ad was shown, BUT it doesn't tell you whether the ad was displayed in a prime spot "above the fold" (the portion of the screen that shows before you scroll down) or far below.

Clicks. How many times someone clicked on your ad, which should bring them to your website or your app's page in the online store.

CTR (Click-Through Rate). The percentage of impressions that produced a click. Higher rates indicate that you have a well-designed ad, you're getting prominent placements for your ad, or both.

ACPC (Average Cost per Click). Online advertising systems award each ad slot to the highest bidder. If you bid 25 cents per click and the second highest bid is 20 cents, most systems will charge you 21 cents (one cent more than the second highest bid) for each click-through to your page.

Be sure to check each deal and make sure they use this system for bidding and don't charge more than the one cent premium.

The ACPC reports the average amount you paid for each click, which can vary based on what screen the ad was on, its page position, time of day etc.

Bid. The maximum you'll pay for each click. If the ACPC you're paying is 22 cents, don't just put in $2.00 to make sure you get the best slot on each page. Someone could come along and bid $1.95 and blow out your budget when the system bills each click at $1.96.

Budget. How much you're willing to spend on a given day (or over a longer period) before your ads stop running. This is an important protection since ad prices and results can fluctuate dramatically.

Always start with lower budgets as you're developing your ads and experimenting with systems. Discontinue any ad that doesn't earn a profit after getting an initial round of clicks, and increase your budget slowly and carefully if an ad is working.

There are many sad stories of new users who thought they were entering $10,000 as a rough guess for their planned annual ad budget. What the system expected, though, was their budget for one day.

Four hours later the money was all gone, spent on clickthroughs of little value from the wrong kinds of sites. Study the system before you use it, and start with very small amounts until you really know the ropes.

Spend. How much you've spent on ads during a certain period.

Sales. The dollar volume in sales you made from this ad. You can then calculate how your Spend compares to your Sales and determine if an ad was profitable.

CoS or ACoS (Average Cost of Sales). The ratio between what you spent on ads and how much money you made. It can be expressed as a dollar amount (a $100 spend yielding 50 units sold has an ACoS of $2.00 per unit) or as a percentage (a $100 Spend that produces $200 in sales revenue would have a 50% ACoS).

5.5.6 A/B testing

Another key method used to gather data and figure out how to improve a product's results is A/.B testing.

The classic (and oversimplified) example is that you are trying to decide whether to make the button that says "Download Now" green or blue.

Using one of several software packages, the team selects 200 random users and shows them the green button. The system selects a separate 200 users and shows them the blue button.

If groups A and B produce a fairly similar number of button presses it may be that there is no material difference between the colors.

If significantly more people press the green button, the team would then make the button green for all users.

CHAPTER 37

The Who (5.6 - 5.7)

DISCUSSING QUESTION 5.6

If you're the passionate creator, who will market and sell the product of your Dream Project?

If you are driven by the financial potential of your Dream Project, how will you create a product or service that inspires passionate customers?

This topic is most relevant for: Everyone

5.6.1 Who's Going to Sell It?

If a project's leaders are passionate about something, users can "feel" that love for the subject or category and equate it with quality and value.

As we've discussed, the world is filled with new products, new services, new books, new songs, new games. Marketing and sales skills are critical to success, and without those specialties even great ideas can die a lonely death because no one ever sees or learns about them.

If you're a passionate product creator, keep these questions in mind as you work:

If I'm not experienced or focused in sales, who will sell the product or service to customers? Is it realistic to think that I can do this all by myself?

How will we get the word out and rise above the background noise of every other message on social media and the Internet?

If you're driven by the business opportunity, not the subject matter, where will you find the passionate product creators to bring that opportunity to life?

DISCUSSING QUESTION 5.7

How will you test your product with real customers to see if it works as well and will sell as well as you expect?

If your Dream Project is a software product, how will you test it to make sure it works as designed, operates in a stable manner and has no significant bugs?

This topic is most relevant for: Everyone

5.7.1 Beyond "People Like Me"

We first touched on this subject discussing the principles of Lean Startups above.

Dream Projects are driven by passion, which makes them very personal to their creators. Filmmakers create movies they'd want to see. Authors write books they'd want to read. App makers create apps they'd want to use.

This passion can drive a team to create something that stands out and rises above the competition.

The danger, however, is that in trying to please ourselves we may not be pleasing anyone else.

Big companies conduct surveys and sponsor "focus groups" to get feedback on potential products, features and competitors. These processes, however, are often too expensive for small startups.

Surveys and Focus Groups are also prone to the rule of "garbage in, garbage out." Poorly conceived questions will produce useless data.

5.7.2 Research and Feedback on a Budget

Here are some ways to do research and get consumer feedback on a budget:

Look at your Facebook friends and your LinkedIn contacts. Make a list of a handful of people whom you respect and who you think would give you honest feedback on your idea (or your sketches, or your demo, etc.).

You don't need many advisors, and if you have more than a few such people save some of them for later iterations.

Invite each friend to coffee or lunch and tell them in advance that you want to ask them for their feedback. Some people will pass, but many will agree.

Share your idea, and be sure to take notes on their comments. It shows your respect for their opinions, and you'll never remember all the details the next day, even if you think you will.

These people know you, so the feedback will not be as impartial as the (sometimes brutal) honesty you see in surveys or online ratings. But I've gotten really useful advice in this way.

It's best to get feedback individually. The dynamics of talking with a group changes participants' patterns of expressing their ideas. Focus group moderators are trained on how to manage these issues.

Find Public Groups. If you live within driving distance of a medium to large-sized city, go to Meetup.com and search for groups that relate to your Dream Project. Try different search terms to describe your craft or business.

It's free to "join" as many Meetup.com groups as you want, which means you'll be notified the next time each group has a meeting. If a topic looks interesting, attending will give you the chance to learn from the speakers.

It will also put you in contact with people who have similar interests whose feedback you can request, either on the spot or in a follow-up over coffee the next week. You'll quickly learn to see the difference between polite praise and the enthusiasm of a person who really loves your idea.

I've also seen entrepreneurs randomly find co-founders and impress journalists at these kinds of meetings.

Meetups may also draw competitors, so use discretion in what you say. But it's rare that a project fails because competitors learned about it.

As Mark Stevens, an influential Silicon Valley attorney, once told me: "Far more startups die from loneliness than from leaks."

5.7.3 Demo Tables

In some meetup groups you can pay $40 to $100 for a "demo table," where you can show your prototype, product or anything else you want to share. A table works well if you want to play a video or show something on a computer, or if your product is large and/or bulky.

You do, however, want to *show* something to people at a demo table, not just stand there and talk about your new business.

Many people at a meetup are likely to wander past the tables to look at what's being shown, giving you the chance to engage them, ask them questions, etc. This is usually part of a company's sales efforts, but is also effective for gathering feedback for a product before it ships.

5.7.4 Online Research

Online research can uncover valuable data that is freely available to everyone, but that most people never find.

Read Competitors' User Forums. Many companies have online support websites that include user forums. These are web pages where users can ask and answer each other's questions as well as interact with the company, and on large websites there will be a high volume of activity.

Competitors' forums can be a gold mine of information. Once you sign up, you'll have the chance to read criticisms, praise and suggested features for your competitor's products, some of which may relate to your product or service as well.

Remember that many users visit only when they have a problem, not to say, "I love your tears-free shampoo!" Long lists of complaints on forums don't necessarily mean that your rival's products have low quality.

Read Topic Newsletters and Websites. Most business categories have specialized websites, both the kinds that offer consumer information and those written for "industry insiders."

I subscribe to three different industry news sites and two different tech newsletters, each with a different focus. Each sends me a daily or weekly email with links to current articles.

It's free to subscribe to many professional news sources, and you'll quickly see which are most useful. You can easily unsubscribe from the rest.

Reviews of competitive products – some full of praise and others disparaging – will give you a preview of how your product may be seen in the eyes of these influential writers. Such data may influence your decisions on which features to prioritize.

Some industry websites offer additional opportunities. For example, if your Dream Project is in Travel and Hospitality, the TripAdvisor website allows you to volunteer to be a "Destination Expert" who is willing to advise travelers planning to visit a certain area or city.

This may seem like "working for TripAdvisor for free" (which it is), but monitoring that specialized topic regularly means you see all the questions that would-be travelers ask about the area. This stream of real-life user data could be invaluable for travel-related projects.

Don't just assume that there are no corresponding sites or forums for your industry or segment. Take some time and search online, because new sites are popping up all the time.

5.7.5 "Quality Assurance" or "Quickly Assassinated"

Note: This section applies to software products, but there are lessons here that can be relevant to other industries as well.

If you're an engineer or have worked on development teams you know that bugs are insidious. Some will show up once in every 100 runthroughs. Some are in plain sight and we all look right at them and don't see the misspelling or the overlapping icons.

You cannot skip steps or get careless with QA, because the punishment is published bugs, which are at least embarrassing and sometimes expensive.

My suggestions below are all standard procedure for projects, and worth the trouble even on very small projects:

Test every milestone thoroughly, not just Alpha's and Beta's. This is part of the Agile development philosophy, and it yields big wins in time savings, budget savings and code stability. If a milestone can't be tested you need to ask yourself, "Did I actually *finish* anything?"

It may seem like overkill to have someone devote a portion of every day to QA, but that time expense is going to be offset by the time that good testing saves for everyone on the team.

Even if someone is focused on QA, the testing process "belongs" to every team member and everyone needs to conscientiously record every new bug that they see.

Deliver regular builds. Testers cannot find new bugs and verify fixes of old ones if they don't get regular new "clean" builds.

Have an organized system. Small teams may be tempted to track bugs through email or Slack. Taking the time to use a spreadsheet with big enough cells to record details or (best of all) a bug tracking system like Jira will pay off. Such systems also make it easier to cull duplicate bugs.

Write a test plan or create a test checklist or matrix. The core of any such doc is a list of every screen and every possible action on that screen, along with any instructions on where problems are likely to occur and limits that need to be tested (e.g. users can't have a birthdate before 1900 or after today's date). In the latter stages of testing, those lists can then be used to ensure that everything has gotten the "once over."

Don't just check off the list. As valuable as a plan or matrix may be, good testers have to be given time to review freely on every build in the same way that users would. Some bugs defy the scientific approach, and good testers have an instinct for "breaking" builds that are supposed to be rock solid and ready to ship.

Prioritize. Even if you're working solo on a project, sort your bug data base items so crash bugs are at the top and "wish we could fix these but may not have time" are at the bottom.

Assign. Write down who is going to fix the bug, and make sure each team member checks regularly for tasks that are waiting for them.

Verify fixes carefully. After I implement a bug fix I'll do a quick check and if it looks like it's working right I'll move on. That's "programmer self-checking," not fix verification. Always have someone other than the programmer review the build to verify the fix, trying to recreate the bug any way they can.

Let testers comment. I have worked with teams that told their testers, "Don't tell me what you think. Just report what's broken." This is a missed opportunity. Testers have to keep comments concise and clear, but they'll give a dev team really valuable feedback on usability.

Yes, it's worth testing that tiny last minute change. Every experienced developer has a story about how "the change that didn't need to be tested" led to a big problem.

Have outsiders test. Even if you're a solo programmer, buy pizza for friends and have them test your product. Better yet, have strangers (who won't worry about your feelings) test for you. "Users doing the wrong thing" produces lots of bugs that a tester who knows the right way to use an app will never see.

CHAPTER 38

The When (5.8)

DISCUSSING QUESTION 5.8

Exactly when and by whom will you be paid?

If you receive money from someone other than consumers, how will those payments be calculated, and by whom?

How far in advance will you know approximately how much money will come in each week or each month?

Will there be any cases where you refund people's money after they've paid for your product or service?

This topic is most relevant for: Everyone

5.8.1 Invoice Terms

When you send anyone an invoice, it's normal to have the "terms" listed on the document. Common choices include:

- Net 30, Net 15, Net 10 (or any other number) – You're asking them to pay you within that number of days.

- Due Upon Receipt – This means you want to be paid immediately.

Of course, just because you state those terms doesn't mean the recipient will comply. In practice, the larger company usually imposes its terms on smaller partners.

I have sent many an invoice marked Due Upon Receipt or Net 10 where I knew that if we got paid in 30 days we should count ourselves lucky.

When small clients and individual customers owe you money there may be more surprises and delays when they have to wait for cash to come in before they can write a check.

5.8.2 Introduction to Business Terms

I'll start this section with an overview of the kinds of payment terms used in contracts, and then describe some of the issues that can arise.

Remember, I'm not an attorney. If there's any doubt in your mind about a contract or business deal or document, an introductory meeting with a lawyer who's specialized in the field is usually an inexpensive way to get good legal advice. You can then decide if you need additional services from the law firm.

I once retained control of a valuable product when a company tried to illegally take it away from us. We prevailed solely because of one sentence that our attorney had advised us to add to the contract. This was many years ago, and ever since that moment I have never underestimated the importance of having an experienced attorney review contracts.

Here are some of the different ways that payment terms can be structured.

5.8.3 Commissions

Many kinds of sales positions, real estate agents, recruiters, talent agents and others are paid a commission when a sale of some kind takes place.

The terms of the business arrangements involved can vary widely, however. Some of those variations are:

Percentage – Commissions in different industries can vary from fractions of 1% up to 50-50 splits, all based on how much value the agent, manager, referring company etc. brought to the deal.

Refundable and Non-Refundable – Let's say that someone buys a used car and then returns it to the dealer a week later. The salesman who sold the car earns commissions that are "refundable," so his commission for selling the now-returned car will be deducted from his next paycheck.

5.8.4 Manufacturers, Retailers and Physical Goods

Selling physical goods to retailers involves different kinds of financial risk than selling apps or services. Whether you're making products or you're a store or website that sells them, you have to understand these issues.

Companies that sell physical goods have to manufacture their items before they can sell them, which means they have to pay for them in advance as well. Many first-time entrepreneurs misjudge how many units of a new product they should order the first time around and end up with a garage full of items they can't sell. Here are other issues to consider:

Timing. Early in my career my boss had me sign a $1 million Letter of Credit, a specialized document which serves as a check in some international transactions. The $1 million paid for the initial manufacturing run of four video games. This payment was nonrefundable, so if we guessed wrong on quantities and all of the games we ordered didn't sell we were going to lose $1 million.

My boss had approved the expenditure, but I admit I was still scared as I signed the deal. The manufacturing process for video game cartridges (now a largely obsolete format) would take months. It could be nine months before we'd know if the games were a success and if we'd make a profit, but I signed away the million dollars today. Every manufacturing CEO understands this risk, not to mention the interest charges if you borrow $1 million for six to nine months!

Re-Orders, Volume Minimums and Velocity Requirements. If a product isn't selling at a store the retailer will give it some time to catch on, but then it will be dropped.

What many people don't understand is that very few manufacturers make money from retailer orders.

Companies only start to make money when they get *re-orders.* **Re-orders mean that a product has "sold through," validating that consumers want the item. When the supply on hand gets low enough, it triggers a re-order.**

But how long do you have to get those sales before you're "delisted" by the retailer and your product vanishes from the shelves? Every chain, category, buyer and merchandise manager is different, but some stores have specific hurdles you have to meet.

Volume Minimums are requirements that you sell through a grand total of a certain number of pieces each month, quarter or year across an entire chain. Some will also calculate the revenue and "turns" (number of times an item sold out and had to be replenished) per linear foot of shelf space. This gives an advantage to items with smaller footprints and most retailers hate oversized items.

Velocity is calculated in different ways by some chains, but usually boils down to "units sold per store per month." If you sell 240 pieces of your product in a 6-store local chain in a given month that's a velocity of 40 (240 units divided by 6 stores).

Big box discount stores like Costco and Sam's Club require much higher velocities than premium retailers like Nordstrom or Williams Sonoma, since the discounters operate on very thin margins. Understanding the volume and velocity requirements of your key accounts is a critical part of your sales process.

Marketing Development Funds (MDF) or "Co-op Funds" and Shelf Space. Different industries handle these costs in different ways, but in general MDF or co-op funds are amounts that manufacturers pay to retailers to subsidize promotion of the manufacturer's products.

As part of the deal, the retailer may also agree to order a larger minimum number of units, to pay a certain price per unit, etc. They may agree to put your products on sale during part or all of the period when you're promoting the product, lowering their margin in order to drive a greater volume of sales. These short-term price reductions are carefully planned and are usually beneficial for both the manufacturer and the retailer.

In the case of an online retail site, MDF will give you the chance to have your product promoted on the website's landing page or a major category page in return for a special discount or fee. The "shelf space" on a website is almost infinite, but space on the major pages that everyone sees when they arrive at the site is very limited and is sold at a premium.

Brick and mortar stores are very different. If you're selling physical products you're haunted by the reality that every store (or chain of stores) has a finite amount of shelf space. Some of that shelf space is actually on a bottom shelf that's located towards the back and may be hidden behind a cardboard display for dog food. That's not very good shelf space if you want people to find and buy your products.

Some of that store's shelf space, however, is in really great locations:

The small item racks by the cash register, where inexpensive "impulse items" can be scooped up while customers wait in line.

The "end cap" shelf on each row that faces the front (ideally) or rear of the store.

A heavy cardboard display (called a "point of purchase" or POP display) with brightly colored signage that fits on the countertop by the register or is configured as a free-standing set of shelves.

If all retail shelf space is precious, those premium locations are like gold. And that's why retailers sell those spots to their suppliers

For example, if you're selling high quality wine glasses through a gourmet cookware chain, the retailer might offer you the chance to spend extra money to do some or all of these things:

- Have your wine glasses included in a sales brochure mailed to all homes within ten miles of each store, with the retailer offering the glasses at a special sale price
- Have your wine glasses featured on the retailer's home page and in an email campaign sent to the chain's mailing list
- Have your wine glasses placed on a shelf at eye level, where they will sell much faster than on a shelf above the shopper's head or at the level of their knees
- Have your wine glasses placed on a POP near the front door, which can dramatically increase sales over normal shelf space
- Have some combination of all of the above promotions, at a discounted price

As one sales executive taught me early in my career, "If you're a retailer, why would you sell products when you can sell shelf space? Products can be returned, but when shelf space is sold, it's sold forever!"

I've authorized credits for $250,000 in MDF to one retailer for a

small number of products for one Christmas season. Big manufacturers working with large chains spend many millions.

The price that retail chains will pay for an item and the quantities
that they will order are sometimes informally tied to MDF programs. If you don't participate at a certain level of MDF spending, a
retailer's orders may top out at a lower level.

In some states there are laws that limit the links between "retailer
incentives," "suggested prices" and order levels. These laws are
designed to avoid price fixing.

Consignment. In some industries products are sold to retailers
and the retailers own them. They do not expect to be able to return
any of the goods they purchase unless there is some kind of defect
in the items. Retailers have sometimes been known to deliberately
damage products in order to avoid this restriction.

In other categories, including toys, software, books and DVD's, the
normal business model is one of consignment. If a product does
not sell the accepted practice is that the retailer can return it for
credit (see below for more details). The practice of insisting on a
consignment model is growing in other categories as well.

Research the trends on consignment in your segment carefully,
since this issue has big financial impacts on your business.

This is why it's critical to understand the difference between the
two kinds of sales for anyone selling physical products:

Sell-In – This is the number of units and wholesale revenue gen-
erated when the manufacturer sells goods to retailers. Sell-In is
shorthand for "sold into the channel." Unless products are sold
on a non-returnable basis, sell-in totals can always be affected by
returns.

Sell-Through –The unit totals and wholesale revenue for products
that have been sold to consumers or businesses by the retailer.
Although there is a small exposure to return of defective units,
once product has sold through much of the risk of returns is gone.

Some companies operate too optimistically, or want to make their sales numbers look good for Wall St. analysts. They offer special deals and sell more units of their products to retailers than could ever sell through, even though they know they will have to take them back.

This often happens at the end of big companies' fiscal years, creating apparent "profits" and allowing executives to earn bonuses. The term for this tactic is "channel stuffing," and it has come under intense scrutiny by government agencies looking to protect investors.

For small companies channel stuffing is usually a matter of over-optimism rather than corruption, but the financial impacts can be just as dangerous.

Credits, Price Protection and Returns. If a retailer operates on a consignment basis and some items don't sell, they will inform the manufacturer they intend to return the goods and will request a "credit," which is effectively a refund. Often the supplier will send them different new products in lieu of cash. Sometimes the retailer will also negotiate that the manufacturer has to pay for shipping both ways on the returned and the new items.

Manufacturers facing these credit requests and returns may instead offer the retailer "price protection." Here's how it works:

Let's say you sell 1,000 alarm clocks to a retailer for $12 each (a total of $12,000), and the retailer than sells them for $25. Sales are disappointing, and after 60 days the retailer has sold only 200 of the alarm clocks and still has 800 on shelves and in the warehouse.

When the retailer says they want to return the 800 alarm clocks, they are due 800 x $12, or $9,600. That means you'd have to give back almost all of the $12,000 you received, plus pay for shipping the clocks back to your warehouse.

To avoid these costs you offer the store price protection, reducing the wholesale price of the remaining 800 alarm clocks to $6.

They paid you $9,600 for those 800 clocks at $12 each. Under price protection you're saying, "Oops, those were too expensive. We'll pretend you only paid $6 each instead of $12 so you can lower the consumer price." You only have to refund $6 per unsold unit (instead of the full $12) to the retailer and you don't have to pay for shipping, saving you thousands of dollars.

If the retailer agrees, they might then sell the clocks for $9.95, less than half the previous price. Often that's enough to clear the inventory, and it's less work for both sides than it would be to send everything back. If the clocks still don't sell, you could offer price protection again to allow the retailer to blow out the ill-fated clocks at a deeply-discounted price.

The lesson here is that manufacturers (who hate refunding money) and retailers (who hate to use a lot of staff time returning items) would rather work out a deal than see a big order shipped back. Price protection allows the supplier to take smaller losses and ensures that the retailer can still make some profit.

Holiday Deadlines. Many retailers register over half their annual sales in the weeks before Christmas, so it's a critical "make or break" time for store chains and for the consumer goods companies who supply them.

If you want your product to be on the shelves for Christmas, what is the deadline by which you have to have it completed, packaged and ready for shipment?

Those deadlines vary by industry, but are real and seldom compromised. For example, in the video games business traditional cut-off dates are often about four months before Christmas.

Why so early in the year? Because some games miss their projected shipment dates. Chains have to plan their Christmas "merchandise mix" far in advance, so they can't risk buying product that never arrives, leaving empty shelves and no chance to profit from them.

5.8.5 The Power of Shelf Space

Shelf space is finite. Big consumer goods companies continually look for ways to take more of it... leaving less space for their competition. Each item in a retail store that has a unique bar code and number is called an "SKU" (Stock Keeping Unit), and companies keep creating more and more of them.

If you walked down the soft drink aisle in an American supermarket 25 years ago you'd have seen a handful of products from Coca Cola, and about the same number from Pepsi.

Walk down the same aisle today and there are five to ten times as many varieties. Three different kinds of diet cola for each brand, with different amounts of caffeine or different sweeteners. Bottled cola imported from Mexico, where it's made with cane sugar. Cherry and vanilla and strawberry flavors. Special holiday packaging, or packaging where every can has someone's first name printed on it, or St. Patrick's Day green bottles.

Yes, some of this variety is intended to appeal to a more diverse audience. But what about all those other brands of sodas that were on the shelf 25 years ago? The RC Cola's and Diet Rite and Tab and Shasta and Faygo and Dad's Root Beers of the world. What happened to them?

They're rarities today because – along with the fallen infantry of failed Coke and Pepsi brands – they are the ones who were pushed off the shelf by the heavily marketed variations that take that space today. After losing more and more shelf space to Coke and Pepsi, many of these smaller bottlers faced a difficult choice: sell their brand to one of the "big guys" or slowly fade from consumers' view. Many brands sold.

The moral of the story: if your business sells through traditional stores, assume that large competitors will try to squeeze your products off the shelf. Plan a strategy that makes your product so valuable to retailers that you're a long term winner in this game of musical chairs.

5.8.6 Service Businesses

Attorneys, accountants, consultants and other service businesses have a very different business model: time. They have to focus on "billable hours," and law firms (as one example) will track each attorney's weekly totals.

In many service companies the professionals are expected to go out and find their own clients to generate their billable hours. A CPA or attorney who is skillful at signing valuable clients will be called a "rainmaker" and earn extra compensation.

Client assignments may be handled in different ways:

Hourly. The professional has a rate per hour. At the end of each month they submit an invoice listing the total number of billable hours spent, and a list of each task and how long it took.

Retainer. The client pays the professional a pre-negotiated set fee every month, under either of two arrangements:

The professional will not count hours, but pre-agrees to do all necessary non-extraordinary work during the month for that fixed price. Some months will be busier or lighter, but it's planned so it all evens out. Big projects are priced and billed separately. Or...

The accountant or consultant does count the hours. If the month's billings exceed the retainer their invoice lists the amount owed. If the retainer were not fully used up, its remaining value is forwarded to the next month as a credit on the account.

5.8.7 Advances and Royalties

Many music, book, movie and game publishers pay the people who create their published works on a royalty basis. Popular authors and big rock stars earn higher percentages, while those who are just breaking in earn less.

Often the publisher will finance the new product by paying "advances against royalties," which are loans that will be subtracted from the royalties earned by the product after it is released. The publisher starts paying cash to the creators only after it has "recouped" enough royalty money to pay back the advances.

For example, a media company might pay a celebrity 15% of the Net Revenue it receives from sales of their book. They could advance the celebrity $200,000 of the money, and then subtract that $200,000 from the royalties before paying them any additional cash.

Advances, like the commissions discussed above, come in two flavors: refundable and non-refundable. Non-refundable advances are in effect a "guarantee," the minimum payment guaranteed in any business deal. If the celebrity's new book sells only 2,000 copies, he still gets to keep the $200,000.

Refundable advances can be "billed back" by a publisher if sales targets aren't met or under certain circumstances. Since those circumstances can be manipulated by companies I never sign any deal that includes refundable advances. I advise you not to sign any such deals yourself.

You'll notice that I said "Net Revenue" is used for calculating royalties, and each contract's definition of "Net Revenue" can be even more important than a difference of several points in the royalty rate.

"Gross Revenue" means the total amount of money the publisher received for the product. This is also called revenue that is "above the line."

"Net Revenue" is what's left after the publisher subtracts expenses allowed under the contract. Each industry has its own "typical" deductions, and what is routinely accepted for books might be an unheard-of deduction for games, and vice versa. Net Revenue can also be referred to as revenue "below the line."

Hollywood studios are famous for subtracting every cost imaginable – and some that are imaginary – from Gross Receipts before they pay producers and actors a royalty on Net Receipts from their films.

Here's a list of some of the items that publishers may ask to subtract from Gross Revenue in a negotiation to calculate the Net Revenue:

- Sales Commissions
- Cost of Goods – The cost of manufacturing the DVD, book, etc., along with the cost of packaging.
- Shipping – If the publisher paid to ship the product to retailers they may subtract it.
- Returns – If a product is returned the publisher will want to subtract the money they received for it before paying royalties. They may also deduct the cost of the return shipping for the item.
- Taxes, Duties, Tariffs etc. – These can vary widely depending on the item, the state or country, etc.
- Marketing — This is a category where companies can be very creative and expansive in claiming expense that they want to deduct from Gross Receipts
- Costs of Currency Exchange – If revenue is received overseas different fees and commissions may have to be paid in order to exchange it for dollars, Euro etc.

In general, a major part of any publishing contract negotiation is defining which of these deductions from Net Receipts are allowed before royalties are calculated, and any limits or caps that may be placed on any category of deductions.

CHAPTER 39

The How Much (5.9–5.10)

Pretend that your business has been operating for a year and you're having some success.

If someone asked you to estimate how much money your business would have in the bank in 30 days from that moment, what would you add and subtract from your company's then-current bank balance to calculate the answer?

This topic is most relevant for: Everyone

5.9.1 Calculating Cash

When I started out as a CEO at my first company, I thought I was pretty good at being conservative with cash.

If a client told us on September 1 that they thought a deal would close by September 15 and we'd have a check by September 30, I'd put that cash in the budget for October 30. That was being conservative.

Then I discovered that in our branch of the software industry it typically takes 90 days for small deals to get from an agreement-in-principle to a final, signed contract. The check that was supposed to arrive on September 15 might come on December 15. Or, as happened recently, the September 15 "promise" turned into a check on February 24 of the following year.

Or, as happens sometimes, the deal falls through and those dollars never arrive at all.

The first thing I'd like you to remember to include in these calculations is:

"If the money is not already in the bank, don't just be cynical about when it will arrive. Be very very super-cynical *because it may never arrive at all.***"**

5.9.2 There's Always a Surprise!

In all my years as a GM and CEO I have almost never had a month in which a significant unbudgeted expense did not appear.

- A computer dies and has to be replaced.
- A client's boss wants a status report and four of us have to fly to Los Angeles and stay in a hotel overnight for a 9:00 AM meeting, then fly back that night.
- It turns out we need specialized insurance for a project and now we have to spend an extra $2,180. Or $21,800.

Stuff happens. Your calculation of how much cash you'll have in 30 days has to include an allowance for those unpredictable expenses.

5.9.3 The "Nut"

There are some things, however, that are predictable:

If you've hired a team, you're paying salaries and payroll taxes every two weeks, give or take a few days. You might be able to stall on replacing that computer or buying that insurance, but payroll and payroll taxes always have to go out on time.

In many jurisdictions businesses can pay their employees either 24 times a year (twice a month) or 26 times a year (every two weeks). If you pay your team every two weeks each paycheck is a little smaller, but in two months of every year you have to make payroll three times instead of two. Those can be extra tough months for a business.

If a payroll date would naturally fall on a Saturday, you may have to release those paychecks a day earlier than usual.

If you've rented an office, the rent is due on a certain date and if it's late you're going to have to pay a hefty penalty. Get too far behind and the landlord will change the locks and you'll be locked out of your own business... with all your equipment and files inside.

You'll typically have to pay business property taxes and quarterly corporate tax deposits. Penalties for not doing so can be steep, and can open a Pandora's Box of legal issues.

This collection of "must do" expenses is often called "the nut," the amount of money a business absolutely positively has to come up with each month. A more genteel term for this, which includes provisions for unexpected expenditures, is "the monthly burn rate."

If you take your current cash and divide it by your monthly burn rate, you'll get a number that represents your "runway," the number of months that the company can currently operate without generating or receiving more cash.

So let's recap:

1. You have to be very skeptical about every dollar of revenue you think will be coming into your business until it actually reaches your bank account.

2. Every month you'll have unexpected expenses.
3. Every month you'll have to cover "the nut," expenses you absolutely positively must pay, no matter what.

Yes, it's not fair. The money coming in is unpredictable, while the money going out is already-committed dollars plus more unexpected costs on top of it.

That's what you need to remember when you forecast the cash in your bank account thirty days from now. Protect your cash and you'll always have a big advantage over your competitors.

5.9.4 The Three Kinds of Cash

Sometimes the defining line between success and failure is painfully simple: those who manage cash carefully are the ones who live long enough to survive their mistakes and make their business a success.

Those who cannot manage cash run out of money and close their doors.

Any Dream Project where you must earn money in order to continue working on it will live or die on how well you manage the cash.

That's why experienced mentors and advisors for startups always teach their entrepreneurs the phrase:

"Cash is King"

That's why we give our accelerator companies lectures about how hard it is to earn cash, and how easy it is to watch it slip away in ways that you never expected.

And that's why you absolutely, positively must understand the three kinds of cash, whether you're a tiny startup or working in a large corporation.

Here's the list:

1. Cash that Someone Else Cannot Take Back

We think of the money in our business and personal bank accounts as "ours" and are used to the idea that so long as we pay our taxes no one can take it away.

In reality, if you're running a business, especially a young business that has not built up cash reserves, it's likely that most or all of your company's cash can be taken from you.

How special is "non-refundable" cash? To appreciate it, read on about all the different ways that cash that should be in your bank account can end up somewhere else.

2. Cash that Someone Else Can Take Back

There are many cases in business where this can happen:

If a business takes out a bank loan it will come with covenants and restrictions. These may include things like maintaining a certain average balance, a certain minimum balance, having a minimum total amount of cash deposited in a given quarter, etc.

If a business falls out of compliance with those covenants the bank has the option (but not the requirement) to "call" the loan, which means you have to pay back all the money immediately. All that loan money in your account is not free and clear. It's money you could have to give back.

As in all of it. As in giving back all of it at once.

The moral of the story: avoid taking bank loans. This is why you hear the phrase, "The only people who can get bank loans are the people who don't need the money!"

Never (and I mean *never ever*) personally guarantee any business loan or lease! It's always better to find an alternate path than it is to guarantee a loan or lease.

If your personal account is in the same bank as your business loan they can take your personal cash without your permission and without giving you notice if the business cannot pay back the bank.

In some jurisdictions they can do this via the fine print in the loan agreement without you explicitly guaranteeing the loan. This is another reason to avoid taking business loans and to maintain strong discipline with cash.

Companies that have raised funds through friends and family, from small "Angel Investors" or from VC's (Venture Capital firms) do so under different kinds of contracts. Some are structured as convertible notes, loans that can be converted into equity in the company by the investor if they wish to do so. Others may be straight stock sales.

With many of these deals, if the investors don't like how the company is doing they can "call the loan." If the loan cannot be repaid some deals give all of the company's property – including intellectual property like patents, copyrights and trademarks – to the investors in lieu of cash. That means that you no longer own the rights to your Dream Project.

In the hands of very aggressive investors such deal terms can be used to take over a promising young company. I have seen ruthless investors engage in such maneuvers, despite giving speeches about how they're supportive of entrepreneurs. Always be careful what you negotiate and don't assume that every investor is trustworthy just because they sound nice and they have money.

Investors are often given voting seats on a company's Board of Directors. If the company does not repay money that investors are owed the board members who hold those voting seats can fire the CEO and take over the company, which gives them control of the bank accounts, physical property and intellectual property.

So all that money that came from investors is not cash that you control. It is money that you could have to give back: Always read the deal terms carefully (the lawyers will give you very long documents), always hire your own, separate law firm to review the deal, and go into the process with your eyes open if you take investors' money.

If you manufacture a physical product that you sell via stores, the payments you receive from those stores often are sold on consignment or come with strings attached, especially until it's been proven that your product will sell.

That means that if one of your products doesn't sell they have the option to return it to you and get their money back.

The IRS and other tax authorities. In the United States the Internal Revenue Service as well as state and local tax authorities can in many cases contact your bank and have them deliver your company's cash to the Government without your permission. If you have not formed the right kind of corporation they can do the same with your personal funds, even if it is the company that owes the taxes. You have the right to appeal if you think there's been a mistake, but in the meantime that cash is unavailable to you.

Not paying any legally imposed tax is a mistake that can snowball into big debts, but not paying employment taxes is often the most punishing mistake of all. Penalties, fines and fees can multiply dramatically in a very short time. Always be fanatical about paying payroll and employment taxes on time.

Checks, Certified Checks and Cashier's Checks. We are all familiar with the fact that checks can bounce, and that if they do so the money we thought we had received will be subtracted from our account.

But cashier's checks and certified checks ought to be OK, right? Unfortunately, even these checks can be forged, so the value added to your bank account can later be subtracted.

3. **Cash You Are Owed or Promised**

Here's a list of things that can happen to money before you receive it. Every one of the problems listed below has happened to teams I've led or advised.

Late Delivery. Even teams that work incredibly hard will sometimes deliver a milestone, a product component or a completed product late. Whether it's a week, a month or a year late, all the money you would have made from that delivery does not come in until the work is completed.

In the software business contracts will define how each segment of an app or program is initially delivered in rough form, and a milestone payment is made for that delivery. If the first milestone delivery is a week late and the second is two weeks late the delays can add up.

Unless you start with a lot of cash in the bank, a small company that falls behind schedule can run out of money before the project is completed.

This always leaves a bad taste in the client's mouth. If they add money to the deal to prop up the team that's late, they can feel as if they've been misled or even blackmailed.

Other clients will add money to the value of the deal, but do so only in exchange for severe concessions on issues like revenue sharing, ownership rights etc. If you're running out of cash some partners will extract very harsh concessions to bail you out.

Late Payment. Some late payments by your partners are deliberate stalling to hold onto cash as long as possible. CFO's in large companies are judged by the average number of days it takes them to pay an invoice, so they're rewarded for delays.

Other times a partner company may have their own cash flow problems. They may be waiting for a big check from somewhere else, and until it comes in nobody outside is going to get paid. Payroll always comes first, and these delays are hard to anticipate or predict.

Currency transfer exchange rates, regulations and delays. If you are being paid by an overseas company or you're a foreign company dealing with a partner in the United States, your bank account and the partner's account will be in different currencies.

The exchange rate for those currencies fluctuates each day. Large banks try to do exchanges at moments when the exchange rate favors them by a few cents. I've had checks that were anywhere from $75 to $7,500 smaller than I expected because of exchange rate fluctuations that were exploited by our bank.

Large wire transfers of some currencies can be delayed by regulators in one or both countries. This may involve collecting data for tax authorities, and some regulators are intent on preventing money laundering by criminal interests. If your money arrives two days later than planned it can cause big problems.

Stalling for advantage. I have seen large companies drag out negotiations with small partners in an effort to induce the other company to use up its cash reserves. Once the small company looks like it's "starving for cash" the large company unveils harsh new conditions for the deal.

By that time the small company may have no choice but to accept terrible terms in an agreement.

If you assume in every negotiation that the other side will try this tactic you'll manage cash, time and negotiations very differently. Never cut off your discussions with alternate partners and clients until a deal is signed, the check is cashed and the money is in the bank.

Real bank error. Like the game of Monopoly, on rare occasions there will be bank errors. Unlike Monopoly, they are often not in your favor, so you are missing some of your money. It can take from 20 minutes to several days for the bank to correct the error. In the meantime that cash is gone.

Change in management. You have a great relationship with a client, with a retailer, with a distributor. Then their CEO is replaced, or the senior executive who oversees the division leaves and they bring in a new person.

Often your deals will continue to operate normally. But other times the new executive may cut away existing products, services or vendors. They may re-negotiate deals on harsh new terms. The revenue you've been receiving from this partner ends, suddenly, with very little warning.

Partner or client acquired by new company. The people, projects and products in the acquired company are perfectly good, but the acquiring company only wants some of them. Everything else is closed down, released or given away.

Your contract or relationship could be terminated. All the money that you were scheduled to receive from that deal disappears.

Bounced Check. When you're dealing with businesses rather than individuals you're unlikely to receive a check that bounces, but it does happen once in a while. In most cases someone just mid-timed when a deposit was going to hit the bank and you get paid 24 to 48 hours later. Or it could be a sign of impending...

Bankruptcy. Sometimes that bounced check is the harbinger of even more damaging news. The company that owes you money could go bankrupt.

When a company that owes you money goes bankrupt there are two tiers of creditors.

- Secured creditors have some form of collateral, like the bank's right to repossess a car for non-payment
- All other creditors are non-secured creditors who get paid only if there is money left over after the company's employees (in many states) and the secured creditors have been paid

I have had a client go bankrupt once in my career. As unsecured creditors we never received a penny. All the cash we had planned to receive disappeared.

5.9.5 Companies Train Managers to Value Cash

When people pitch to big companies like Microsoft, Google and IBM, I often hear the phrase, "I'm going in and asking for top dollar. They have tons of money!"

This is actually a terrible approach. Here's why:

Large firms know that managers might be more generous with cash when everyone knows there's plenty in the bank. To offset this psychology, they make spending and budgeting controls *more* rigorous than those at a typical firm. Managers have to work extra hard for every budget dollar.

When you inflate your prices for the rich company, they know you're bidding high and you're less likely to get the deal.

5.9.6 Don't Sell Yourself Short

There's a flip side to this story of how much to charge customers and clients.

Many of us tend to sell ourselves short. We say things like, "They'd never pay me that much per hour," even though we know that our rate is normal for this assignment.

Underpricing high quality work makes us look like we lack confidence in ourselves.

So how do you figure out what to charge so you're neither greedy nor self-defeating?

Do your homework. If you don't already know, research the typical rates for the services you provide at your level of experience. Do online searches. Talk to people you know in the industry.

Make that research a continual process, so you track changes based on the circumstances of different deals.

If you do a good job on every project you'll be also able to raise your rates gradually over time.

5.9.7 Lessons from Las Vegas

The classic model of going to VC's to raise millions of dollars does work. But most venture-backed companies raise money only after they've risked a lot of their own time and money proving that they had a great idea.

The allure of all these Silicon Valley success stories ignores the tragedies of people who mortgaged their homes to raise money for their startup, and whose new company ran out of cash before they made the business profitable.

If someone is going to Las Vegas you may hear them say, "I've budgeted $200 (or whatever number) for gambling. If I lose it all then the gambling part of my trip is over."

That same principle works well for how much of your own money to risk in a Dream Project. As they say in Vegas, "Don't bet more than what you can afford to lose."

Often an entrepreneur turns out to risk far more than they intended to risk. Success seems to be just weeks away, or a pending deal suggests that a short term loan will quickly be repaid. The Founder steps in, writes a check from her savings account, and everyone marches on.

Too often, all that happens is that the deepening financial crater swallows more and more of the entrepreneur's personal and family resources. Don't do this.

So, if I'm warning you about all these perils, how can I be so optimistic about encouraging you to explore and launch your Dream Project?

Because there are many ways to launch a Dream Project without taking these extreme risks.

5.9.8 A Million Ways to Build a Dream

Here are some alternate ways to build your Dream Project that don't require that same (and often ill-advised level) of personal risk.

Some will apply to the kind of work you do, others won't match your personal situation. Use them all, however, as inspiration and idea-starters.

Pitch to Investors and Raise Money to Fund Your Project. If you watch the American TV show "Shark Tank" this may sound like a good place to start. As a frequent judge at pitch competitions in San Francisco and Silicon Valley I've seen that this is the right path for only a small percentage of worthwhile and promising Dream Projects. I'll explain why in a later chapter.

Start with a Paying Client. If your business performs a service, you can reduce risk by not striking out on your own until you have one or more paying clients.

A pair of attorneys, for example, may not start their own new law firm until they have commitments that each of them can bring in two sizable companies as paying clients in the first 30 days.

There are rules in different states about how attorneys and other professionals can and cannot "bring clients with them" when they leave a firm. In many other businesses and industries there are employment agreements that firms require employees to sign on their first day of employment. If you carefully read your employment agreement and there is any question in your mind about what's allowed, you'll want to talk to an attorney.

Start by Doing "Work for Hire." Software developers often have ideas for great new apps, but creating the program and bringing it to market would take too much time and cost too much money.

One way to buy time to complete that great new app is to do other paid projects for clients. Typically the business terms of such deals mean that the client owns the Intellectual Property ("IP") in the app, which means they own the final product.

This is why such projects are called "work for hire," because the team that builds the app does not own it. In some deals the team may receive a royalty or bonus if the app sells well.

The danger of work for hire deals is that a small team may never have time to work on their own app. This can produce a vicious cycle where a group that wants to do a Dream Project is always stuck chasing their next contract and never earning enough to have time to do what they started their company to do.

How do you break that cycle? By learning how to better schedule and bid based on the results of every project. Most top teams also use strong project management processes, whether they be "Agile" or some other system.

Use Your Vacation as a test case. For the first few years after graduating from college I was a teacher and had ten weeks off each summer. Although I got my Master's Degree during that time and then taught at Claremont Graduate University (where I shared a classroom with the legendary author and Professor Dr. Peter Drucker), I used some of those summer breaks to co-author a text-book and write fiction for a major magazine.

If you're a teacher or have a job where there is a longer break each year, you have the perfect opportunity to experiment.

Spend part or all of the time working on your Dream Project. See how you feel and what you're thinking after completing the goals you set for this block of time.

Take a Sabbatical. If you work in education or in some large companies, every few years you qualify to take a sabbatical and be paid during your time off.

Some organizations define what you can and cannot do during the sabbatical, since the idea is that you use the time to learn something that you bring back to share with the team. But you may be able to meet these requirements and make some progress on your Dream Project as well.

Start Out Part-time. As we've covered in depth, this can be an especially effective strategy. By not giving up your primary job you avoid the worst financial risks of a new venture.

The schedule of when you do the work doesn't matter. What does matter is:

- The time you're spending is not adversely impacting your personal relationships and family life in a significant way
- The time is not chain reacting into negative effects on your performance at your primary job if you need that job to pay the bills
- You can make enough progress each week and month that you feel it's realistic that you will complete work that you are proud to have done

Never finishing anything feels awful and makes every day torture. But finishing just a few of the right things part-time, if you're really proud of them, can feel downright wonderful.

Enter a Contest or Competition. If you're writing a book, composing music, creating art or producing a new app or game it can help increase your visibility and grow support.

Many kinds of contests are listed online, and the winners can label their product and the website, "Winner, Spring 2018 Best New Company Award." Winning a number of such contests can support the message that your product has high quality and is unique.

Turn Your Student Project into a Business. Many universities with undergraduate and graduate programs in engineering or media-related fields have students work as teams on major projects. This allows them to work in the same kinds of teams they'll join as they launch their careers.

In general, I think it's best to start our careers by working for great established companies and soaking up all their best practices and intuitive principles of leadership.

When students talk to me about jumping directly from school into starting a Dream Project I share with them how the years I spent working on great (and good-but-not-great) teams prepared me for starting successful companies.

In that context, I have seen a number of successful small companies launched when a student project was so strong that the team turned it into a shipping product and formed a business.

There can be a catch, however. Depending on the university, student projects have different kinds of status:

- The project may belong to the students themselves, and the team is free to do whatever they want.

- The IP (Intellectual Property) rights may be owned by the university, since the project was created under faculty direction using school facilities. The team is free to make it a commercial product, but they may have to pay a royalty to the university based on the income they receive.

- The university may both own and control the project. The students cannot commercialize it without first getting permission to do so and negotiating a royalty agreement with the school.

- In some cases university policies may prohibit the commercialization of student projects. This is done to keep students' focus on the learning, experimentation etc. and avoid the distractions of money.

If you're considering turning a school project into a business, be sure to check with your program's Director to understand what rules apply at your institution.

Do Something Traditional to Earn the Money to Do Something Revolutionary. Your Dream Project is to publish a book of the 50 state flowers, each shown growing in the wild in beautiful landscapes in their home state.

That project will cost a lot of money to do, and you have to do all of the travel and all of the work and spend all the money for cover design, typography and printing before you ever sell your first book. It's a high-risk kind of project, since you only start to make money – and to find out how much you'll make — at the very end of the process.

If you know how to shoot weddings and have done a few events for friends, you might start out building your own business by specializing in wedding photography, which can be very profitable. You could start part-time and then work up to a full time practice.

Is it your Dream Project? No. But the money you earn and the experience you get bring you one step closer to starting your Dream Project.

DISCUSSING QUESTION 5.10

How much cash will you have to start with in order to cover all of your Dream Project's expenses until it starts producing positive cash flow and pays for itself?

This topic is most relevant for: Everyone planning to work full-time on a Dream Project

5.10.1 Your Initial Funding

Most entrepreneurs find that as a company gets up to speed their initial estimate of cash requirements was low. If you have an experienced advisor or friend in the industry, ask them to look through your spreadsheet to catch omissions and overoptimistic budget items.

In the pages that follow we'll discuss how to build a basic Business Plan, which will give you a much better projection than any "guesstimate" spreadsheet.

What's the classic Silicon Valley advice? "Take your first, best guess. Then double it."

5.10.2 Your First Company Budget

Making a projected budget for the first time may seem intimidating, but it's actually a straightforward process.

You can find a variety of samples to work from by doing a Google search for "sample company budget." Be sure to look at several different examples from different websites, because each may have unique categories you want to include in your plan.

If you've done lots of internal budgets at established companies that's a great start. But there are lots of expenses that are buried in the "Overhead" line on those budgets that you'll need to break out for your own business plan.

What is overhead, as defined in business accounting?

- Product development cost is considered to be all the costs that go into creating your game (and operating a live team if necessary), including the salaries of the people on your team
- Everything else is considered to be overhead: rent; equipment; salaries and expenses for marketing, sales, HR, finance etc.

It is critical that as you make your budget you make a column for each month of expenses, because they're not evenly divided throughout the year. There are bulges, often at the end of each quarter, where more money is going out the door. Some annual expenses that cannot be broken down into monthly payments will also produce spikes in spending.Your expenses are not evenly divided month to month. There are bulges, often at the end of each quarter, where more money is going out the door. Some annual expenses that cannot be broken down into monthly payments will also produce spikes in spending.

Since every company has unpredictable expenses, define a reserve or contingency fund amount for each month to cover these unexpected items. Do your best not to spend that reserve, but having it will make it easier to work from a realistic budget.

For your first budget, treat everything as a simple expense, since this works best for managing cash flow. Later you can work with your accountant to "capitalize" large purchases for tax purposes.

Be sure to research all the different kinds of taxes and fees you'll have to pay, and budget them into the months when the money will need to be spent. There may also be multiple certificates, licenses or permits you need to acquire, and these costs should be budgeted as well.

Lay out your projected revenues on the same monthly basis that you used for your expenses. Be very conservative about when money will come in, remembering all the ways we discussed above for payments to be delayed.

You'll then be able to track your "cash flow," which consists of:

Cash at start of month + Cash received this month
– Cash spent this month

This lets you project how much cash you'll have in the bank at the end of each month, quarter and year.

In the first drafts of your budget it will be routine to see that your month-end cash goes down to zero at certain points in the year. You'll need to cut or postpone expenses to get past those choke points, and it's best to do so from the very start of your planning.

As noted above, it's tempting to spend a lot of money up front to get your office, warehouse or storefront set up perfectly. Focus on doing things well, not perfectly, and always preserve as much of your cash as possible.

CHAPTER 40

Looking at Both Sides of the Coins (5.11-5.12)

DISCUSSING QUESTION 5.11

What will you do if you complete your Dream Project, offer your product or service to the world... and it doesn't sell?

This topic is most relevant for: Everyone

5.11.1 Living with the Dark Side

I've said at several points in this book that I'm here to encourage you and share lessons I've learned about building Dream Projects.

The first reason for asking, "What if we fail?" is that you may answer, "That would really suck, but I'm controlling the risks so life would go on and I'd find a way to build a Dream Project again."

You may have a different answer, and we'll discuss a range of these issues below.

Having a project or business fail can be heartbreaking, even if the lessons learned later prove to be valuable. Considering failure and concluding that the downside is an acceptable risk is a step that encourages us to keep trying, to keep moving forward.

Note: In a later chapter we'll discuss "pivoting" when the original plan doesn't work out.

5.11.2 All Sorts of Answers

The second purpose for this question is to consider failure and make sure we're making decisions based on all of the available information.

For example, some reasonable answers would be:

"I'd have to go look for a new job. And I'd have to do it while I had enough savings left to make sure we were covered financially while I looked, since finding a good job takes longer than finding any old job."

"I'd go back to blowing glass as a hobby and keep an eye on what's selling in the stores. If I see a good opening I could always try making it a part-time business again."

"I'd take a long hard look at what I needed to change about the product or how I'm selling it. But it's just part-time and I'm not spending much money on it. I can tolerate the cost for another year, keep experimenting and see what happens."

If it's something you want to do, there will always be another Dream Project you'll want to work on. As the investors of Silicon Valley will tell you, "Failures are where you learn what you needed to know to finally achieve success."

5.11.3 When We Lose Perspective

On the flip side, here are some answers to "What if the idea fails to make money?" that set off fire alarms and sirens in my head:

"I'd borrow $100,000 against my house (or $5,000 against my car, etc.) and use that money to fund the company so we can keep going."

If you didn't know what disease you had and nothing the doctor prescribed was working, would you spend $100,000 to buy more of the same medicine? Please don't do this.

"I'm putting in the last cash I've got so we can keep going, and if we fail I may have to declare personal bankruptcy."

If things are going this badly why would we keep going? In fact, it's clear that we should not keep going, because doing so will only make things worse for you.

"I can't give up. I have to go all in, put up every dollar I can get my hands on. I've come too far and this is my only chance. If I don't bet on myself, how am I ever going to get someone else to bet on me?"

Not all of our ideas are going to work out, and we all get more than one chance. If other people think it's a bad bet for them it may very well be a bad bet for you, too. Instead of going all in, it may be time to take the chips you have left, cash them out and look for a time when you can sit down at a better table where you're likely to win.

You may say, "Who'd mortgage their house (or borrow against their car or sell their late mother's engagement ring) to chase an idea nobody else believes in?"

My answer: Someone who's worked so hard and so long and is so determined that they've lost perspective. They stop thinking and are ruled by passion and commitment.

And it happens to intelligent, thoughtful, experienced people all the time.

That's another reason why I ask this question. Sometimes talking about the consequences of failure opens our eyes and stops us from doing something foolish.

DISCUSSING QUESTION 5.12

What will you do if you sell something to someone or provide them with services, but then they refuse to pay or ignore you?

This topic is most relevant for: Everyone

5.12.1 Forewarned is Forearmed

I told the story above of "The Chess Game," a fictionalized case based on several real-world problems, where a major corporation refused to pay a small company as required by a contract.

How can you avoid the same thing happening to you? You can't avoid all risk, but here are my suggestions for reducing your exposure:

On all but the smallest transactions, take the time to negotiate and sign a written agreement that makes the terms of the deal clear. If most of your deals are similar you can pay an attorney to give you a "boilerplate" contract (one with the most common terms and conditions already spelled out) and then only pay for legal advice in the future if you make changes to its provisions.

Honorable partners almost always accept when you say, "We like getting everything clear in writing so there can't be any mistakes or misunderstandings that will get in our way later."

The other party may ask you to start with their contract draft instead of yours for the negotiation, which is common and reasonable if they're the larger company.

If the deal is of any scope and the other side wants to avoid a written contract, walk away from the deal. As bad as that sounds, what follows when you work without a contract will be much worse.

5.12.2 Letters of Intent

If a contract negotiation looks like it will take a long time you can suggest a Letter of Intent (often called an "LOI"). An LOI states only the major terms of a deal, and says that the parties will negotiate a full contract in good faith later. It can define basic steps for each party to follow, and payments that will be made.

For big, slow-moving companies that are dealing in good faith, this kind of Letter of Intent is done all the time. They'll often help you get one signed quickly to get the deal going and buy time for the contract negotiation.

Although a Letter of Intent may look simple and straightforward, you still want to have it reviewed by your attorney.

Even if it says, "This LOI is not binding upon the parties..." there are exceptions in how that word "binding" is interpreted, so don't let those words stop you from involving your lawyer.

If a company that is moving slowly says, "We don't do Letters of Intent," proceed with caution. They may be playing the stalling game to try to delay the real negotiation until you've depleted your financial reserves.

There are also some cases where an LOI can work against you. An LOI that gives you a little money but prevents you from negotiating with anyone else (a common provision) can put you in a worse position than you'd be in without the LOI. This may be part of a larger strategy, or the other side may be using stalling tactics to gain leverage over you if your cash is being depleted as negotiations go on.

Use your common sense, and in sizable deals do research on the people with whom you're dealing. If someone makes you worry that you'll never get paid, insist on being paid via escrow or via a wire transfer before you give them anything of value, and don't accept a cashier's check or certified check that can be forged. If you're selling a physical item of any kind this is essential – Craigslist sellers all have sad stories of scams that fake buyers used to rip them off.

If your intuition is telling you not to trust someone, it's usually best to follow those instincts and proceed very carefully, or not at all.

Don't automatically trust big, well-known companies. They may, like the "Chess Game" client I described, have a few rotten apples on their well-respected tree.

If you have not been paid for your prior work and the payment is overdue, do not conduct or deliver additional work. In many professions it is standard practice to decline to perform services for clients until they have no outstanding invoices that are more than thirty days (or 60 or 90) past due.

In the software business we often are paid in a series of installments on large projects, so as each major segment of work is completed a payment is made. If payment has not been made for a prior delivery the development company does not give the client any further completed work until the past-due payment is made.

Get paid for direct costs up front. Building contractors normally are paid at the start of the project not just for their first period of work, but for all of the wood, steel and other materials they'll have to buy to begin the project. This same principle should apply to any initial up-front expenditures you'll be required to make.

CHAPTER 41

Businesses, Plans &amp Business Plans (5.13-5.14)

Have you ever written a Business Plan? Do you already have one for this Dream Project?

This topic is most relevant for: Everyone

5.13.1 Writing the Right Plan for the Right Reasons

If I heard someone talking about writing a business plan 30 years ago, I knew they were working on a planning document to make sure their company got off to a good start. In a few cases those plans would also be submitted to Venture Capitalists as part of a funding pitch.

Today when I hear first-time entrepreneurs talk about Business Plans the exercise may be very different. If they're looking to raise money the primary purposes of the plan are to a) generate an estimate for the amount of money they'll need to raise to found their business, and b) produce an amazing set of projected revenue and profit numbers to impress investors.

That pitch deck is a valuable tool if you're raising money, and we'll cover it in a later chapter. But a Business Plan serves you in many other important ways.

5.13.2 Starting Over with the Definition of Business Plan

A Business Plan is a document you write to help plan the founding and the running of your new business. Its most important purpose is to help you budget intelligently, develop an effective strategy, and maximize your chances of success.

There are several good sample outlines available online, including those listed on the Inc. magazine website. (Note: I am a 3-time Inc. 500™ CEO, but I have no business relationship with the company.) A google search for "business plan template" or "sample business plan" will produce a number of choices.

If you're creating a part-time one-person business, the plan won't be long and complex. If you are planning a large-scale startup that you'll pitch to investors, your document will be longer. In particular, it will include far more detailed financial estimates, projections and analysis.

The building blocks of a strong Business Plan are:

Define what kinds of products or services the company will create, the audience to whom it will market its products, and how it will make money from those customers. You've already answered all of these questions as you've worked through the sections of this book.

Describe, step-by-step, each important phase of organizing and funding the company.

Then describe each step of creating your Dream Project, testing and launching it, and acquiring customers and revenue.

Define who will carry out each of the steps you just listed, a summary of how they will do it, a schedule for when they will do it, and what the company will have achieved or acquired after those steps are completed. If this is a small, part-time project this list will serve as your personal action plan.

Estimate the costs involved, and when those expenses will have to be paid.

Estimate projected revenues, and when they are expected to arrive.

Combine those two projections into a single spreadsheet that compares the month-by-month revenue and expenses. This will show if the current plan will produce a profit or a loss, and how much cash you'll need up front to get to profitability.

Early drafts of any plan are very likely to show a loss. You'll also want to examine cash flow, which is usually tracked by looking at how much cash you expect to have in the bank at the end of each month. Many plans that show a company as being profitable after two years will also show the company running out of cash after fifteen months, a fatal problem.

You'll need to revise your plan or increase your funding to ensure that your available cash never runs out, and that you never miss important commitments like paying team members' salaries and benefits, taxes, rent etc.

This may seem like a lot of work, but it will save you even more work later on.

A good Business Plan doesn't have to have a lot of fancy language and long justifications for what you're doing. It only needs to summarize all of the steps listed above and do so concisely. You need only enough detail to confirm that everyone involved agrees on the plan.

The plan should neither be overly aggressive nor artificially pessimistic. It may include alternate financial estimates on the aggressive and on the conservative side.

Finally, you have to sincerely believe that you can do what you write in the Business Plan. It helps no one if you make up a story to impress an investor, and such fantasies will become readily apparent in any pitch.

You don't have to write your Business Plan all at once – it's often better to assemble it piece by piece over time as you experiment and figure things out.

If you look back at your answers to the previous questions in this book, you'll see that some of them can be copied right into your Business Plan, because many of my questions are driven by the need for solid planning.

DISCUSSING QUESTION 5.14

What would the best possible financial result be from your Dream Project?

Is your ideal to sell the company for millions within three years and walk away wealthy?

Or do you picture success as building a company that will pay you the salary you need to live comfortably while doing work you love, so selling the company isn't a big goal?

Is there some other ideal financial goal you're picturing?

This topic is most relevant for: Everyone

5.14.1 Begin with the End in Mind

The heading for this section is a famous quote from Stephen R. Covey in his book, *The Seven Habits of Highly Successful People*.

Not long after I founded my first company I was talking with the commercial real estate agent who was showing us small offices to rent.

I told her about how we wanted to build great products, but that software developers like us who got too large often had financial problems. Looking at that history, I told her, made me want to keep our headcount and company size under control.

"So, is this a lifestyle company?" she asked me.

I was embarrassed. I didn't know what a lifestyle company was. "No better time than now to learn about it," I thought, so I asked her.

The woman grinned. "They're common in the real estate business. A lifestyle company is a firm that somebody founded so they can be in charge and do work that they love to do. They can make a good living, be the boss and do what makes them happy. But they never expand, because they don't want all the headaches of running a big operation."

I was talking about this a few days later with our attorney, who is also a good friend. I told him about what she'd taught me.

"She described it really well," he told me. "That's a lifestyle company, and investors hate them. The founders never want to sell until they're ready to retire. If you invest in startups you're taking a lot of risk. When a company does well investors want the founders to sell so everyone (including the founders) can earn their profits. Investors don't like to leave the money at risk for years."

That's why investors hate lifestyle companies. It's like gambling at a Las Vegas casino where you can never cash out your chips.

Investors don't keep their money invested in the same companies year after year. They're looking for an "exit strategy," a way to make money and then take back those profits to bet again in a new company. So they value CEO's who have an exit strategy of their own.

If your Dream Project involves starting a new company, choosing how big it might get and how much you'd want it to grow is an important decision.

Your choices, whatever they may be, will attract some potential allies and repel others.

PART VI

RISK AND REWARD

CHAPTER 42

Risk and Reward: The Questions

QUESTION 6.1

Do you have a paying job you're giving up, or can you pursue your project in your spare time?

Please take your time, write down your responses, and answer fully from your deepest thoughts. Think only about your own opinions, not about what others may want you to think or do. Do not look ahead to other questions until you have finished this one.

QUESTION 6.2

If you're starting out in your spare time or working part-time, how many hours a week can you devote to your Dream Project now?

How much of your income (if any) will this loss of time impact?

How much will the additional time impact your family and social life?

Please take your time, write down your responses, and answer fully from your deepest thoughts. Think only about your own opinions, not about what others may want you to think or do. Do not look ahead to other questions until you have finished this one.

QUESTION 6.3

If you're starting out in your spare time and plan to go full time on your Dream Project later, what are the criteria for making the jump to full time?

If you feel you're ready to make the jump now, what is it that makes you confident that this will be a good move?

QUESTION 6.4

How much money do you need to bring in FOR SURE each month in order to keep up with your bills (including taxes)?

If you're factoring living off of savings to any degree, how long can you live on this "minimum income" before those savings are exhausted?

Are those savings intended to be used for something else? What is the impact and what are the potential risks of using them on your Dream Project?

If you're not factoring for savings or other sources of money, what is the minimum monthly income you need in order to be OK?

Note: Please do the research, study your bills and take the time to really understand your financial position. It's critical to making good decisions.

Please take your time, write down your responses, and answer fully from your deepest thoughts. Think only about your own opinions, not about what others may want you to think or do. Do not look ahead to other questions until you have finished this one.

QUESTION 6.5

How many people depend on your income?

Did you factor their needs in your total monthly financial obligations?

Please take your time, write down your responses, and answer fully from your deepest thoughts. Think only about your own opinions, not about what others may want you to think or do. Do not look ahead to other questions until you have finished this one.

QUESTION 6.6

How does your partner feel about the financial risk?

How does he or she feel about how this will affect your personal schedules and the free time you may have for social or home activities?

If you don't have a partner right now, how could working on your Dream Project affect your likelihood of finding someone? How do you feel about the issue?

Are there any other risks that are a source of concern?

Please take your time, write down your responses, and answer fully from your deepest thoughts. Think only about your own opinions, not about what others may want you to think or do. Do not look ahead to other questions until you have finished this one.

QUESTION 6.7

Have you ever worked on a team that created a product or service that started out to be one thing and ended up being another?

QUESTION 6.8

Have you ever "pitched" a big project to a client or boss in order to get budget approval and a formal signoff?

If so, how well do you think you did?

Please take your time, write down your responses, and answer fully from your deepest thoughts. Think only about your own opinions, not about what others may want you to think or do. Do not look ahead to other questions until you have finished this one.

QUESTION 6.9:

Have you ever pitched to investors or company management and tried to raise money for a new company or project?

If so, how well do you think you did?

Is raising money part of your plan for your Dream Project?

QUESTION 6.10:

_____

Have you ever tried using Kickstarter, Indiegogo or other crowdsourcing website to raise money for a project?

Is that part of your plan for your Dream Project?

Please take your time, write down your responses, and answer fully from your deepest thoughts. Think only about your own opinions, not about what others may want you to think or do. Do not look ahead to other questions until you have finished this one.

_____

QUESTION 6.11:

_____

What's the biggest risk your team faced on the largest project you've ever worked on?

_____

QUESTION 6.12:

What were the three biggest risks at the start of your most recent project?

What were the three biggest remaining risks when your team was nearing completion on its most recent project?

Please take your time, write down your responses, and answer fully from your deepest thoughts. Think only about your own opinions, not about what others may want you to think or do. Do not look ahead to other questions until you have finished this one.

QUESTION 6.13

Does your product have any elements that require govern-ment approvals, health or safety certificates from industry groups, documentation relevant to import or export controls, etc.?

Please take your time, write down your responses, and answer fully from your deepest thoughts. Think only about your own opinions, not about what others may want you to think or do. Do not look ahead to other questions until you have finished this one.

QUESTION 6.14

How will you handle it if something goes wrong with your product?

CHAPTER 43

My Story: Re-Launching the Sinking Ship

When you go through something traumatic early in your career it sticks with you.

Electronic Arts is now one of the largest game publishers in the world, but when I joined the company in 1983 we were an endangered startup, with our market threatening to disappear beneath us.

EA was founded in 1982 by Trip Hawkins as a game publishing company. While Atari, Mattel and Coleco fought for the multi-billion-dollar console games business, EA set out to establish its beachhead in computer games, a far smaller market with only a few entrenched competitors. If we gained the #1 position there, we reasoned, we could then move on to challenge the bigger players.

But it was the first generation of video games and something went wrong. Sales peaked in late 1982 and started to plateau. The toy store chains concluded that video games were a fad and that they would soon fade away. Retailers started marking down prices and offering game blowout sales on discount tables.

Soon there were newspaper headlines that read, "The Video Game Boom is Over!"

I was Director of Game Development for Mattel's Intellivision console, the #2-ranked video game system in the world. In a period of nine months in late 1982 and early 1983 we went from generating over a billion dollars in annual revenue to being able to sell almost nothing.

Atari and Coleco went bankrupt. Mattel Toys went through a "crunchdown" that gave control of the company to investors in return for the capital infusion needed to save the company. All but five of the 1,200 people in the Mattel Electronics division lost their jobs.

I was very fortunate that Trip Hawkins recruited me into EA. The computer games business, where Electronic Arts was focused, had weathered much of the storm affecting Atari, Mattel and Coleco. EA sold products through computer stores rather than toy stores, but the bad publicity from the toy business wasn't helping.

We had another problem at the young EA. The company had predicted that the Atari 800 home computer would be the best-seller of 1983-84, but the Commodore 64 was the runaway winner on the sales charts. Atari, beset by the toy store disaster, ran far behind.

We did what today in Silicon Valley is called a "pivot" and redirected most of our resources to adding new Commodore 64 games to our lineup.

By early 1984 much of our original investment cash was gone, and we were still operating at a loss. Trip called everyone in the company into a conference room – about 50 people — and announced that we had a hiring freeze, a spending freeze, and any other kind of freeze that would help save those remaining dollars. It was a very tight year.

Fortunately, the pivot worked. More Commodore 64 games came on line and we produced new hits. We started to earn a profit. We all started breathing normally again.

As an advisor to startups today I see many cases where an initial idea doesn't work and the company needs to pivot.

Some CEO's consider moving into completely new business models in different industries, changing every detail about their product.

I always remind teams not to look for a random new idea if their original concept doesn't get traction.

"The category you already know is where you'll have the greatest strengths," I'll tell them. "What would you do if you could start from scratch, take advantage of what you've learned, leverage or re-use existing work, and harness your team's passion?"

That strategy worked for us back then at Electronic Arts, and it can work just as well today.

CHAPTER 44

What to Do with Your Answers (6.1-6.3)

"YOU SHOULD NEVER DOUBT
WHAT NOBODY IS SURE ABOUT!"

— Willy Wonka

If you have not yet written down your answers, please go back and do so. Writing your thoughts down – even when you're the only one who'll ever read them – will produce far more insights than just answering silently to yourself in your head.

DISCUSSING QUESTION 6.1

Do you have a paying job you're giving up, or can you pursue your project in your spare time?

This topic is most relevant for: Everyone considering a full-time Dream Project.

6.1.1 Limiting the Downside

This is a central and critical question, one you've heard me discuss in several different contexts in this book.

If you plan to go full-time on any job where you may not be paid enough to support yourself and your family, the risk to your personal financial health is the biggest risk in pursuing your Dream Project.

Working from a pre-defined budget that you can stick to and be OK is far better than "spending money you can't afford on an initiative that may not earn it back," which I will absolutely, positively warn you not to do!

There's no harm in saving up a war chest of "money you can afford to risk." But before you spend that war chest, I want you to consider every other alternative.

As we've discussed, the simplest and most universal option is to work on your Dream Project part-time so you can keep your existing income.

For many people this is fulfilling and as far as they want to go. Others will be seeking that moment where they can jump to full-time, but in the meantime they can learn a lot about what works and doesn't work by trying out their Dream Project part-time.

Can all Dream Projects be pursued part-time? No. If you're trying to build the next Apple or Google, you'll need to build a team and work full time on the project. But until you've raised enough money to support your team, be sure to explore how far you can get part-time until that moment comes.

DISCUSSING QUESTION 6.2

If you're starting out in your spare time or working part-time, how many hours a week can you devote to your Dream Project now?

How much of your income (if any) will this loss of time impact?

How much will the additional time impact your family and social life?

This topic is most relevant for: Everyone except those with the financial means to self-fund a full-time project without incurring significant financial risk to themselves and their families.

6.2.1 The Different Costs of Time

If part-time work is the path you're considering for advancing your Dream Project, look at the number of hours you think you can spare. Then consider the financial and personal impact of that time.

The money part of the equation can be calculated on a spreadsheet.

The personal costs of working extra-long hours, days and weeks, if that's what you're considering, are more complex and call for a different kind of evaluation:

Family: Will the extra work time invade the parts of each day or week that you most enjoy sharing with each other?

If you have kids is there a way to schedule your work on your Dream Project so it does not impact your time with them unnecessarily?

Social: How much time do you spend with friends and on outside activities, and how important is that time to you? Will your part-time Dream Project inhabit those same time slices each week? If you're used to being social, placing yourself in work-imposed solitary confinement may be a bad way to proceed.

Physical: For some people working on their Dream Project is like having a hobby. It doesn't feel like work, so the time flies by. For others the extra hours, no matter how fulfilling, start to wear them down. Eventually the routine steals all the joy and a Dream Project turns into a nightmare. Could that happen with your Dream Project?

Health: If your Dream Project has you sitting at a desk, is there still time for you to get enough exercise to support your health? Do your moods change when you don't get a chance to engage in physical activity, as happens for many people? Or will the extra work be physical and wear you down over time? Any of these issues can affect your physical health, or the emotional health of your most important relationships.

DISCUSSING QUESTION 6.3

If you're starting out in your spare time and plan to go full time on your Dream Project later, what are the criteria for making the jump to full time?

If you feel you're ready to make the jump now, what is it that makes you confident that this will be a good move?

This topic is most relevant for: Everyone who plans to eventually go full time on their Dream Project.

6.3.1 Decisions Based on Something More than Faith

There are many different ways you might answer this "when will I go full time?" question:

- "I can go full-time right now, because we've been lucky and achieved a level of financial security where I can commit fully to my Dream Project without risking my family's financial future."

- "When I've worked out all the details in the plan for my Dream Project, and I have time to pursue it, and everything is in order on the home front so I can dedicate the time needed to make this a success."

- "When my part-time income from my Dream Project reaches $X, so even if that's all I make I can still pay the mortgage and put food on the table."

- "When the kids have all graduated from college, so we have more financial freedom."

- "When I've saved up enough to fund the initial costs and a few months of runway, so I can give the idea a fair chance to succeed."

- "When I've raised enough money from investors to give us a twelve month runway."

- "When I feel like I'm finally ready to let go of my old job."

- "When my Dad is feeling better and we don't have to spend as much time helping my parents."

- "Never, because I love this project as a part-time activity, but I realize that I'd never want to do it full time."

- "Never, because I realize now that I'm not as committed to the idea as I thought I was."

What matters is that you've considered this question both logically and emotionally. That's how you give your ideas and feelings a chance to gel and become clear.

As with so many questions in this book, the only one who knows the correct answer is you.

6.3.2 My Baseball Friend

Early in my career I wrote computer games as a hobby, before there was a video games industry. When the industry began I became one of the original five game programmers at Mattel Toy Company for their new Intellivision console.

46 years after my first primitive program I'm still designing video games. Sometimes your hobby can turn into a wonderful career.

But that isn't always the case.

When our sons were young we collected baseball cards together. There was a baseball card shop in our area where a really nice older man would treat kids kindly, and the boys and I would stop by once or twice a month to buy some cards.

Over the course of two or three years I noticed that the owner progressively got more and more serious. One day I stopped in by myself and there were no other customers in the shop.

"How are you?" I asked the owner.

He looked up at me from behind the desk where he'd always sit, and he just said, "I'm tired."

"Long day?" I asked.

"Long day. Long week. Long year. Bratty kids who steal stuff. Grown men who argue about how a $50 card is only worth $20, then walk out without buying anything."

"That would drive me crazy," I told him, and it was the truth. I'd be miserable dealing with those issues.

"Baseball cards used to be my hobby," he said. "Every time I looked at them they brought me joy. Three years of doing this as a business... Now all I want to do is go home and watch TV. Right now I think I'd be happy if I never saw another baseball card again."

I've always remembered that conversation. If your Dream Project is turning a hobby into a job, both the upside and downside have to be considered.

My college hobby turned into a wonderful career.

My friend in the baseball card shop had his hobby turn into a nightmare.

CHAPTER 45

The Money Side (6.4-6.6)

DISCUSSING QUESTION 6.4

How much money do you need to bring in FOR SURE each month in order to keep up with your bills (including taxes)?

If you're factoring living off of savings to any degree, how long can you live on this "minimum income" before those savings are exhausted?

Are those savings intended to be used for something else? What is the impact and what are the potential risks of using them on your Dream Project?

If you're not factoring for savings or other sources of money, what is the minimum monthly income you need in order to be OK?

This topic is most relevant for: Everyone

6.4.1 Your Minimum Acceptable Income

This is a key part of the spreadsheet you'll build that shows how much money you need for you and your family to be OK, and how much (if any) you'll spend on your Dream Project.

If you have a partner or initial team members who are joining you on this project they will need to ask themselves this question, too.

This step has no emotional component. It's all about numbers, money, costs and obligations. Please don't manipulate the spreadsheet to make it say something you want to hear if that projection really isn't true.

I hear people say, "Well, my monthly expenses are $3,500, but I can probably get by on $2,500 if I just stall out some payments." After late payment fees and interest charges and lowered credit ratings, they could turn a $3,500 monthly "nut" into $4,000. Instead of getting by on less they could be spending even more.

Avoid self-sabotaging approaches like, "I've got a lot of room on my credit cards. I can run them up and gain a few extra months." There are lots of ways to get work done if you plan in advance, and do so without running up your credit cards until you start drowning in debt.

For every dramatic story I've read about someone launching a company using credit cards, I've heard many, many sad stories of financial disaster and broken families. Using credit cards or retirement savings to "just get past one last hurdle" almost always doesn't work. Please don't do this.

When you're calculating all of these numbers, be sure to research all the taxes you'll have to pay if you found a new business or are working for yourself. In the U.S. this can include self-employment and "minimum required" taxes of different kinds for all levels of government.

6.4.2 The Even Bigger Picture

I cringe when I hear someone say they're borrowing from their retirement account (or their kids' college fund) to fund any kind of project.

401-K's, IRA's and other systems work because putting in comparatively small amounts of tax-free money for *decades* adds up to enough to give you some retirement security in a challenging economic world. The money you put in when you're young has a long time to grow, and even the money you add in middle age adds up to a lot more than it would have in any other way.

College funds work because you may start with a nest egg from family members and then add to it for fifteen years or more. The money has time to multiply and to rise with inflation if necessary.

Any experienced investor will tell you that most new ventures fail to make a profit.

If you take money from your retirement fund to risk on a new venture, you're not just losing money. You're paying extra taxes on what would have been tax-free income.

If you use your kids' college fund, you may be adding risk to their entire working lives, not just their college years. In a society where technical training often has a dramatic impact on personal income the chain reaction can be even worse.

Worst of all, you're making a bet with low odds that doesn't represent "money you can afford to lose." $20,000 in retirement money when you're 38 years old may equate to $200,000 or $300,000 when you really need it.

Would you borrow that much money from your parents' limited savings and then make a low-odds bet with it?

Borrowing that money from your older self or from your kids is just as bad an idea.

Would you borrow that much money *anywhere* for a bet where the house usually wins?

You can create and launch your Dream Project without taking these risks. It will take longer and represent more work, but there are ways to do it and we've discussed many of them.

If you don't fund your Dream Project the wrong way there's another benefit. You won't have to face yourself or your family years from now and regret being careless with money that had a more important mission in your lives and that can never be recovered.

6.4.3 Don't Get Caught Betwixt and Between

If you use savings, raise money from family or friends, or turn to outside investors, three commonly held rules of Silicon Valley (and any other valley!) apply:

1. Don't raise or spend significant amounts of money until you've fully developed your ideas and your plan
2. Don't raise more money than you need
3. Don't raise less than what it will take to get your business to the first stage of "success" (under your personal definition of the word "success")

Let's break down each of these three guidelines and cover what they mean:

Don't raise significant amounts of money until you've fully developed your ideas and your plan. Many people come up with good ideas that could be a successful product or business. They can give you a 30-second summary that sounds great.

But if they haven't gone through the kinds of steps I discuss in this book, they're not ready to start spending significant amounts of money... nor to be borrowing money from others and placing more people at risk.

Research, experiments, planning and all the stages of preparation I discuss here take a lot of time, but for most businesses they don't have to take a lot of cash.

Spending on a business project before it's fully planned is like buying expensive tickets to a Broadway show that hasn't been written yet. Not only do you not know much about the show, you don't even know who the stars will be and whether it's a musical, a comedy or a tragedy where everyone dies in Act Five!

Don't raise more money than you need. Needless to say, most of us won't have this problem. If a company's founders have a great track record and they're entering a hot category, however, VC's may actually offer more than the company needs.

Why not take it? As we'll discuss below, nothing comes for free. Taking more money means you're selling a higher percentage of the company – and giving up more control – without getting a major benefit in return.

Don't raise less than what it will take to get your business to the first stage of "success" (under your personal definition of the word "success"). For startups that plan to grow to be more than a small business, larger amounts of money are required to reach the point where a company is consistently self-sustaining. And note that being *consistently* profitable is a far more difficult objective than *becoming* profitable!

Let's say that you've invented a great new kind of toy robot that will play with your dog and keep it company when you're away at work. It's a simple design, so it will cost "only" $2,000,000 to hire and pay your team, set up a small office, fully design the robot, test prototypes, carry out a marketing plan and manufacture enough units to prove that they will sell and be popular.

You don't raise the money until you have detailed and mature plans. Check!

You don't raise more than you need. Check!

But maybe you're having a hard time raising the money. Or you could want to get the best possible deal from investors, so you're trying to take in as little capital as possible and retain a higher share of ownership in the company.

So you raise $1,000,000, hire a team and start work. Everything is going great, but you know that in a few months you'll have to raise more money or your cute dog robot will never ship.

Raising money for your startup is a very time consuming process, and many entrepreneurs spend long hours on this one task alone, often more than half their time. You can make a lot of pitches (and learn a lot of valuable lessons) before you get your first "yes."

That's time you can't spend interviewing potential hires, leading your team, supervising the robot design, finding the right overseas manufacturer and negotiating the right contract, or any of a hundred other important things. Without you spending time on these key tasks the company may fail even if it raises the money.

But if you get half way through your project and you can't raise that second half of the money, all the money that you and your allies have invested will be lost. You'll have to lay off all your team members. Your company will close, and all of your time will have been wasted, because you raised too little money to have a chance of succeeding.

As I'll discuss below, there are natural stages of investment and companies don't raise all the capital they'll need at once.

But when you raise (or invest) money at any stage of developing a business, it has to be enough to carry you until the next natural window of investment opens.

DISCUSSING QUESTION 6.5

How many people depend on your income?

Did you factor their needs in your total monthly financial obligations?

This topic is most relevant for: Everyone

6.5.1 Timing is Everything

Have you factored into your plans the financial needs of those who are dependent on you, such as kids, older family members, etc.? If not, please go back and adjust your chart or spreadsheet now.

There was a time in my career when my wife and I were both working long hours supporting ourselves and our two kids. Those children were depending on us.

Later in my career our sons were grown and off on their own. The list of people we supported was a lot shorter.

The simple fact is that if other people are dependent on our income, our financial options for pursuing a Dream Project are reduced.

If no one else depends on me and I risk my well-being chasing after a dream, then I'm the only one whom I place at risk. Even if I make foolish choices, I'm the one who'll face the consequences.

In my view, if kids or others depend on me I need to put their well-being first whenever I have the power to do so.

This doesn't mean that Dream Projects have to be abandoned. It does mean that sometimes they have to be pursued more slowly and conservatively, and that some risks will need to be postponed.

DISCUSSING QUESTION 6.6

How does your partner feel about the financial risk?

How does he or she feel about how this will affect your personal schedules and the free time you may have for social or home activities?

If you don't have a partner right now, how could working on your Dream Project affect your likelihood of finding someone? How do you feel about the issue?

Are there any other risks that are a source of concern?

This topic is most relevant for: Everyone.

6.6.1 Talking About the Risks

How you manage your communication with loved ones is solely between you and them. In that context, I'm going to share some personal experiences for you to consider.

There are two stages of thinking about setting out to build Dream Projects, which I like to refer to as the dreamy stage and the serious stage.

The dreamy stage is where we consider something without thinking it through. Every time my wife and I go to Hawaii we think about saving up and buying a condo there. By the time we've been home for a week we remember that not going to Hawaii as often as we'd like makes it more special.

I don't think you need to talk with anyone about dreamy thoughts unless you want to do so. You're just sorting out your feelings.

Once you get to the stage where you're seriously considering any major project, however, my opinion changes. If this could dramatically affect someone who loves you, someone who's dependent on you, then I think you need to talk to them before you put dreams into action.

How you respond to their feedback is up to you.

If no one else depends on you emotionally or financially and no one else is responsible for your debts then the only one who can be hurt is you. In that case I'd still ask a close friend or family member to provide critical feedback on your plans.

If you have not yet discussed your Dream Project with anyone else, I hope you'll do so before you put any of your dreams into action.

CHAPTER 46

Pivots and Pitches (6.7-6.8)

DISCUSSING QUESTION 6.7

Have you ever worked on a team that created a product or service that started out to be one thing and ended up being another?

This topic is most relevant for: Everyone

6.7.1 To Pivot is Human

Silicon Valley has re-invented many of its traditions over the last twenty years, and coined a number of new terms to describe patterns that have emerged for startups.

One of those terms is "to pivot." A startup executes its original idea but has limited success. They have a strong team, no one has panicked, and they still have money in the bank.

Instead of continuing on a suicide mission until they run out of cash, the team uses its remaining resources to create a different product. They leverage the team's passion, expertise and the lessons learned on the first pass. If the new idea works, the company "pivots" to follow its revised strategy.

Some legendary pivots that worked out well include:

- YouTube — Started as a dating site
- Flickr — Began as a role-playing game
- Twitter — A side project for a podcast network

6.7.2 Pivoting in the Right Direction

A team builds a new app that helps truckers efficiently plan their routes. But Waze beats them to market and they can't sign up any customers. All the truckers are very satisfied with Waze and not looking for a new product.

They brainstorm a new plan to which they can pivot. Three engineers adapt the software to help people find the most bike-friendly routes for their commute or for weekend rides. Despite the very different product audience, they are re-using over 75% of the code they've already written and debugged.

The CEO's experience, however, is in "B2B" (Business-to-Business) software. He learns that new shipping containers are being designed for larger cargo vessels, creating a need for software to plan the optimal loading of the mega-ships.

An engineer on the bike routing app tries to demonstrate their progress, but the CEO barely looks at the screen. "I have something else to discuss," he tells her.

She listens respectfully as he describes the cargo ship loading app.

"I'm sorry," she says, "but the engineers you've hired here are specialists in geo-location, path analysis and AI. What you're describing is a packing optimization problem. If I can just show you how the bike..."

"This isn't a B2C (Business-to-Consumer) company," he tells her. "We sell to businesses. We don't know how to sell to bike riders."

The CEO is focused on his specialty, not on the expertise of his team. As I discussed above in *Re-Launching the Sinking Ship*, the best pivots are those that leverage the team's strengths and passions — and the valuable lessons and assets from the original product.

6.7.3 A Near-Perfect Pivot

Pokemon Go is one of the highest grossing mobile games of the last several years. The team started out at Google developing a game called Ingress, which had a big budget and lost a lot of money. They were spun off into a separate company called Niantic, where they needed to create a profitable game or shut down.

Ingress was a science fiction adventure game where you played by going to real places in your home town or current location, where special gameplay sequences would be triggered on your smartphone screen. In addition to being fun to play, it was designed to get you to exercise.

Google has a tradition of putting up a fun or interesting image on its home page every day, with many of them being interactive. One such link was a game where Pokemon were scattered on your Google map and you could go out into the real world to search for and collect them. The game turned out to be one of the most popular mini-projects the company had ever done.

The Niantic team recognized the potential of this idea. They didn't start from scratch on a completely new full-scale version of the Google Maps game. Instead they took all of the real-world geographical locations used in *Ingress* and turned them into *Pokemon Go* related sites, saving months of work and producing a large new game with a relatively small team.

When *Pokemon Go* became a runaway hit they had problems keeping up with the massive player demand, issues they eventually corrected. That part of the story doesn't change the fact that Niantic and Google pulled off a near-perfect example of how to pivot.

DISCUSSING QUESTION 6.8

Have you ever "pitched" a big project to a client or boss in order to get budget approval and a formal signoff?

If so, how well do you think you did?

This topic is most relevant for: Everyone, because the leader of any Dream Project has to make pitches in different settings to different audiences.

6.8.1 Becoming a Star Pitcher

You may be...

• Networking to get colleagues inside your current company excited about your great new idea

• Trying to sell something you've made with your own two hands to a potential customer

• Looking to raise money from investors

• Talking to journalists about your new product or service

These are all very different situations, but the one thing they all have in common is that you'll be making a "pitch" and hoping to get a positive response.

We will deal with pitching to Venture Capitalists and other financial investors in another section below. You'll find that most "pitching" you do is actually for other important purposes, which is why we'll deal with the general topic first.

There are entire books written on how to create and present pitches, especially those to investors. In the pages that follow I'll give you a top level crash-course, but there are many more resources on the Internet and in the library.

In recent years the American television series *Shark Tank* has focused on the pitches that entrepreneurs give to investors. Unfortunately, the judges' celebrity status changes the value of any company in which they get involved. Just getting featured on the show boosts sales, and being partnered with a "Shark" brings massive promotional value that real investors cannot bring

The conversations on that show are very different from those you'd have with potential investors in "real life" situations, because the sharks know that they have extraordinary leverage in every negotiation – their only competition is each other. Apart from the on-screen drama, many of the on-screen deals fall apart when they sit down to negotiate the details.

6.8.2 The Compelling One Sentence Summary

Many websites with advice for startups skip this first step, but in my experience it's vitally important.

You've already created a first draft of this summary, back when you answered the questions in Section 1 of this book!

6.8.3 The 30-Second Summary

In addition to your one-sentence pitch, you need to think about a version that lasts about 30 seconds.

This is sometimes called an "elevator pitch," based on the idea that if you bump into a potential partner in an elevator you can get her or him interested in your project before they reach their floor and get off.

If you were pitching the original Star Wars movie and had just 30 seconds to do so, you could say something like:

> It's a science fiction epic that stars Academy Award winner Sir Alec Guinness and a strong cast of young actors. The Director, George Lucas, has won a Golden Globe.
>
> It has amazing special effects, with wild looking aliens, cute robots and the biggest starship you've ever seen.
>
> The heroes are people you'll want to cheer for, and the villain is imposing, ruthless and frightening.
>
> And it has some of the best music and sound effects you've ever heard.

Compared to a single sentence, this description is richly detailed. Yet once you sit down to write your 30-second summary you'll discover how hard it is to fit within that tiny time limit.

6.8.4 The Two-Minute Summary

The 30-second summary is what you'd say if you met someone in an elevator. But what do you do if they get off the elevator with you and ask you to keep talking?

The two-minute summary is what you'll use when the 30-second pitch gets someone interested.

If you ever compete in pitch competitions with very short time limits – and I've judged many in the one minute to five minute range – the two-minute version will often form the basis of what you do.

It gives you the chance to describe the highlights of your project, and it's good to go back to the basics:

• What problem it solves or what new benefit it brings

• Who will be the customer?

- How big the product's potential market will be

- How well the product or service has been received thus far

- Why your team's experience qualifies you to build this Dream Project

6.8.5 Crafting a Pitch Deck

A pitch deck is a slide show, one that's usually created with Microsoft Office PowerPoint (if you use a PC) or Apple Keynote (if you use a Mac).

There are many different books and articles about these presentations, and you can Google "how to build a pitch deck" to see multiple well-written examples.

Here's a concise summary of key things to remember:

You should have no more than ten to twelve slides in your "initial presentation" deck. The objective is to get someone interested in your Dream Project, not to cover every detail and nuance.

You should be able to present the full pitch deck in as little as five minutes, or as much as 20 or 30 minutes. You'll decide the pacing based upon the audience.

In a one-hour meeting much of that time will be consumed by questions you're asked and by discussions that follow. Allow time to listen to feedback and suggestions. That means planning a presentation that lasts 20 minutes (and can stretch to 30) for a 60-minute slot.

Guy Kawasaki's famous font-size rule is, "Find the oldest person in the room, then divide their age in half. That number is the smallest font you should have in your presentation."

My personal not-so-famous font size rule: "Regardless of the audience, 30 is the smallest acceptable font size, because anything smaller means you have too many words on one screen."

You want the audience to listen to your voice, not read ahead on the slides. Include bold photos. Use headlines and short bullet points, not full sentences. If they want details you can follow up.

You can embed video if it is of high quality. Keep it short — 60 to 90 seconds is good. Just be aware that videos often fail to run when installed on different computers. If you're not using your usual laptop, leave time to test it before the meeting and have a back-up plan if it doesn't play or has no audio.

Apart from your video, don't use music or anything that will compete with the sound of your voice as you deliver your pitch. Don't talk over the video: let it do its job.

Assume that some people will arrive late for your meeting, and don't let it throw you off. The meeting host will tell you when to start and whether you need to cover anything a second time.

Assume that some people will leave before you're done. They may have been bored or they might have had another meeting. Don't beat yourself up about it and just keep going with your confident presentation.

6.8.6 Pitch Decks to Raise Money from Investors

There's a perception that Silicon Valley VC's have started to standardize what they're looking for in a pitch deck. The good news is that this makes it easier to know you're doing it (more or less) right.

The downside is that following the usual sequence can make your pitch predictable, and predictable doesn't command attention.

Since VC's see far more pitches than I do as an advisor and pitch judge, I can only imagine how often they think to themselves, "OK, next will be the 'hockey stick' sales curve slide."

Here's what I recommend, an approach that I learned from several brilliant Silicon Valley leaders:

Stop showing the standard slides in the standard order. Cover the same ground, but tell a fascinating story that happens to be about your company, using your slides to illustrate it. Make the story so interesting that they'll want to get involved in the next chapter.

In that context, here are the most common must-have items to include in your slides. If there's a good reason to do so, move things around in the sample order below.

Title Page. I like to have a striking image on the page, and to make sure that the project or company name is very easy to read.

The Vacuum You're Going to Fill. Most great startups serve a hungry audience that jumps at the chance to use the product or service. It's critical to clearly communicate the nature of that vacuum you've discovered.

The Brilliant Way You'll Fill That Vacuum. You'll just have a few written words in bullet points, so use your voice to paint a clear picture of how your Dream Project will make some part of our lives better. Some people call this "the product vision."

Why You Can Do This When No One Else Has Done It. Maybe you have great new tech. Maybe you've assembled the world's best team. Maybe you've invented a way to be profitable at a price 38% lower than the competition. Convince people that you can actually pull this off.

If you have assembled an all-star team on the project, you might elevate the slide about your team up to the spot prior to this slide.

How You'll Make Money. Share the business model for your Dream Project and describe who will pay you, what they'll get in return, and how you'll receive the money. Tell the story of how you'll execute your Dream Project and meet financial goals as well as serving your audience.

Who's the Competition. Give a concise and balanced summary of the current top competitors. Avoid the mistake of saying, "We're unique and we have no competition!" The first television station in the U.S. had no competitors, but still had to compete for advertising dollars with radio, movies, newspapers, magazines and more.

Leadership Team. Display a head shot and short bullet-point bio for the top people in the company. If a person's background is evidence that you have a special team or they cover a critical function, include her or him. Otherwise, omit them.

Financial Projections and Other Really Impressive Stats. This is often called the "hockey stick slide," since VC's are looking for teams that will return hundreds of dollars in value for every dollar they invest. If you look at a hockey stick, its silhouette looks like a sales chart where revenue starts slowly and then skyrockets.

You'll need to have a budget spreadsheet that matches the chart of your future success, because a potential investor will want to see it. Double check that the assumptions and projections in the spreadsheet feel reasonable and possible, not exaggerated.

Identify Key Performance Indicators (KPI's) for your business segment. For example, for mobile apps and websites the critical KPI's are:

- CPI: Cost per Install — Cost to acquire each new user (all marketing expenses divided by the number of product downloads).

- LTV: LifeTime Value — Average revenue received per user who downloads the app. LTV must exceed Cost per Install to be profitable.

- Conversion Rate: If the app is free, the percentage of people who pay money to upgrade, add extra features, eliminate ads etc.

- D1, D7, D30: Retention Rate — The percentage of users who are still using the app a set number of days after the initial download. D1 is the next day, D7 is after a week, and so on.

If the early usage patterns on your app were encouraging, you might include this data on the Financials slide:

CPI: $4.77   LTV: $27.31

This tells investors that you're operating at a gross profit of $22.54 per user. All your expenses have to get paid out of that number, but it's encouraging.

Wonderful Progress You've Already Made. This is the slide where you share the "traction" you've achieved.

The "Ask" and What You'll Do with the Money. The "Ask" is how much money you want to raise from investors. You may also share the minimum amount that any one investor has to invest in order to buy into the deal, since it's impractical (and in some cases illegal) to accept small investments from inexperienced investors.

You may decide not to place it on the slide, but be prepared to discuss the "pre-money" and "post money" valuation of the company, which determines how many shares the investors will receive if they agree to put up the cash.

If you're raising $100,000 and willing to give up 20% of the company in return for that cash, that means that the pre-money valuation is $500,000 (since $100,000 is 20% of the total). The post-money valuation is $600,000, the sum of a) the $500,000 pre-money valuation, and b) the $100,000 in cash they company received.

See the discussion of Valuation below for more details on this topic.

"Thank You" slide with contact info. If they want to follow up we want them to know where to find you!

Contingency slides. When you end a presentation you'll leave the thank you slide on screen until the meeting wraps up. You can go back to any previous slide that someone might want to see again.

You can also place extra slides at the end of your deck, after your thank you slide. If the right question is asked, you can say, "Yes, we've thought about that. Let me show you a slide that has that chart."

Or, "Yes, we considered the effect of a 2% increase in the Fed rate over the next 18 months. I'll show you a chart of how that affects our numbers."

These contingency slides are a way to support longer discussions with potential allies. They also can impress investors with how well you've studied the market and how thoroughly your plans have been prepared.

6.8.7 Longer Presentations with Your Pitch Deck

We've covered several different kinds of short presentations. Once you're ready to deliver a concise pitch you've done much of the necessary work for longer presentations, prioritizing and polishing your message.

Many pitches that I see fail to describe the company's product or service in a clear and precise way. *Your one-sentence description solves that problem.*

Many pitches go on for several minutes without ever clearly describing why anyone would want to pay money for the product. *Your 30-second pitch will make this clear.*

Many pitches wander through various facts, features and claims, with some that are important and some that are close to irrelevant. *Your two-minute summary will hit just the most important high points and nothing else.*

Once you've been through those key highest-priority two minutes, I like to practice both a 5-minute and the 20-minute "complete pitch deck" version.

Be sure to apply the same discipline to these longer presentations that you used with the shorter formats. Include only the highest priority information and images. Cut ruthlessly any bullet, slide or image that does not directly support a key element of your new product or service.

6.8.8 How to Perfect Your Pitch

You may be pitching to investors or pitching to recruit volunteer coaches for local Little League teams. The key to perfecting any pitch is simple, yet most entrepreneurs at pitch competitions don't follow it.

After you've prepared your short pitches and your pitch deck, here are the steps behind the "secret" of mastering your presentation:

Practice delivering each version of your pitch alone, ideally in front of the mirror. Use note cards or a written outline if you feel you need it. You'll feel self-conscious for a while, but this will pass.

Do this a few times a day, at whatever point you have the time. When you start to get tired, take a break or stop for the rest of the day.

Practice until:

- You don't need the note cards,
- You can talk about your Dream Project at a moment's notice, providing the right level of detail for any situation, and
- You hit all the right high points. You'll miss something small in one talk or another, and that's not a big deal.

Next, practice with a family member or friend who interrupts you periodically with questions. Answer the question, then work the conversation back to the content of your pitch. These interruptions happen all the time in real pitches, and it will keep you from getting flustered when it happens for you.

Stop practicing *before* **you memorize word-for-word each ver-**

sion of the pitch (other than the one-sentence summary). If you find yourself reciting word-for-word from memory, deliberately work to change things up.

Memorized presentations sound canned, rather than sincere and spontaneous. Your audience can feel like they're listening to an actor instead of a passionate presenter.

If your Dream Project is something that can be demonstrated, like hardware, software, clothing items, kitchen tools etc., be sure to include a demo in your full-length pitch deck presentation. If the demo is simple enough, integrate it into your shorter presentations as well.

If your product is a grain harvester, an oversized robot or a self-driving car that's hard to demo, prepare a high quality video. Rehearse how you'll integrate it into your talk and when you'll let the visuals and the music take center stage. Never "compete" with your own video for users' attention.

When you know in advance you'll be giving a pitch, take the time to research the people and company to which you'll be pitching. LinkedIn profiles may identify companies you've both worked for, schools you both attended or shared interests that you can mention in your meeting. Establishing common ground with people you've just met can accelerate the process of building trust.

If there are recent press releases from the company or news items about them, this information will allow you to tie this into your pitch, as in, "I know that you just announced your big initiative to open new markets in South America, and one of our key advisors is based in Argentina."

There's another critical skill we need to practice for these longer meetings. And it's one that many program never teach.

How would you feel if someone came over to your house to visit and then they did nothing but talk about themselves for an hour?

I'd start wondering how long it would be until they left.

Once you're outside the boundaries of "a brief pitch to see if you're interested," we don't just want to be doing a presentation.

We want to be having a conversation. We'll encourage questions and comments. We can ask our own questions of the group.

The objective here is not just being a polite visitor. If there's a good fit between your ideas and the opinions of your audience, an open and dynamic discussion will be the fastest and most compelling way to find it.

Not to mention the fact that it will make your presentation far more interesting to the people you're trying to impress.

6.8.9 Don't Sabotage Your Pitch

After delivering years of pitches and judging many pitch competitions in the United States and Europe, I've developed a list of "things you shouldn't do." Some are gaffes, others are clichés, others are mistakes I've personally made and learned from.

Mistake: Not Arriving Early. Arriving right on time for a pitch meeting means you're late.

If you're showing slides or doing a technical demo, arrive a half hour early. Ask if you can have early access to the meeting room to set up and make sure everything works. Even if you have to wait to set up, it demonstrates that you prepared in advance, and many companies plan for visiting teams to have early access to conference rooms.

If it's been confirmed that this is more of a discussion than a pitch and that no slides will be shown, have your computer ready with your slide deck just in case.

Even with no demos to set up, always arrive fifteen minutes early – add more of a safety margin if there's a long drive and traffic could be bad. It shows that you're prepared and reliable.

If you're flying to another city for a morning meeting, don't take an early flight that morning. If it's delayed or cancelled by weather, you miss your meeting time. Even if the bad weather was all over the news, you still look bad for not anticipating the problem and avoiding it.

In these cases it's better to fly into town the night before and either stay with friends or accept the extra cost of a hotel within a reasonable drive of the meeting site. If that expense is too great, it may mean that the meeting isn't worth scheduling at all.

Mistake: Running Long. There's always a time limit for a discussion, whether it's a spontaneous conversation (you can tell when people get bored or have to leave) or a scheduled meeting. Pace your presentation so you come in under that time limit.

A few years ago I was at a conference where ten of us each gave a three minute "flash presentation" on one idea. A very loud buzzer would sound when time was up. Only two of the ten speakers finished on time, so that the audience didn't have to hear the annoying buzzer. We were the two highest-rated speakers at the session.

I've judged pitch competitions where the time limit was one minute, two minutes or five minutes. Almost every entrepreneur runs long and has to be cut off. Even with these ridiculously short time slots it makes them look unprepared.

In the super-short versions of your pitch you're not trying to tell your whole story. You're just trying to get people hooked so they want to learn more.

Mistake: Apologies, Self-Criticism etc. Modesty is charming, but when you're standing in front of a room and pitching your job is to demonstrate confidence.

"Please excuse me, I'm not very good at this."

"Sorry, I'm really nervous."

"Sorry, I forgot something important."

As natural and honest as it is to say these things, a pitch meeting is not the place to do it.

You'll make mistakes. I do it, everyone does it. But you have to remember what they teach actors in the theatre:

"No matter what happens, pretend it's all in the script and that everything is fine. Stay in character, and improvise until everything is going right again."

Even if you're convinced that people can tell you're nervous, don't apologize or acknowledge it. The longer you practice this, the less nervous you'll become.

If you recover graciously and confidently when people notice that things went wrong, you'll earn bonus points for being able to handle adversity under pressure.

Mistake: Reading Your Slides. As I covered above, your slides should have very few words on them, with just the most important bullet points. If you read your slides aloud it makes you look unprepared and bores the audience, since they can read the words all by themselves without your help.

Mistake: Typos. You want your audience to believe that you are committed to quality. You want to convince them that you'll pay attention to every detail.

If there are misspelled words, grammatical errors or mis-aligned images and text on any of your slides, it undermines those messages about quality.

Mistake: Cliché Phrases. Here are some of the worst:

"Have you ever tried to [do something that's much harder than it ought to be]? Wasn't it frustrating? Well, we got tired of pulling our hair out and decided to fix the problem!"

This "identify with the audience through a shared feeling" approach is excellent. The trouble is that it's been taught this way for years, so I hear this gambit at least twice at any pitch event.

"As you can see, this is a $12 billion market! With just 1% market share in three years, we'll have sales of $120 million!"

This cliché is a running joke in Silicon Valley. As she listens to this the VC thinks, "If it's that easy, why didn't you pick a $50 billion market so you'd have sales of $500 million? Or a $100 billion market so you'd sell $1 billion?!"

This argument only makes sense if you're an insider who has done it before:

"Video production for retail point-of-sale is a $1 billion business. Our team has worked in the space for over 10 years, and in our last full year in-house we accounted for $26 million in sales. That's a 2.6% market share in our segment just for our three co-founders."

"How many of you learned to bake with your Mom back when you were a kid?"

The presenter waits, sees fewer hands than he expected. He looks frightened but carries on.

This "raise your hand if..." approach creates more cringes than any other pitch cliché. If I attend a competition I'll usually see it done more than once, usually with a poor response.

To avoid the cliché he might have said, "Last year I visited an old friend. When I arrived, he and his wife were having a great time baking with their kids. I remembered how much fun I had learning to bake with my Mom, so I created these kits called, "Come Bake with Me, Mommy!"

Mistake: The Infomercial Pitch. "Ladies and gentlemen, I am going to present to you an idea that has such great business potential that it won't just interest you, it will excite you! What would you say if I told you that there was an industry where they're still using the same kinds of web technology that they were using twenty years ago?"

My heart sinks. I am listening to an Infomercial Pitch, and I can't wait for it to be over. The speaker has energy and enthusiasm, but soon you realize that what you're seeing isn't passion for his product. It's showmanship.

At one pitch competition one of my fellow judges interrupted to say, "But wait., there's more! Now what would you pay?" It was an embarrassing moment.

Mistake: "We Can Be Anything You Want Us to Be!" I went to college with a guy who would walk into the dining hall in the morning and ask us, "Do you like my shirt? Yes? No? I can go back upstairs and change it if you want!" It was annoying.

Here's what this mistake usually sounds like in a pitch meeting:

CEO: We're planning to do major updates to the website on a quarterly basis.

Investor: Wouldn't it be almost as easy to do them monthly and have all the content be more current?

CEO: I... Well... We studied the patterns of the price changes, but... Yes, we could do them monthly. If you think that's a good idea we could do them monthly.

Here's a better answer:

CEO: We studied the patterns of the manufacturers' price changes over the last two years. All but a couple of the smaller suppliers were doing their updates on a quarterly basis, so we synchronized to their schedule.

Investor: What if a major new product line is introduced?

CEO: If it's big I think we'd do a manual update the same day we had the pricing data. If it's something small, we'd just wait for the quarterly cycle.

Investor: I think that's fine for functionality, but for user retention I think you need more frequent cosmetic updates to your website.

CEO: (Pausing to write this down as a note.) Thanks, that's worth thinking about.

In this latter example the CEO listened to the suggestion and considered it, but didn't automatically agree with the investor. He did not act defensive, and professionally explained the rationale behind their thinking.

Mistake: Arguing and Defending. You wouldn't imagine that entrepreneurs would go into meetings, investor events or pitch competitions and argue with the people they're trying to impress, but it happens all the time.

Usually – though not always — it's a mistake. The CEO feels like she's expressing confidence, but what she's really doing is sounding defensive.

The VC's in the room are thinking, "If the CEO is this argumentative now, what will she be like when they're facing a problem and we're trying to help fix it?"

Instead of arguing or defending your position, listen carefully, write down the comments and say something like, "Let me think about that," or "I'll do some research on that," or "That's not what we were thinking, but we should discuss it with the team."

A pitch meeting is not just where you present your product or service. You're also presenting yourself as a prospective partner, and everyone you pitch to will be evaluating you in this way.

Mistake: Contradicting or Interrupting Team Members. It's routine at pitches, especially those made to potential investors, to have co-founders or key team members in the room with the CEO. These team members may take the lead in discussing topics like technology, sales or pricing.

Potential partners value this approach because it gives them the chance to evaluate not just one person, but the leadership team as a whole. They can also get a feel for how well you work together.

Inevitably someone on your team will say something that's not quite right, or not as eloquent as the way you express it. As the leader of the team your natural instinct is to cut in and explain the point more clearly.

Don't do it. The people to whom you're presenting may start to wonder why you publicly disrespected your team member, or why you didn't prepare the team well for the meeting.

Whatever problem the misstatement created, you'll have a chance to fix it somewhere down the line. Interrupting on the spot will almost always make things worse.

Mistake: Not Taking Notes. We get so caught up in rehearsing and setting up that it's easy to forget something as important as having a way to take notes. Yet there is no easier way to communicate to people that you're there to listen and learn, not just to talk.

CHAPTER 47

Pitching to Investors (6.9-6.10)

DISCUSSING QUESTION 6.9:

Have you ever pitched to investors or company management and tried to raise money for a new company or project?

If so, how well do you think you did?

Is raising money part of your plan for your Dream Project?

This topic is most relevant for: Everyone planning to raise money from investors (or from internal management) for their Dream Project.

6.9.1 What You Must Know about Pitching to Venture Capitalists

The world is full of hype about Silicon Valley, assumptions that people who work in the Valley recognize as BS.

There is one key fact that you need to understand before you ever try to pitch to VC's or any other sophisticated investor who is not a member of your family:

To do these pitches you need to have:

- A product that you are already selling for real money to real customers
- A complete core team that is already working together
- Experience in leading teams or (ideally) successful startups

If your startup has not met these three key milestones it will be very hard for you to get meetings with high-end investors.

If you do get the meeting (often through an introduction by a friend or mentor) you are gaining valuable experience but it's very unlikely that you'll earn an investment. The meeting was probably done as a favor for someone else rather than because they were interested in investing in you.

If you're pitching to VC's, the problem you're trying to solve must be a big one.

If you're not looking to raise several million dollars, you're wasting your time talking to most VC's.

VC's usually don't consider any startup that can't grow to be worth hundreds of millions of dollars at a minimum, and they don't consider investing less than a few million in those top-flight early stage companies.

The one exception: Some VC's have started "Seed Funds," from which they make smaller investments in very early stage companies. But their long-term expectations are still that any portfolio company will grow to be very large.

The VC firms' results – like those of many other businesses — are calculated on a formula called "Return on Investment" (ROI). If you take $100 and put it in the bank for a year and earn 1% interest, your ROI is 1% per year. If you buy a stock for $100 and two years later sell it (after commissions) for $110, your ROI is 5% per year, your 10% profit divided by two years.

Venture capitalists are spending very little of their own money when they make investments. They raise cash from investors who want a higher ROI than they could get from bank deposits, bonds, real estate etc. These banks, insurance companies, pension funds and wealthy individuals back VC teams who convince them that the VC's partners can spot great young companies that can grow and generate that ROI.

Venture Capital firms may have multiple "funds" operating at one time, and the results of the investments in each fund are pooled together for the benefit of the investors in that fund. Each fund invests in many companies, most of which fail.

To succeed they have to try to earn back $30 to $100 or more for every dollar invested in that rare successful company, so it can pay for all the failures and the fund can still generate a combined ROI high enough to make the investors want to come back and invest with the VC team again.

This explains why high-end investors only invest in top teams whose products are already being sold to real customers for real money.

6.9.2 The Risk Reward Ratio

There is one master issue that drives how you, your supporters, potential investors and even your competitors make business decisions: the balance between risk and reward. This is called the "Risk-Reward Ratio."

Formally, the Risk Reward Ratio is a mathematical formula used by financial traders to evaluate the downside and upside of buying something at a given price with the idea of later selling it for a profit.

The term has entered broader use in business, however, and can be applied to any deal or investment. If you consider flying to New York from Los Angeles for a pitch meeting, you're risking the cost of the trip and at least two days of lost time you could have spent building your project. Against that risk you evaluate the potential reward if you secure the deal and it benefits your team.

There is no precise way to turn these disparate factors of cost, time and probability into a precise formula, but you'll hear people say, "I'm trying to weigh the risk-reward ratio of making the trip."

If you look at a lottery ticket in a mini-mart you know that it risks $1 of your money, but it could reward you with millions if the right numbers come up.

If we spent money based solely on logic we would never buy a lottery ticket, because the odds are so overwhelming that we're going to lose the dollar we're risking. But the reward, however unlikely, is so compelling that we risk the money anyway.

This illogical behavior highlights the fact that our analysis of risk and reward is often driven by emotion rather than logic. This issue is discussed in Nir Eyal's book, *Hooked: How to Build Habit-Forming Products*, which I recommended in a prior chapter.

When we ask people for a sale, an investment or even their time we don't want to present a spreadsheet to convince them logically. We want to tell a story that engages their emotions and spurs them to action by inspiring them to support our team.

6.9.3 The Stages of Investment

Standard terms describe each stage at which a startup might seek a round of investment. The descriptions below are general and there are always exceptions, but here are the basics.

The "Friends and Family Round" often represents money raised before there is any product or service to evaluate. Former associates, friends and family are investing in the people who make up the company and betting on their ability to produce a successful product or service.

They should only risk money that they can afford to lose if things don't work out. Many states have minimum net worth requirements for "qualified investors" to prevent people without the necessary resources from overcommitting.

The Friends and Family Round could be as small as $2,500 from Mom, Dad or a retired family member. CEO's who have been part of highly successful startups may have multiple associates who are now wealthy, and their Friends and Family Round could be much larger.

Once you have started working with your initial customers and can demonstrate traction you are now ready for the "Seed Round," where you pitch to people outside your circle of friends and family.

The Seed Round is critical because (barring unusual special cases like Google and Twitter) you have to raise enough money at this phase to be able to run the company until it becomes profitable. If the money you raise in your Seed Round does not get you to profitability it will make it very hard to raise additional funds, and the terms for what you can raise may be highly unfavorable.

Your Seed Round is likely to include some **Angel Investors**, people who have built up enough savings that they can invest $50,000-$250,000 in high risk ventures. "Super Angels" may invest even more. They also are likely to want to invest via "Convertible Notes," which are loans that can be converted into equity on pre-established terms if the company does well. To learn more about Convertible Notes see the link I discuss under "Valuation" below.

There are also organized groups of Angel Investors who collaborate to evaluate, recommend and research companies for potential investments.

If your company has rapid growth and has reached scale and profitability, the door opens to raise a "Series A" round of financing. At this point you are at a size where the amount of money you're raising is probably in the millions, and you're far more likely to be dealing with Venture Capital firms than with Angel Investors.

The Series A investors are also likely to require that they receive a "preferred" class of stock that gives them extra priorities and privileges in the event that the company's fortunes rise or fall dramatically.

Of the companies that successfully raise a Seed Round of investment, only a small percentage ever raise a Series A. Some fail, some plateau at a smaller size, others try for the A Round but don't represent a compelling opportunity. Some especially strong startups are acquired before ever reaching an A Round. This is why making your Seed Round money last is so critical, because it can take time to rack up the strong performance needed to earn a Series A.

Companies that are having continuing success may have a B Round, a C Round and so on. If the money is being raised to position the company for a high-margin buyout or IPO, this is a good thing.

But each time that a company marches down the alphabet in a C or D Round, the odds that the news is bad go up. Why is the company still having to raise money? Why can't they survive on their own cash flow? What are they doing that scares away potential acquirers?

The higher the letter attached to a round of investment for a company, the more likely it is that this is a "down round," which means that the later investors pay less per share than the earlier investors. This makes those early investors very unhappy, since it sends them the message, "You paid too much! The value of the company is going down, not up!"

If a company needs money badly the later investors may require that the firm creates another new class of preferred stock that effectively lowers the value of all the other stock. This "dilutes" the earlier investors, employees and founders, even those with other classes of preferred shares.

**If the value per share of the old stock is diluted and pushed
sharply lower, the round is called a "crunchdown,"** because the
earlier investors see their ownership percentage lowered dramatically in order to give a higher percentage to new investors.

6.9.4 Accelerators and Incubators

These two terms, once clearly different, are now often treated as
synonyms in Silicon Valley.

In traditional use, an "accelerator" is a program where promising
early stage startups trade an equity stake in their company (I've
heard of everything from 1% to 7%) for:

- A small infusion of cash (usually less than US $50,000)

- A training program with established industry mentors and advisors

- Office space where companies in each "cohort" go through the
  process together

- Introductions to investors interested in their segment

- A formal pitch day with a wider group of investors

Business "incubators" were originally founded by governments to
foster new business growth and the jobs and tax revenue it could
create. Corporations also created incubators to find, nurture and
acquire innovative new products. Incubators were unlikely to give
cash or take equity, though they might provide contract work to a
team.

The differences between these two kinds of organizations have
now blurred, so I often hear, "If you're looking at accelerators and
incubators, you should remember that..."

So, should you seek out a slot at an accelerator or incubator? Only
you believe it will benefit your company more than it distracts or
dilutes it. Here are some questions to ask:

- What successful companies in your category were nurtured at this accelerator?

- What do alumni companies say about this accelerator?

- How much equity will they take? How much working cash do companies receive for that equity?

- How long do companies remain in house? What is the script for what they do while they're there?

- How many of their alumni companies are operating successfully? How many have been acquired, and in which categories?

- Who are the most active mentors and advisors? Are they people whom you'd love to work with?

- What investors and funds have historically invested in their companies? In what segments?

- Finally, considering all of the above, how do you picture your future being different if you go through this program?

6.9.5 Negotiating Valuation

Note: If you reach the point where you're negotiating valuation with investors, it's time to involve an experienced corporate attorney.

I'm raising this topic because to many first-time CEO's the process feels more like mind-reading than metrics. Here are key things you need to know if you're a CEO who's raising money:

Founders will try to set the company's valuation as high as possible, while still closing an investment. That's because the higher the total valuation, the fewer shares of the company they have to give up (the less "dilution" the founders experience when more shares are issued in the company) for the same amount of cash they receive.

Good founders will negotiate hard but not be self-destructive in the deal they try to strike.

Investors will always try to set the company's valuation as low as possible when they make an investment. That's because the lower the total valuation, the more shares of the company they receive for the same amount of cash.

Good investors will negotiate hard but not be materially unfair, because they know that this could damage the company's likelihood of success.

There's an old Silicon Valley saying, "Pigs get fat, hogs get slaughtered." Trying to make as much money as you can in a deal is fine, but being greedy and not sharing the rewards with partners and team members can lead to the loss of key allies.

A "term sheet" is a short document where a company or individual summarizes a deal they would be willing to make with you. The valuation of the company will be a critical component of any investment term sheet.

There are lots of term sheet templates on the net, but I think that by far the best resource is the "WSGR Term Sheet Generator" from Silicon Valley law firm Wilson Sonsini Goodrich and Rosati.

A Google search will give you a link to the program, which allows you to play around with different values and see how investment deals can work. They have two variants of the program on their website, one for equity investments (where the investor purchases stock in your company) and another for convertible notes (where the investor gives your company a loan that can later be converted to stock.)

The moment when any prospective investment truly becomes serious is when the investor gives you a term sheet. Investors and VC's like to encourage entrepreneurs, but they only invest in a tiny percentage of those whom they encourage.

Until you see a term sheet, assume that the deal remains a long shot, and don't allow your team to become too optimistic.

The first investor or firm to commit to investing in your firm

is called the "Lead Investor," and they will usually negotiate the initial valuation with you. If the Lead Investor is respected the investors who follow will often accept the valuation you set with the Lead Investor without putting you through another negotiation.

The Lead Investor will also do the bulk of the "due diligence" on the deal (a thorough review of financials, products and the team) before they invest. It's critical that everything you present in your pitches to investors and other potential partners is accurate, and that your projections are defensible as being reasonable, since it will all be carefully reviewed as part of due diligence.

Make sure to raise any significant potential problems early in your discussions. The famous recent example is Yahoo's failure to disclose major data breaches to Verizon during negotiations for the sale of the company, which ultimately lowered the valuation they had negotiated and almost scuttled the deal.

If you receive a term sheet, pick your corporate attorney wisely. You'll normally use a law firm that's in your area, but there are exceptions. If you were doing a deal with a film or television company in Southern California you could hire a respected law firm that specializes in entertainment and whose offices are in that region. The same is true for many tech firms in Silicon Valley.

These deals close much more easily if you use "one of the usual firms" in your business segment. Such attorneys can predict how the negotiation will unfold and close because they deal with each other regularly.

Look for similar companies to yours that are well-established but not direct competitors. Call them up to ask who their law firm is. Many companies will answer this question readily.

Look at the websites of conferences in your business segment, ideally events that are taking place or took place in your area. Look for law firms in the list of event sponsors. This suggests that they do a lot of work in your field.

Never just hire a famous firm. Meet with the specific attorney who would be your key advisor, and interview him or her the way you'd interview someone working at your company. If you think the firm is great but don't hit it off with that person, ask them respectfully if you can speak to someone else and describe the qualities you're looking for (e.g. "Irving was great to talk to, but I'm looking to work with someone who has closed deals with companies headquartered in Japan.")

Do not hire that guy who went to school with your dad. If you take him to lunch, however, it will placate your dad and you'll probably get some smart business advice!

6.9.6 Dilution

A company's shares are not issued all at once when you organize and launch the company. Good attorneys or advisors will walk you through how many shares to give yourself as founders stock, how many to reserve for investors, how many to reserve for stock option pools for co-founders and for other employees (which they earn gradually over a period of years if they stay with the company and/or they meet key goals) etc.

This plan will produce a spreadsheet where the original founders will see their percentage of ownership gradually drop as investors and key employees are brought in. If things go well, that dilution will be more than offset by the increase in the value of each share in the company.

If the founders have a total of 2,000,000 shares between them and you then sell 200,000 shares to an investor, the founders are "diluted" by 10% in that deal.

This kind of dilution is normal, and getting that first investment means you accomplished something most startups never do. Many first time CEO's are horrified by dilution from investment because they are preoccupied with the percentage of the pie they own. The winners of the game focus on the size of the pie, and evaluate their share in that context,

As your lawyers will doubtless tell you, it's far better to own 10% of a billion dollar company than 100% of a million dollar company. Experienced lawyers will have wise counsel on these issues.

6.9.7 Stock Options and Vesting

Note that I'm not an attorney and I'm omitting many details in what I describe below. There are variations in laws and rules in some states, and in many of these cases there are tax considerations for both the company and for the stock option recipient, which is why you'll want to be guided by a good lawyer.

Stock options give someone the right to buy a predetermined number of shares in a company at a predetermined price, usually a price that will be very favorable in a few years if the company does well. They are given to key team members, who often work for below-market salaries in the early days of a company.

Owning shares in a company means you're part owner of the company, the same way that you would be if you bought shares in Apple or Google. Shares are often referred to as "equity," another term for stock. "Having an equity stake" means the same thing as "owning stock."

Co-founders may have a stock pool with special terms for those who joined the company at the start, when the venture is most risky. They may work for dramatically low salaries in order to earn more stock.

If the firm is a big success the option holders will have the chance to earn much more money by selling their vested stock than they could ever have received in salary and bonuses elsewhere. Higher risks yield a higher potential reward.

Stock options do not give all the stock to the person at once. Instead they have:

A Term: How long the person has to stay with the company in order to earn the right to buy all the shares awarded in the option. In my experience the most common term has been four years.

A Strike Price: The price at which the person has the option to buy each share. They are not obligated to do so. Options do not give team members shares for free. They only give the right to buy a set number of shares for the Strike Price.

A Blackout Period: A period at the start of the option where the option is completely cancelled if the person leaves the company, in which case they have the opportunity to buy no shares. In the four year options I normally see, the most common blackout period was six months, though in recent years I've seen a lot more 12-month blackouts. If a new hire does not stay with the company until the end of the blackout period they do not earn any shares.

An Execution Date: The date when the Term of the stock option begins. This can be a team member's first day of work, can begin after they have worked with the company for three months or a year, or any other date that the company chooses. The team member also has to sign a document accepting the stock option, since there can be tax hassles (along with great joy) if the company is successful.

A Vesting Formula: This determines how many shares the team member earns the right to buy based on how long they stay with the company, or upon hitting clearly defined goals. Each time a team member hits one of the milestones, they "vest" a certain number of shares, which means they earn the right to buy them at the Strike Price.

My favorite vesting system is a "trickle formula." Let's say that Susan is a key early team member at Acme Inc. and is awarded a 48,000 share four-year option, and that for Acme this represents almost half of 1% of the company.

The trickle formula I prefer is that the team member vests 1/48 (just over 2%) of the assigned shares each month for four years. In Susan's case that is an easy to calculate 1,000 shares per month.

If the blackout period is twelve months, Susan vests no shares for the first year after she receives the stock option. On the first day of the thirteenth month, she vests thirteen months of shares: the twelve months of vesting that were during the blackout period, plus the shares she vests in the thirteenth month. After that she vests 1/48th each month for the rest of the four years.

If Susan leaves after four months (voluntarily, laid off or fired), she'll have vested no shares and will not have the right to buy any shares.

If she leaves after 26 months she'll have vested 26,000 shares, and has the right to buy them at the Strike Price if she wishes to do so. The rest of the shares in her option are cancelled.

An Expiration Date: The date when the option expires if the team member does not exercise it and buy the shares. After this date the option to buy the shares at the Strike Price is lost. I've seen different periods, but the most common is ten years.

6.9.8 Cliff Vesting, and Why to Avoid It

There's another vesting system, called "cliff vesting."

Sometimes when people use the term "cliff vesting" they're really just talking about the Blackout Period described above, especially if it's a full twelve months. As part of the system described above I believe it's a viable format for companies.

But there's another kind of cliff vesting, and it can be manipulative and insidious. Under this system there are no small monthly sets of shares that Susan would vest. Instead she might vest 5,000 of her 48,000 shares all at once after one year, 10,000 more shares all at once after two years and the last 33,000 shares all at once after four years.

Some companies that practice this system have regular layoffs. People who are close to vesting a major block of shares are more likely to be cut from the payroll in these layoffs. If they miss the vesting date by even a day, they lose the right to buy what could be very valuable stock, and Silicon Valley is full of bitter stories that are rooted in this system.

I would never work for a company that offered me this kind of back-loaded cliff vesting, and I would never impose it on the people working with me to build a company.

6.9.9 The Catch 22 of Compensation

Cash compensation is an issue that drives strong emotions, because it has such a big impact on our lives and on our pride and confidence levels. My opinions are below for you to consider, but every experienced manager ends up working out their own pre-ferred set of practices. Your personal values and experience should drive your decisions on these issues.

Researchers have proven over and over again that a big majority of people feel they're underpaid at work. In some cases this is because, well, because they're underpaid at work.

But there's a psychological element to compensation, too. As humans we are driven by deep instincts to always try to do better tomorrow than we did today.

- We want our kids to have a better life than we did when we were young
- We want more reserves in case there are layoffs
- We want to make family arguments about money go away
- We want to finally be able to afford that vacation (or that new car, or that bigger apartment) we've always wanted
- We want to feel proud of ourselves, not just for the money but for the validation that we do important work

I have thought all these thoughts and felt these drives to earn more money throughout my career.

Once you have the final call on what people get paid in a company, this normal psychology becomes a Catch 22. Even when you're working your heart out to be fair, a majority of people are likely to be dissatisfied with their compensation.

And you have to learn to live with it, even as you work to make your system even more fair next month and next year.

Salaries and Raises. Once your company is well established, you'll want to have access to industry salary data from The Croner Co. or another data provider. You can use public surveys like those done by websites like Indeed.com, but the respondents reflect a random cross-section that may not account for geographical deltas. As a result, numbers may be significantly higher or lower than real averages. (Note: I do not have a current business relationship with The Croner Co., but have previously been a client of theirs for many years.)

Team members generally receive a written evaluation and a salary adjustment once each year. It's best to stagger these around the year based on start dates – the companies that evaluate everyone at the same time face big all-at-once increases in costs rather than a gradual increase.

Bonuses. The great things about giving someone a bonus are:

- You can tell the person exactly what they did that was great to earn the bonus (which will make them want to keep doing that same thing)
- You can provide fast positive reinforcement for doing something outstanding, rather than having to wait seven months till their review
- A bonus can be used instead of a stock option to reward someone for their key role in building a super-successful product – and you can wait to determine that bonus until it's clear who made those critical contributions

- If the great performance doesn't continue no one should be surprised that you don't pay another bonus
- You can pay bonuses when the company is making money, and scale them back when things are tight
- It's a one time expense, not one that recurs and builds from year to year
- If it feels right you can give an impact player a bonus several years in a row, so long as they understand that it's never a guarantee and is performance based
- Having more small "spot bonuses" for more people can work better to motivate teams than fewer, larger bonuses

Different states, countries and different cities have different laws about salaries, taxes, bonus etc. Once your company has more than a few team members it's wise to review your practices with an attorney.

DISCUSSING QUESTION 6.10:

Have you ever tried using Kickstarter, Indiegogo or other crowdsourcing website to raise money for a project?

Is that part of your plan for your Dream Project?

This topic is most relevant for: Those considering crowdfunding for their Dream Project.

6.10.1 Crowdfunding Basics

Kickstarter, Indiegogo and similar websites offer creative people with great ideas the chance to earn pre-orders that will fund the creation of their Dream Project. Some groups have raised millions of dollars with promises of exciting new products.

Some of those products ultimately shipped and found success. Other teams, however, never delivered a finished product, and under the original (now modified) rules of Kickstarter they were not required to refund any money to their backers.

The cold shower of skepticism brought on by these failures has made it harder — but not impossible — to use crowdsourcing to fund at least part of your Dream Project.

The two biggest services in the space are Kickstarter and Indiegogo. Both are websites where users sign up for the option to review and support projects.

Kickstarter is significantly larger and has more traffic than Indiegogo. Indiegogo is a worldwide service that covers any kind of fundraising. Kickstarter specializes in creative projects of all kinds and is focused primarily on North America and the U.K.

In practice, most successful Kickstarter campaigns allow buyers to pre-order special editions of a new product in return for pledging their payments for those items several months (or even years) in advance.

Kickstarter screens the people who try to raise money on the platform. This is not a priority at Indiegogo.

If a campaign fails to reach its funding goal on Kickstarter, the effort is canceled and no money is collected from the people who pledged funds.

If an Indiegogo campaign fails to reach its goal it offers organizers the option to keep the partial funds, but charges a significantly higher commission.

As of this writing, Kickstarter charges a 5% commission plus a small funds processing fee. Indiegogo charges 5% to successful projects (and a credit card takes another 3% or so for processing), and 10% to those who keep a partial funding total.

Indiegogo uses credit cards, and has dropped the option to use PayPal. Kickstarter uses your Amazon account to accept the payment.

6.10.2 How Crowdfunding Campaigns Work

Let's say that you're shooting a documentary about the lives of the descendants of the people who built the Golden Gate Bridge, featuring oral history that they were told by their families as they were growing up.

To create your film you'll interview people on camera, collect and digitize historical photos and drawings, and shoot different angles of the bridge as it looks today in different lighting and weather conditions. Finally, you'll edit it all together, add a narrator's voice-over, and layer in original music, old photographs and graphics. The total budget for your film might be $25,000.

But first you need to prepare for your Kickstarter campaign. Your page will be up for 30 days, and if you meet your goal the project will be funded. If not, you'll get nothing, even though you may have spent many hours and thousands of dollars creating your Kickstarter page.

You'll write ad copy describing the wonderful documentary you're about to shoot. You'll hire a graphic designer to create illustrations. You'll shoot two interviews and vistas of the bridge and create a video trailer.

You'll need to set up tiers of attractive rewards for people who pledge money to support your project.

Actual campaigns may have ten to fifteen tiers of "rewards," but for our sample project you might say:

$10: Your name will appear under the heading "Special Thanks" in the final credits of the film.

$25: All rewards above, plus a DVD of the completed film.

$50: All rewards above, plus a unique Golden Gate Bridge T-Shirt.

$500: All rewards above, plus a ticket to the premiere showing of the film in a local theatre and a collectible statue of the Golden Gate Bridge bearing an engraved brass plate with your name and the word "Sponsor."

$2,500: All rewards above, plus you get to spend one day on the Golden Gate Bridge with the camera crew and receive an "Executive Producer" credit.

These categories seem simple, but a lot of work is required to follow through with your backers if you meet your goals:

- Collecting hundreds of names and making sure they're spelled correctly for the credits
- Sending out 122 DVD's to 122 different addresses after you stuff them in padded envelopes that cost $1.16 each. Plus $1.75

postage. You earned about $2,850 from those donors, but you'll spend $500 on the rewards.

- Designing, printing and sending out 62 T-Shirts after you find out what size each person needs.

- Buying twelve Golden Gate Bridge sculptures, mounting brass plates engraved with the exact spelling of each name, then shipping them to the right addresses.

- Ironically, the big gift is the easiest: you work with four untrained crew members for a day on your shoot.

The sad truth is that you'd probably have to raise $30,000 this way in order to have $25,000 left to create your film. It's been common for creators to misjudge costs and spend too much of the money they raised on rewards instead of on the product.

6.10.3 The Missing Link: Marketing

Thousands of crowdfunding projects are launched each year. The majority never are backed by passionate fans and fail to reach their targets.

Like any other online product, if you don't make the world aware of your great new project before it becomes available, nothing will happen when you try to open the gates and welcome in customers.

In this mature crowdfunding market many projects raise funds elsewhere to develop part of their film, book, device or other product. With samples to show and previews to share, they can then use crowdfunding to raise the remaining cash required to complete the full project.

Projects may spend months before the launch of their 30-day campaign preparing their product and promotional materials. They build Facebook pages and collect fans, create Twitter accounts and collect followers, write press releases and pay a wire service to publish them. Some hire specialized marketing advisors.

Once the 30-day period begins, tending a major campaign is a full-time job for at least one person unless your funding budget is quite small. There are lists to build, backer questions to answer. Organizers have to post constant updates – as many as one per day – adding details to the information about the project. The Facebook and Twitter and press networks have to be fed a steady diet of new content, new photos, etc.

Study the successful campaigns on Kickstarter and Indiegogo and you'll see this pattern of support.

It's essential that the first few days of the campaign go well and show buyers that you're on track to reach your financial goals. A project that starts slowly appears doomed, discouraging potential buyers.

That said, I've seen a friend's campaign that appeared doomed do a PR push during its last three days that raised $8,000 to power it past a $25,000 goal. There are good reasons to not give up too easily.

6.10.4 Stacking the Odds in Your Favor

About one third of Kickstarter projects succeed. The patterns I see are:

It's a lot easier to raise a small amount of money for a more basic project than to raise a bigger budget for something with lots of bells and whistles.

It's super hard to sell an app or anything else that's ephemeral. Mobile games, for example, have a dramatically lower success rate than board games or boxed computer games. Even if your reward items are collectible, people still want a product they can hold in their hands.

Don't sell a product, tell a story. It's not "The world's greatest fly-swatter!"

It's "There I was, deep in the jungle, holed up in a rotting cottage at the abandoned plantation. The flies were everywhere, bloated with dengue fever and seeking exposed flesh. How could I fight them off? I looked down and saw the coil of galvanized wire on the pockmarked floor. In just minutes I had woven it into a tapered frame and wrapped it with the waterproof cover from my camera. It worked! Minutes later I crushed the last of the flies that lusted for my blood. Now you, too, can own the fly-swatter that saved my life..."

Use lots of images, lots of video, and have quality music on the video. Shoot your own video to tell your story and take the time (or hire a film student) to edit it well.

Unless your budget is huge, don't hire expensive crowdfunding experts. Use Google to find stories like "How Exploding Kittens Raised Millions" on the web.

Selling something completely new is hard. Nostalgia drives many sales for comics, books and video games. What familiar story could your product spring from?

CHAPTER 48

Managing Risk (6.11-6.14)

DISCUSSING QUESTIONS 6.11 AND 6.12

6.11: What's the biggest risk your team faced on the largest project you've ever worked on?

6.12: What were the three biggest risks at the start of your most recent project?

What were the three biggest remaining risks when your team was nearing completion on its most recent project?

These topics are most appropriate for: Everyone

6.11.1 How the Best Teams Assess and Control Risk

I believe that a vital part of training every manager in companies large and small should be the continual and routine assessment of risk. Yet I see many management training programs that spend little or no time on the subject.

Why do I believe it pays off to routinely monitor risk, even when no major issues are brewing?

Because that's the best way to keep major issues from brewing. The small amount of time that routine risk reviews take is more than made up if you avoid just one significant problem a year.

It took me far too long in my career to drum this wisdom through my thick skull, but I see continual reminders of its importance.

6.11.2 A Weekly Routine

You can buy entire books on this topic, but here's a top level summary of a risk management process that takes just a few minutes a week.

Each week the team's leaders review a list of the three to five greatest risks currently facing the company (or project, or division etc.). For each risk they list:

- The likelihood that the problem will occur,
- The scope of the potential impact, and
- Actions we can take *now* to prevent or reduce it

For example:

Risk: Bad weather causes flights to be canceled so we miss one or more of the key interviews on the press tour.

- Likelihood: Low for Western and Eastern U.S. flights in July, Moderate in Midwest and South.
- Impact: Meetings in LA, Chicago, Dallas, New Orleans and especially New York are critical. Cannot reschedule easily since we'd miss other commitments.
- Steps We're Taking Now: Jen will pre-book a backup flight for each critical segment if bad weather is expected, then cancel and pay the penalty if we don't need it. For DC-JFK flight we'll reserve backup rental car so if necessary we could drive and still get four hours of sleep before meeting. Worst case scenario is

that we cancel DC and go Atlanta-JFK a day early.

If the weather forecasts were all favorable as the press tour began, they'd push the risk down to a very low level, but they'd still have a backup plan in place.

Once managers have learned the system and written the initial risks, most weekly reviews are quick check-ins that take very little time.

(Question 6.12 is also covered by the text above.)

DISCUSSING QUESTION 6.13

Does your product have any elements that require government approvals, health or safety certificates from industry groups, documentation relevant to import or export controls, etc.?

This topic is most relevant for: Everyone whose Dream Project is a product.

6.13.1 Rules Aren't Always Obvious

If your Dream Project is in an industry where you've worked for much of your career, this was probably an easy question to answer.

But remember, rules are always changing. I always recommend doing a series of Google searches like:

"FCC approval needed to" for articles on the latest FCC requirements for electronics.

"Underwriters Laboratories approval procedure" for anything that uses electricity.

"[City Name] health inspection" for any community's requirements for restaurants, food trucks, retailers etc.

"Required fireproofing children sleepwear" for regulations on kids' clothing.

"U.S. export restrictions" and "U.S. import restrictions" for information on technology products.

"Shipping hazardous materials" to get the regulations for the U.S.

Postal Service as well as each unique shipping company's rules (e.g. UPS, Fed Ex, DHL, etc.)

Try many different wordings for your search, not just one or two. More than one government entity may have jurisdiction over what you do, and they may use different terms within their regulations.

DISCUSSING QUESTION 6.14

How will you handle it if something goes wrong with your product?

This topic is most relevant for: Everyone

6.14.1 Once Bitten, Twice Shy

Everyone who works in any kind of product development function has stories of products that were thoroughly tested, released... and then turned out to have major flaws.

The Hubble space telescope was launched over 30 years ago. After it was in orbit they discovered that its images were all blurred because the measuring device used to grind its mirror was misaligned by 1.3 millimeters. A rescue mission had to install corrective hardware into the satellite to produce its current spectacular photographs.

A tiny change to a mobile phone app isn't thoroughly tested, and after its release the product crashes within two minutes for every user. By the time a correction is placed in the app store and available for download, over 25,000 users have abandoned the product.

A disgruntled employee deliberately sabotages a software product so it will display disparaging text about the company to users after two hours of activity. The hidden message is discovered by the company, but the story has already spread around the world on social media. The company's reputation for developing sophisticated technology is badly damaged.

The moral of this story: test everything in your product, however simple, and test everything all over again after any change is made.

If you are not vigilant on every version of every product you'll have your own sad stories of quality problems that damaged your company.

PART VII

NEXT STEPS

CHAPTER 49

Next Steps: The Question

QUESTION 7.1

For my last question in this book I'm going to ask you to use your imagination.

A magical genie has decided to reward you for all the good deeds you have done.

You are transported back to your old home, the place where you lived when you were twelve years old. It is late at night and everyone else is asleep.

You are not alone in the room. Sitting across from you is your 12-year-old self. Even though you are both the same person, the adult you and the 12-year-old you can talk to each other in the same way that any two people can talk.

The genie will allow you to tell your 12-year-old self three things about your grown-up life, and see how "you" react at age 12.

Tomorrow morning the 12-year-old version of you will have no memory of this conversation. But for tonight you can share the three things that you would have most wanted to know back then about your future life.

And you'll get to see how you as a child would react to knowing those three facts.

What three details about your life do you share?

How does the 12-year-old you respond?

Please take your time, write down your responses, and answer fully from your deepest thoughts. Think only about your own opinions, not about what others may want you to think or do. Do not look ahead to other questions until you have finished this one.

CHAPTER 50

My Story: Thanking a Man Named Ethan Allen

We're used to thinking of certain kinds of Dream Projects as "doing good in the world."

Providing clean drinking water to remote third world villages. Offering high quality medical care to inner city children in the U.S. Developing more efficient and cleaner kinds of renewable energy.

Those are all wonderful and noble missions, and I have great respect and admiration for the people who carry them out.

But they aren't the only kinds of Dream Projects that can impact peoples' lives.

In Section 1's "My Story" chapter I wrote about how I re-designed a board game called *All Star Baseball* back when I was 15, but as a teen-ager never thought of submitting my work to the big game company in Chicago.

As an adult I've always remembered that experience, and reminded myself to never give up on pitching my ideas and giving them a chance.

I had no way of knowing it back then, but that work I did as a teen-age hobby laid the foundation for my career. As an adult I led the design on several major baseball video games.

All Star Baseball was invented by a former Major League player named Ethan Allen (no relation to the furniture stores or American patriot of the same name). The game had already been on the market for over twenty years before I discovered it as a young boy.

Allen died in 1993, and I deeply regret never tracking down his address and writing to him after I became an adult. If I had done so, part of the letter might have read like this:

Dear Mr. Allen:

I wanted to write to thank you for inventing the All Star Baseball board game, which I played constantly when I was in junior high and high school.

First of all, I'm a big baseball fan and I loved playing your game because I felt like I really was managing my favorite players.

But your game was much more important to me than just the fun I had while playing.

I grew up in an alcoholic family, and most evenings things got loud and difficult around our house. I would retreat into my room and play All Star Baseball and try to block out everything that was going on around me. Your game was my escape.

I know you created the game so that kids and families could enjoy managing baseball teams. But for me your game did far more than just provide fun. It provided a haven, a safe zone where I could study baseball in a far kinder fictional world than the real world around me.

You helped me get through some very tough years, and I'll always be grateful to you.

— Don Daglow

I now hear similar stories from people about how they got through tough times by playing my game while they were growing up. A couple who met in an online game I designed fell in love "in the real world," got married and had a baby.

It's a great feeling. And it's something that can happen with all sorts of Dream Projects, not just books, games and movies.

I've used a lot of different sample Dream Projects to discuss various issues in this book.

The person who designed and sold unique leather purses could get letters from people who carried those purses through critical meetings around the world.

The team that coded an app to find the nearest coffee shop might get letters from couples who first met when they noticed they were both using your app.

The family that started a native plantings nursery could get a thank you letter from a family because their grandfather's garden is in bloom again after years of drought because of the nursery's recommendations.

Almost any Dream Project can have a wonderful positive impact on other people's lives in ways we can never fully anticipate.

If you're weighing whether you want to pursue your Dream Project, keep this phenomenon in mind.

What kind of thank you letter would you like someone to send you?

CHAPTER 51

What to Do With Your Answer (7.1)

"THE WORLD IS IN PERPETUAL MOTION, AND WE MUST
INVENT THE THINGS OF TOMORROW.
ACT WITH AUDACITY."

— Madame Clicquot

DISCUSSING QUESTION 7.1

For my last question in this book I'm going to ask you to use your imagination.

A magical genie has decided to reward you for all the good deeds you have done.

You are transported back to your old home, the place where you lived when you were twelve years old. It is late at night and everyone else is asleep.

You are not alone in the room. Sitting across from you is your 12-year-old self. Even though you are both the same person, the adult you and the 12-year-old you can talk to each other in the same way that any two people can talk.

The genie will allow you to tell your 12-year-old self three things about your grown-up life, and see how "you" react at age 12.

Tomorrow morning the 12-year-old version of you will have no memory of this conversation. But for tonight you can share the three things that you would have most wanted to know back then about your future life.

And you'll get to see how you as a child would react to knowing those three facts.

What three details about your life do you share?

How does the 12-year-old you respond?

This topic is most relevant for: Everyone

7.1.1 Returning to The Beginning

The Passion-Process-Product method I describe in this book isn't a road map leading from one place to another.

It's a pyramid, with your passions as the foundation. The process we evolve and the product we launch are supported by that foundation, without which they're just a set of inanimate building blocks.

That's why we always have to come back to our passions. And why I chose to end this book with a unique question.

A quote (which I've seen attributed to both Peter Graham and Thomas M. Disch) states, "The Golden Age of science fiction is 12." That's when your mind is still open to the exciting what-if of science fiction, but has become sophisticated enough to consider adult challenges.

To me, 12 is that crossroads age when you have real dreams for your life, but you have no idea what's really going to happen.

If I could go back and tell that 12-year-old me three facts about my life now, I'd probably say things like:

1. "Everything turned out OK, despite all the rough times I went through as a kid."
2. "I married a wonderful girl and we have two great sons and three grandchildren whom we adore."
3. "I've spent most of my career leading teams, designing and producing video games and doing work I love. I've been teamed with people whom I care about and respect."

Considering how badly I felt about myself back then, I think I'd have been overjoyed to hear those things.

How would the 12-year-old version of you react to your career choices and your Dream Project?

How do you feel after thinking about the discussion with the 12-year-old you?

If all of these thoughts and feelings align reasonably well with your plans, it's all good. If you've developed new dreams as an adult, that's great as well. Lasting passions discovered at age 25 or age 50 are just as valid as those discovered in childhood.

If something about this dialogue between the young you and the adult you doesn't connect to the dream you're chasing, however, don't just push the feelings under the rug.

Look back at the answers you've written — just for yourself — to the questions in this book. What could you change about your plan that would make you feel better?

Don't worry if every detail doesn't feel exactly right. I've had times in my life when it took me a year or more to fill in important blanks in my plans.

Figuring out what we *really* want to do, what we *deeply* want to do, can take time.

But it's worth it.

CHAPTER 52

Epilogue

"WHAT THE STEVE JOBS MOVIE MISSES, WHAT ALL THE
BOOKS ARE MISSING, IS WHAT I REMEMBER MOST
ABOUT STEVE. HE HAD THIS INCREDIBLE ZEST, THIS
INCREDIBLE DRIVE TO GO OUT AND CREATE THINGS.
"WHEN I HEAR HIS NAME I THINK,
'LET'S GO BUILD SOMETHING GREAT!'"

— David Grady

EPILOGUE

I close this book with the quote above because it connects the legend of one of our most respected entrepreneurs with the heart of everyone who has ever had a Dream Project.

David Grady has spent over 20 years at Apple and before that worked at Next, another Steve Jobs startup. David and I worked together at Electronic Arts from 1983-87, and this quote comes from a conversation at an EA reunion.

It really made me think about why it is that we pursue Dream Projects.

I've worked in creative startups for over 30 years. You know there's a financial upside, the potential for a big win. You also know that it could all go nowhere and end badly.

The mood in all of the successful new companies I've seen, however, is not the quest for riches. It's not the hunger for respect and fame. It's not the fear of failure.

The emotion that fuels winning startups is the desire to build something great. The nature of that Dream Project may be different for every one of us, but the passion that drives it is the same.

If you've felt it, you know what I mean.

I hope this book helps you act on those feelings and to create your Dream Project. I hope that the questions I've asked have inspired answers that are all your own.

I wish you much success and even more happiness.

Acknowledgements

Special thanks to Raj Lai, Cynthia Lee and the Stanford Graduate School of Business Igniters program as well as Dr. Vijay Sathe of The Drucker School of Management at Claremont Graduate University for their feedback, guidance and support on this book. Meggan Scavio, Stephan Reichart, Tobias Kopka, Frank Sliwka, Thomas Dlugaiczyk, Dr. Jörg Müller-Litzkow, Francesca Fanini, Giovanni Barbieri, Steve Hoffman and Naomi Kokubo also gave me the chance to hone these ideas with great audiences.

The list of mentors and teammates who taught me the lessons in these pages is very, very long. In partial payment of my debts of gratitude, the list below includes one major influence from each job in my career.

Gabe Damico, Principal of Claremont High School, gave me my first entrepreneurial job after my friend Terry Morrison and I went into the community to market our Adult School Spanish classes. He taught me that with a small budget you can still make a difference.

Claire Gray, a fellow teacher at Rancho Cucamonga Middle School, taught me how planning and process could make a complicated job feel simple. Her advice freed me to work both creatively and efficiently, and transferred readily when I moved from classroom to business,

Dr. Chris Arce, Superintendent at Cucamonga School District, gave me my first full-time management job. He role-modeled an intense, unselfish commitment to quality that didn't change with every political micro-climate.

Gabriel Baum, VP of Applications Software at Mattel Electronics, gave me my first executive position as Director of Intellivision Game Development. He taught me how companies were different than schools, and channeled my occasional "excess passion" in productive ways.

Trip Hawkins recruited me into a startup that grew into a major international company, and taught me how Silicon Valley entrepreneurship was different from traditional corporations. Many other people on the EA team also taught me lessons that have benefited me ever since.

Doug, Gary and Cathy Carlston at Broderbund Software taught me how to put a family twist on the hard-edged business lessons I'd learned, and reminded me about the power of believing in my natural management style.

I learned a lot from many great teammates over 20 years at Stormfront Studios. Bob Wallace, our Chairman of the Board, gave me a years-long master class in management that is reflected throughout these pages.

At The Strong National Museum of Play, now-retired CEO Dr. G. Rollie Adams and his successor Steve Dubnik both demonstrated that a non-profit could have as effective an operation as any other kind of company.

Finally, my wife Marta and our sons Michael and Christopher and their families have shared every step of this journey with me. It is the lessons of life that we've all learned together that are the most important, and without their constant connection and support I would never have learned much of anything at all.

About the Author

3-time Inc. 500™ CEO Don Daglow has held multiple startup CEO and leadership positions in a career that covers much of the lifespan of Silicon Valley. Teams under his leadership have shipped games with an aggregate of over $1 billion in retail sales, and his work has been honored with a Technical Emmy® and recognized by the Lemelson Center for the Study of Invention and Innovation at the Smithsonian Museum of American History.

Don advises a wide range of startups and established international companies, coaching both new and experienced CEO's, executives and teams facing the challenges of team-building, management, product development, industry growth and competition.

He is also Senior Director for Strategic Partnerships at The Strong National Museum of Play in Rochester, NY; serves as an advisor and mentor at the Founders Space accelerator in San Francisco; and is the volunteer President of the Academy of Interactive Arts & Sciences Foundation, the charitable wing of the Academy.

Daglow has delivered keynotes and speeches at The Smithsonian Art Museum in Washington D.C., BAFTA in London, the Biennale in Frankfurt, Medientage in Munich and many international games conferences.

Originally trained as a playwright, Don began his career as a teacher and writer. Starting in 1971, he wrote mainframe computer games as a hobby before the introduction of Pong and home computers, and entered the games industry early in the first cycle of home video games.

Starting as one of the original five Intellivision engineers at Mattel Electronics in 1980, he became Director of Applications Software for what grew to be a billion-dollar business. In 1983 he joined a small Silicon Valley startup called Electronic Arts, which went public and became a major international corporation. After working as an executive for Broderbund, which was sold to The Learning Company for $416 million, he founded Stormfront Studios, which he led for 20 years.

In 2008 Don accepted a Technical and Engineering Emmy® Award from the National Academy of Television Arts and Sciences for his creation of Neverwinter Nights, the first graphical MMORPG, which paved the way for the multi-billion-dollar World of Warcraft.

He lives in Marin County, California with his wife Marta.

His professional website is www.daglowslaws.com, and the email address for his consulting work is ddaglow@gmail.com.

Index

www.ingramcontent.com/pod-product-compliance
Lightning Source LLC
Chambersburg PA
CBHW031805190326
41518CB00006B/198